# birth

# birth

## *Facts and Legends*

## by Caterine Milinaire
### REVIEWED FOR MEDICAL ACCURACY BY
### JOSEPH BERGER, M.D.

HARMONY BOOKS
A Division of Crown Publishers, Inc.
419 Park Avenue South
New York, New York 10016

*HARMONY BOOKS
A DIVISION OF CROWN PUBLISHERS, INC.
419 PARK AVENUE SOUTH
NEW YORK, NEW YORK 10016*

*COPYRIGHT © 1974 BY CATERINE MILINAIRE
LIBRARY OF CONGRESS CARD CATALOG NUMBER: 73-92289
PRINTED IN THE UNITED STATES OF AMERICA.*

*PUBLISHED SIMULTANEOUSLY IN CANADA BY GENERAL
PUBLISHING COMPANY LIMITED.*

*THE ARTICLE ENTITLED "CATERINE MILINAIRE: HOME BIRTH" WAS
ORIGINALLY PUBLISHED IN THE JANUARY, 1971 ISSUE OF VOGUE
MAGAZINE UNDER THE TITLE "HOME BIRTH: A FEAST OF JOY." IT IS
COPYRIGHT © 1971 BY THE CONDÉ NAST PUBLICATIONS, INC.*

**Seventeenth Printing**

# acknowl- edge- ments

*Without the good help and kindness of mothers and fathers who contributed their experiences, the smiles of children, the patience of companions and friends, the advice of doctors and midwives and the encouragements from the Harmony team, this book would still be an obsession. I am forever grateful to all of them for giving their time towards the realization of this work.*

*Besides all of the people mentioned in this book, particularly in the "Birth Experiences" chapter, I would like to thank: Moun and Ian ☆ Henri ☆ Gilles Emanuella and Galade ☆ David Rosensweet, M.D. and Ricky ☆ Colette and Peter ☆ Reno ☆ Barbara and Mike ☆ David Padwa ☆ Bruce and Susan Harris ☆ Linda Sunshine ☆ Maria Iano ☆ Stephanie Tevonian ☆ Ellen Leventhal ☆ Helene Nelsen ☆ Sam Clapp ☆ Eva Robinson ☆ Josy ☆ Joaquina ☆ Christina and Howard ☆ Ben and Yannick ☆ Fred and Indiana ☆ Vicky McLaughlin ☆ Lynn Beck. And thank you to Dr. Joseph Berger for giving me a better appreciation of the medical profession.*

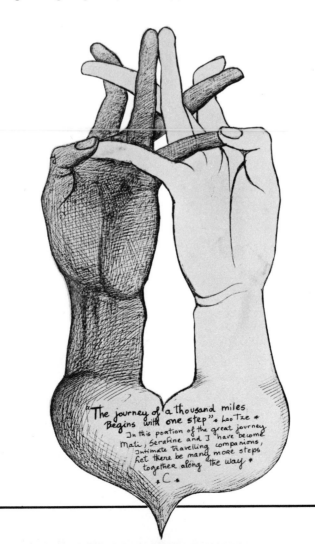

"The journey of a thousand miles
Begins with one step" ☆ Lao Tze ☆
In this portion of the great journey
Mati, Serafine and I have become
intimate travelling companions,
let there be many more steps
together along the way ☆
☆ C ☆

# DEDICATED
## TO
## ALL THOSE
## WHO
## BECOME ANOTHER
## THROUGH
## BIRTH

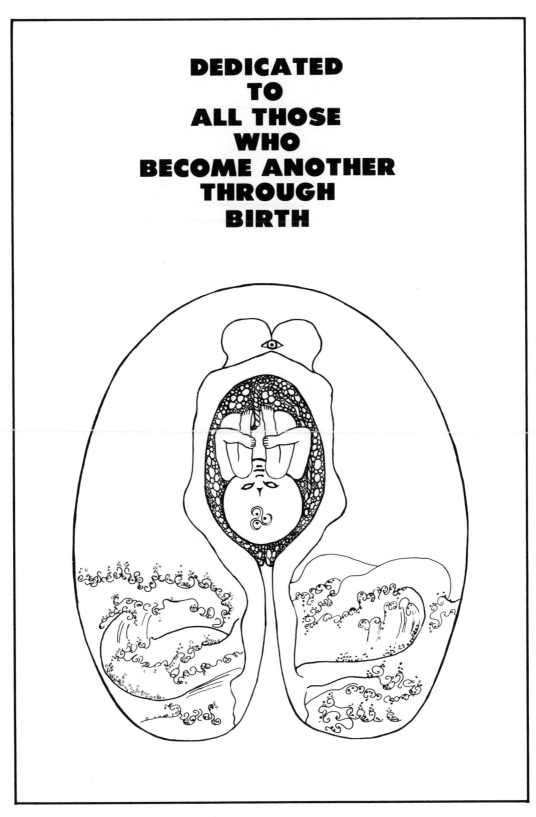

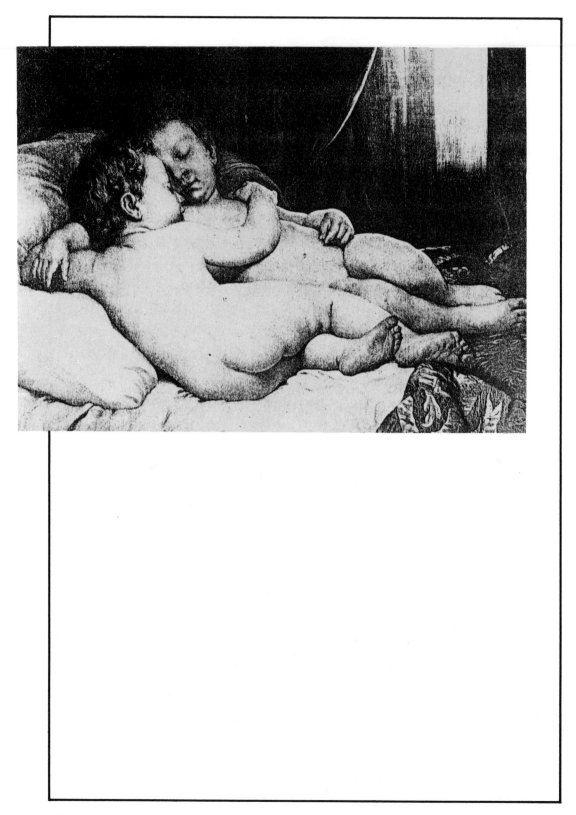

# contents

X

# fore-thoughts

Think deeply—a baby—think about it . . .What a joy, but what a commitment!

Every woman (and man) in this world thinks about having a baby at one time or another. Some think about it more often, even to the point of obsession. It does not mean that all women wish to become pregnant. Changing life-styles have made it hard for many women to bear and raise a child. It is a long term commitment that involves devotion, patience and strength (mental and physical), among other qualities. Childbearing in a world of exploding population is becoming a smaller part in women's lives. This is especially true in countries where contraception and abortion are readily available (which in turn help focus attention on the quality of prenatal care, birth and childcare). There is no more rushing into having children; there is plenty of time to prepare for this special experience.

Giving birth is life's most powerful realization of a miracle. It is so fantastic an event that it is always surrounded with the greatest expectation. Yet men and women never feel quite well-informed enough to let go—to give fully—to be carried away by the exploding forces of new life, to relax and let nature take its course at birthtime.

Birth is still the taboo event of human life. Only recently have women and men begun to probe, expose and seek alternatives to the birth-consciousness that has been imposed upon them for centuries. Today it seems as though men and women are seeking knowledge about every phase of childbearing from friends, doctors and parents. It is only through expanding their knowledge of childbearing that people can fully understand and celebrate the miracle of birth.

A great deal of material can be found on the subject of physical development during pregnancy and the different phases of giving birth, all written by professional people and experts in the field. But little has been recorded, in written or visual form, about people's personal experiences and about the spiritual preparation essential for a high state of mind during pregnancy and actual delivery. This is the fundamental focus of BIRTH: parents' stories in which they relate their personal experiences with pregnancy, birth and childbearing. We learn best how to cope with birth from listening to our body, our friends, our doctors, mostly from men and women who have gone through the birth experience. From their stories we shape our expectations. There are many different ways to choose from, and we want to know as much as possible; the good, the bad, spoken in everyday language. The subject of birth is exciting and, in many respects, vastly unexplored. To anyone with a little curiousity it becomes a fascinating probe. After all, this is where we all started, and to give someone else a good start in life is the least we can do.

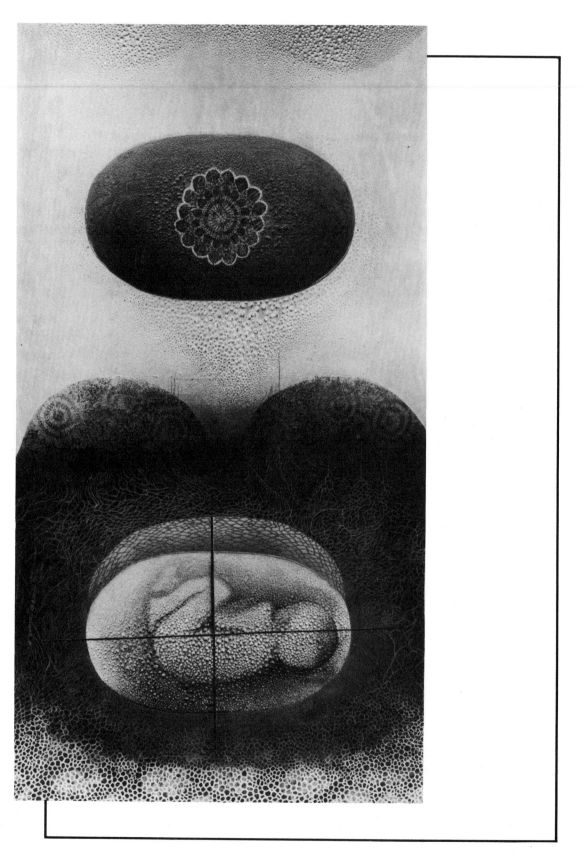

# *Forethoughts*

This book does not advocate that the best way to give birth is at home, in the hospital, with or without drugs. It merely says that you have a choice; each has its advantages and drawbacks. Birth does not belong exclusively to the medical domain, which for all its knowledge still does not know how to transform the impersonal, depressing, blank environment of its hospitals. There is much to be thankful for in the progress of modern obstetrics and great empathy for a person who has studied long years to achieve such skills. However, this is no excuse for the almost mechanized treatment received in the large medical establishments. On the other hand, birth at home with all its personal care, relaxed atmosphere and lack of hospital germs can quickly turn into a drama if a serious complication arises endangering both the life of the mother and the child for lack of equipment that is on hand in a medical delivery room. A pleasant environment and the freedom to follow one's own birth rhythm is important, but so is the assurance that all possible safety measures are readily available.

More than ever babies of the future will be conceived in joy, rather than out of a sense of duty, as a burst of emotion transforming the meeting of two spirits into a new life. Pregnancy becomes a transition, a passage so special it requires a great deal of patience, humor, self-love, good nutrition and physical care. Finally, childbirth can be a pleasure, a time of sensual fulfillment, a gathering of unknown forces and pure creation.

Birth, however eventful, is always an act of love. Whether we choose home or hospital as a location, the idea is to be well prepared and to have a totally positive experience.

In describing the baby's development within the mother's womb we will use the word "it" to identify the fetus, the embryo, the growing individual. The English language has beautifully provided neutral ground for description with the pronoun "it," which encompasses both the masculine and feminine gender.

A warm, human "it" defined from the start as a person will elude misinterpretations.

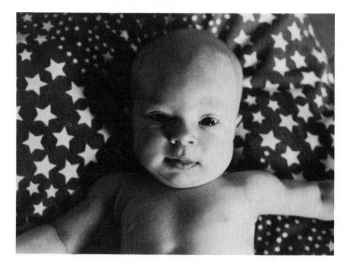

# inside stories

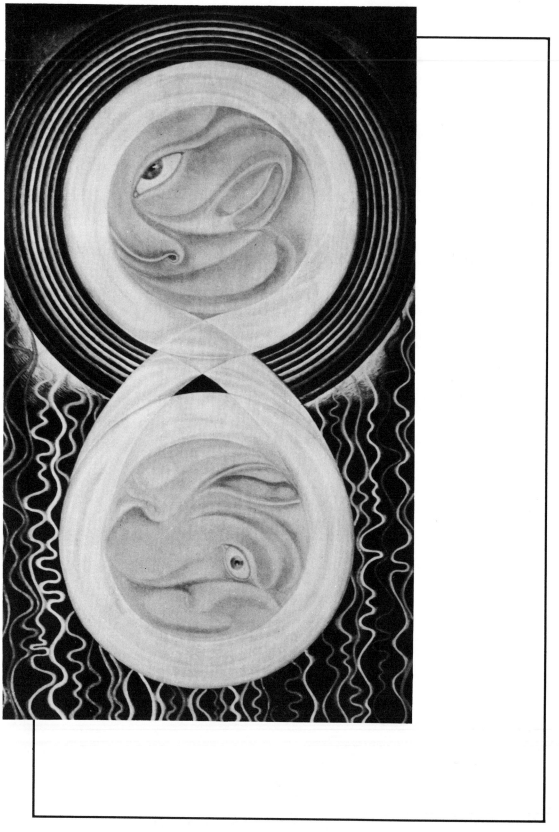

**AS A THREAD IS SPUN
ON A SPINDLE
THE BODY SHE SPINS
AND WEAVES.**

**t**HE BEGINNING
OF A
NEW PERSON
STARTS
AT
CONCEPTION
WITH
THE MEETING
OF
THE EGG AND THE SPERM
IN
FERTILIZATION
WHICH
IS
THE UNION
OF
THE FEMALE & MALE CELL
INTO
ONE
THE BEGINNING
OF A
NEW PERSON

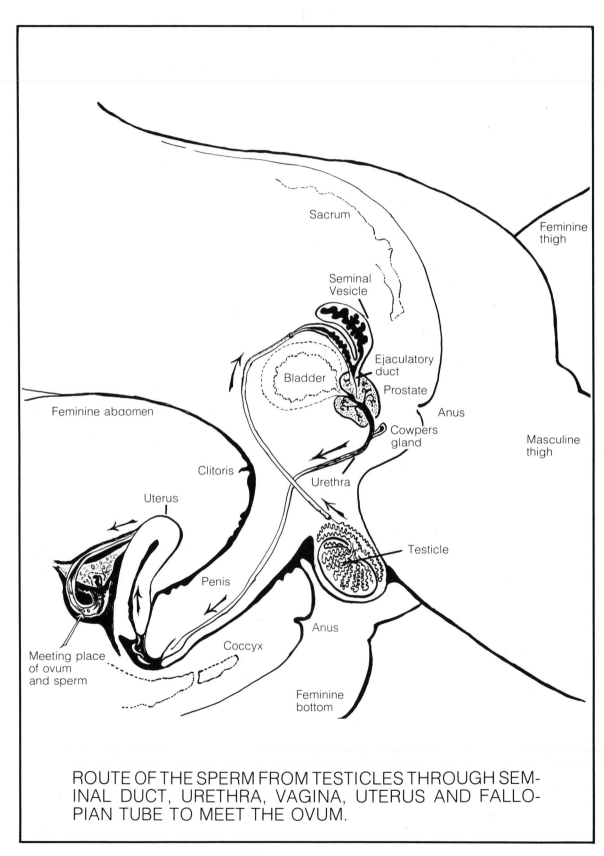

ROUTE OF THE SPERM FROM TESTICLES THROUGH SEM-
INAL DUCT, URETHRA, VAGINA, UTERUS AND FALLO-
PIAN TUBE TO MEET THE OVUM.

# inside stories

## DETAILS OF THE PARTICIPATING CELLS AT CONCEPTION

**Female Germ Cell** or the egg, also called ovum. One egg is ripe every month in the egg storage: the ovaries. The pituitary, a small gland situated at the base of the brain, secretes stimulating hormones into the blood. This causes the follicle, a protective bubble for the maturing egg, to burst. The ripe egg falls away from the 250,000 immature eggs stored in the ovaries since birth and is pulled towards the abdominal cavity by the seaweed-like ends of the fallopian tube. The egg floats through one of the tubes, alternating between one and the other each month. It is moved slowly by little hairs called cilia towards the mother's womb: the uterus, the nest.

The egg can be fertilized in the fallopian tube six to twenty-four hours after ovulation.

**Male Germ Cell.** The sperm (short for spermatozoon) is much smaller than the egg and is effective for approximately forty-eight hours. The male cells are produced in the testicles; twenty to five hundred million are released with each ejaculation. Only a small number reach the environment of the egg. A few will manage to peel off the protective membrane of the egg; but only the first one that reaches the center, the nucleus, can fertilize the egg.

Fertilization takes place in a little more than an hour.

**The Two Germ Cells.** Magnetically drawn together, the two germ cells fuse. The 23 chromosomes of the female cell blend with the 23 chromosomes of the male cell to shape a new cell. In the following brief half-hour a great deal of the new person's physical and mental attributes are established. They are drawn from the inherited characteristics of each parent and their ancestors.

## THE NEW CELL

Made up of 46 chromosomes, the new cell begins to move wildly, as if agitated by a great force. It becomes so violent a rumble that an explosion follows and the fertilized egg divides into two cells of the same type. This is the start of embryo growth.

**The Division of Cells.** The cells continue to divide; they become smaller within the original envelope. Slowly, they are moved down through the narrow fallopian tube by liquid secretions and little hair-like projections. Three to five days later the tiny cluster has reached its nest: the uterus, where it will wander in the salty fluid for a few days. By approximately the sixth day, the cluster of one hundred and fifty cells resembles in formation the mulberry fruit (or *morula* from Latin) and is the size and color of a tiny freckle.

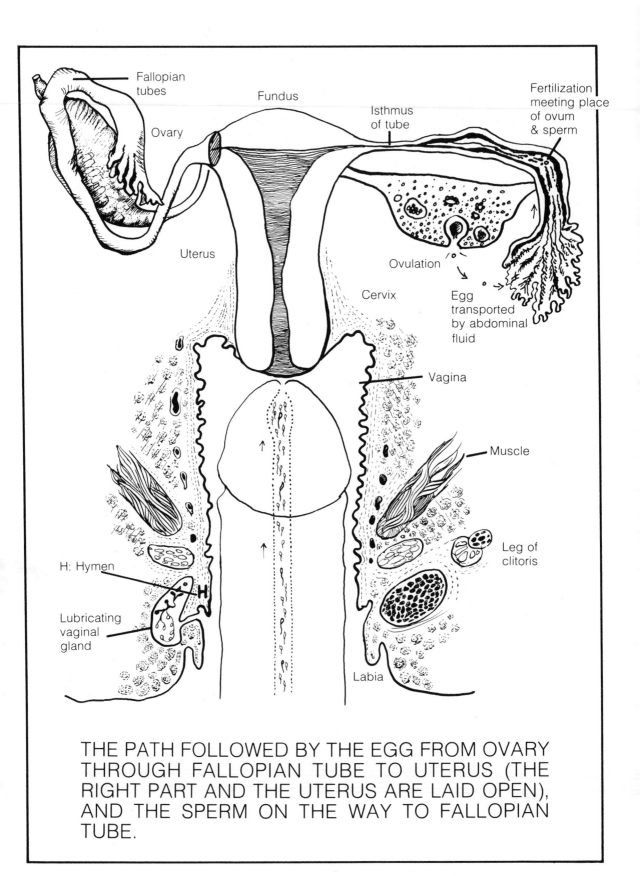

Fallopian tubes

Fundus

Isthmus of tube

Fertilization meeting place of ovum & sperm

Ovary

Uterus

Ovulation

Cervix

Egg transported by abdominal fluid

Vagina

Muscle

Leg of clitoris

H: Hymen

Lubricating vaginal gland

H

Labia

THE PATH FOLLOWED BY THE EGG FROM OVARY THROUGH FALLOPIAN TUBE TO UTERUS (THE RIGHT PART AND THE UTERUS ARE LAID OPEN), AND THE SPERM ON THE WAY TO FALLOPIAN TUBE.

**The Embryonic Vesicle.** A liquid secreted from the center of the cluster pushes the cells away, leaving a hollow space and a multi-layered envelope called the embryonic vesicle. The vesicle is composed of two different layers of cells. The external layers eventually become the food vehicle for the embryo in the form of placenta and bag of waters. The inner layers will shape the body of the child.

**Lining of the Uterus.** Meanwhile, the uterus has been preparing itself, as it does every cycle, to receive and feed the fertilized egg by building up a thick spongy lining of nourishing tissues. When fertilization does not occur, the cycle ends with menstruation, the shedding of the uterine lining.

**Nesting.** By the seventh day after ovulation the fertilized egg is ready to nest in the prepared wall of the uterus.

The aggressive external layer of cells eats away and absorbs a section of the fresh lining, breaking tiny blood vessels and preparing a space for the entire embryonic vesicle. Finger-like projections (villi roots) grow from the tiny vesicle-embryo in order to anchor the cluster securely as it sinks deeper into the uterus.

**The Feeding Circuit** is established between mother and child through the villi roots. They will also function as lungs and digestive organs until the embryo grows further and the cord and placenta are formed. All forms of the child's nourishment received from the mother's blood filter through the walls of this structure, as does the sterile waste matter which moves in the opposite direction.

**Growing From Cell to Embryo.** The nesting cluster of cells multiplies and transforms rapidly within the vesicle envelope. It is now buried deep under the surface of the uterine lining. By the second week after fertilization, groups of cells begin to look very different from each other. Large and small cells take up their position in shaping the human being. Brain cells, bone cells, blood and skin cells start to form. The large cells are shaping the embryo which resembles, at this stage, a small disk of tissues. A transparent sheath starts to grow around the embryo. This is the amniotic sac, or bag of waters, which will contain the fluid to cushion, warm, supply drink and provide a wading pool for the fetus.

**The Embryo Elongates.** By the third week, the embryo is tubular shaped; it is growing a spinal column of sorts and then bending over upon itself. The large rounded head-end almost touches the tail. The brain and nervous system are developing. The head shows traces of eyes and sprouting ears. The cheeks and jaws often look like gills at this stage. Shortly, by the fourth week, a basic structure pulsates and pumps blood through an independent microscopic circulatory system. The digestive tract is a little tube that begins at the mouth and goes into the developing stomach and intestines. On the embryo's side, tiny buds of fin-like shapes appear, soon to be arms and legs.

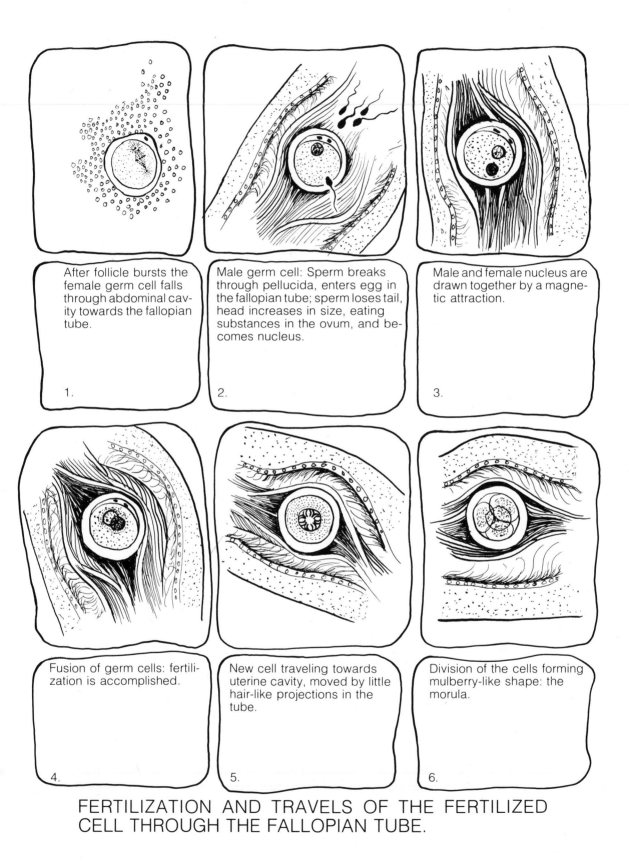

1. After follicle bursts the female germ cell falls through abdominal cavity towards the fallopian tube.

2. Male germ cell: Sperm breaks through pellucida, enters egg in the fallopian tube; sperm loses tail, head increases in size, eating substances in the ovum, and becomes nucleus.

3. Male and female nucleus are drawn together by a magnetic attraction.

4. Fusion of germ cells: fertilization is accomplished.

5. New cell traveling towards uterine cavity, moved by little hair-like projections in the tube.

6. Division of the cells forming mulberry-like shape: the morula.

FERTILIZATION AND TRAVELS OF THE FERTILIZED CELL THROUGH THE FALLOPIAN TUBE.

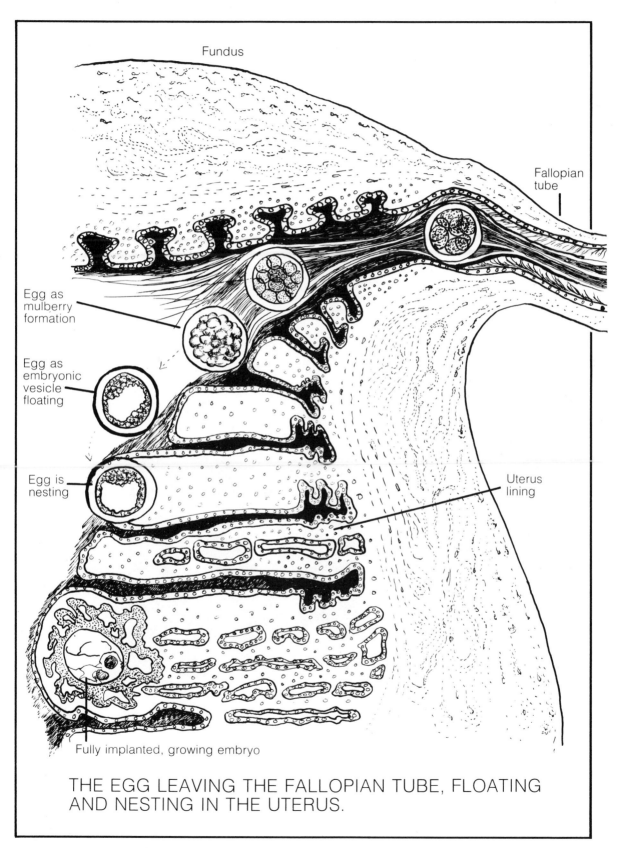

Fundus

Fallopian
tube

Egg as
mulberry
formation

Egg as
embryonic
vesicle
floating

Egg is
nesting

Uterus
lining

Fully implanted, growing embryo

THE EGG LEAVING THE FALLOPIAN TUBE, FLOATING
AND NESTING IN THE UTERUS.

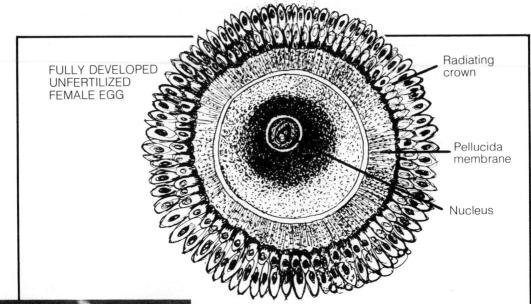

FULLY DEVELOPED
UNFERTILIZED
FEMALE EGG

Radiating
crown

Pellucida
membrane

Nucleus

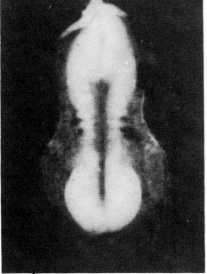

EMBRYO (DORSAL ASPECT) AT APPROX-
IMATELY 21 DAYS; SIZE, 2.1 MM.

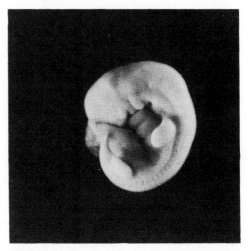

EMBRYO AT 34 DAYS; SIZE, 8 MM or 5/16
INCH.

**As the First Lunar Month Ends** the finely structured creature is a quarter of an inch (5 mm) long; it is growing into a recognizable human being at an incredibly fast pace.

By this time the first period is approximately two weeks late. The embryo is one month old fourteen days after the first missed period, since conception usually only takes place ten to fourteen days after menstruation. This is based on a regular 28 day lunar cycle. However, the physician will start counting the pregnancy from the last day of the previous period.

Since the memory of each evolving cell—and we all started as one cell—is the story of all that has transpired universally; it is interesting to think about the possibilities of having first evolved through the various species . . .amoeba, fish, snake, turtle, boar, tiger, etc . . .before modifications and specialization formed us into the genetically coded human body.

**Recommendation:** Almost needless to say is that it's important to be super healthy at this stage. The embryo, growing at a speed it will never again repeat, is drawing from the mother the basic elements for its structure and is very susceptible to communicable diseases.

In addition, x-rays during this (or any other) stage of pregnancy are strictly taboo. Even if you only suspect that you are pregnant, be sure to let your doctor know. This includes dental x-rays as well. In absolute emergencies, a dental x-ray may be performed if the abdomen is shielded, but even this should be avoided if possible.

## SECOND LUNAR MONTH

The embryo's nest is now well covered with tissues and roots. The embryo feeds through a primitive umbilical cord and the little body floats in the amniotic sac. Currents of gelatinous cells modify and specialize into the nose and ears, the arms, elbows, fingers, and, a while later, the legs, knees, feet and toes. The sex organs are apparent (sixth week) but not distinct enough to differentiate as either male or female. The eyes are getting their pigmentation; a dark circle is forming and above that is the vague indication of an eyelid. The tail is still quite prominent but will soon disappear. The internal organs, the stomach, liver, and kidneys are getting ready to function. By the eighth week the embryo is covered with a thin layer of tissue and a transparent layer of skin. The little body is one inch long (2.54 cm) and weighs about one thirtieth of an ounce (1 g). The heart has started to beat.

**Abortion.** Even though you may have planned this baby, there may be some strong emotional or financial reasons that have recently occurred to make you doubtful about continuing with the pregnancy. If you feel you want to have an abortion, it is best to have it now, via suction curetage. It is a simple, fast method that can be performed up until the 12th week of pregnancy. After this period of time the methods become more emotionally taxing, tedious, painful, expensive and hazardous.

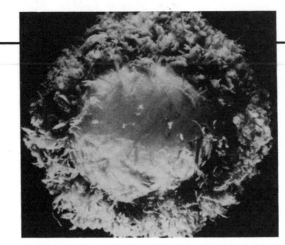

EMBRYO AT 5 WEEKS WITHIN ITS EMBRYONIC
VESICLE.

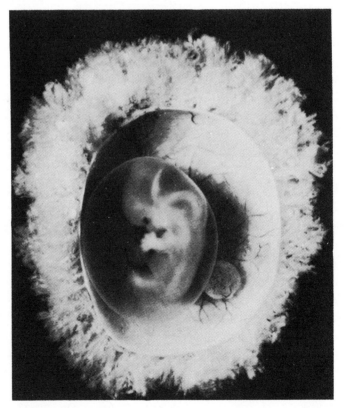

42 DAY FETUS ½ INCH LONG.

## THIRD LUNAR MONTH

The offspring (translation of fetus from Latin) is now refining; cells are transforming the cartilage of the skeleton into bones. Finishing touches such as nails appear as a fine membrane on the fingertips; teeth sockets are laid down in the jawbone. Externally, the sexual organs are strikingly alike. Both have the same glands and similar skinfolds — a slit and tissue folds on either side with a small round bud in the middle. It remains almost the same for the female sex. The clitoris bud stays small and the folds surrounding it become the labia. Development continues for the male sex; the bud grows into a penis, the tissue folds join and swell into the scrotum. The internal reproductive organs already contain a few primitive eggs or sperm cells. By the twelfth week the eyelids close over the eyes only to open again around the seventh month. The mother does not yet feel anything as the fetus only weighs an ounce (28 g) and its muscles are not big enough for strong movements.

## FOURTH LUNAR MONTH

The major systems are now developed even though there will be many little changes before birth. The main process from now on is for the baby to grow strong enough to be able to live on its own. The fetus is now about six inches long (15 cm) and neatly secured in the amniotic membrane. Surrounded with beneficial fluid that keeps renewing itself, the fetus is cuddling up to the growing placenta. The baby is growing so fast now that when it stretches the mother may feel the movement faintly. It spends its time drinking, floating about and sleeping. The little oxygen needed by the baby is carried in the red blood corpuscles from the placenta through the umbilical cord to the little heart which pumps it through the entire body. The placenta, rooted in the lining of the uterus, is now the same size as the fetus. A dark red mass of tissues and arteries, the placenta performs the important task of digesting the necessary materials for the child (proteins, vitamins, minerals, fats) and releasing the amount needed in a simpler form. The placenta also produces the progesterone hormone in sufficient quantity to maintain pregnancy and prepare for the milk. A fine downy growth of hair (called lanugo) develops as a covering over most of the fetus, almost all of which will be shed before birth.

## FIFTH LUNAR MONTH

The baby's heartbeat is now loud enough to be heard through a stethoscope. The baby is very sensitive to noise and may respond by vigorous kicking if very loud music or other noises disturb it. The scalp and eyebrows are more marked. Eyelashes appear and nails harden. Breasts shape out with pale pink nipples.

By the 20th week the average fetus weighs one pound (500 g) and is 12 inches long (30 cm). It is making the mother's abdomen protrude

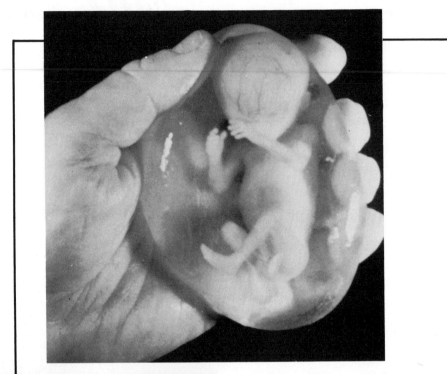

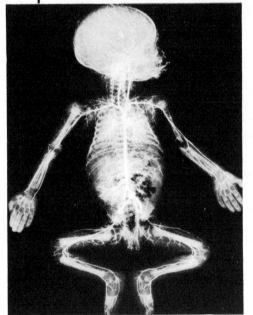

(ABOVE) 12 WEEK OLD FETUS IN AMNIOTIC SAC, SHOWING SIZE RELATIVE TO ADULT HAND.

(LEFT) CIRCULATORY SYSTEM OF 30 WEEK OLD FETUS.

(BELOW) SEVEN MONTH FETUS, UMBILICAL CORD AND PLACENTA.

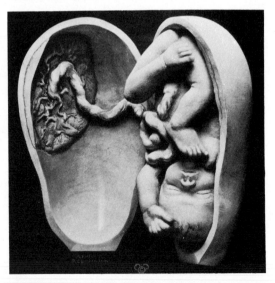

externally because the uterus needs more room to expand. Some spotting or bleeding may occur even at this advanced stage in pregnancy.

## SIXTH LUNAR MONTH

The miniature baby can grip firmly with its hands and suck its thumb. It is small enough to turn around completely in the womb. The skin is wrinkled and red; there is not quite enough of that tissue underneath the skin which gives babies that plump look. To protect itself against abrasion, through long submersion, the skin secretes a greasy protective varnish, similar to cream cheese, called vernix (from the original Latin word).

## SEVENTH LUNAR MONTH

The baby is now two-thirds grown in the uterus. Born prematurely, one in four can survive if there is enough stored fat, if the liver, kidneys and lungs have matured enough to function independently and if it is kept in an incubator. The amniotic fluid that has been increasing steadily will now start decreasing in order to make room for the growing baby who will weigh two and a half pounds (1 kg) by the end of this month. Enclosing the baby in the amniotic fluid is the amnion, a thick shimmering membrane. It is water-tight and hermetically sealed around the umbilical cord. The cord starts at the baby's navel, travels through the waters and the amniontic membrane to the placenta which functions outside the sac. The amniotic fluid is renewed completely every two hours. The cells of the amnion continue to divide from the original layer and grow along with the baby.

The baby exercises, stretching arms and legs in all directions. These movements the mother feels as slippery slides and little kicks.

## EIGHTH LUNAR MONTH

Most of the body hair has been shed by now, but the hairs on the head and eyebrows are lengthening. A little fat has accumulated and the skin has a smoother appearance. The eyelids have reopened. All the organs are sufficiently formed to function independently. Contrary to certain old superstitions, if born prematurely now, it has an even better chance of survival than it did the month before; but it definitely needs all the growing it can get inside of the uterus for health and strength. Towards the end of the month, it is a big 16 inches (38 cm). On rare occasions, it can still do sommersaults but usually it only moves from side to side. At this point, it might settle in a head-down position, crowned by the pelvic bones.

## NINTH LUNAR MONTH

Still perfecting and growing, the mature infant sleeps and eats quietly. When it changes position, the mother may see bulges moving around her abdomen which may be an elbow or a knee. The neatly folded legs are

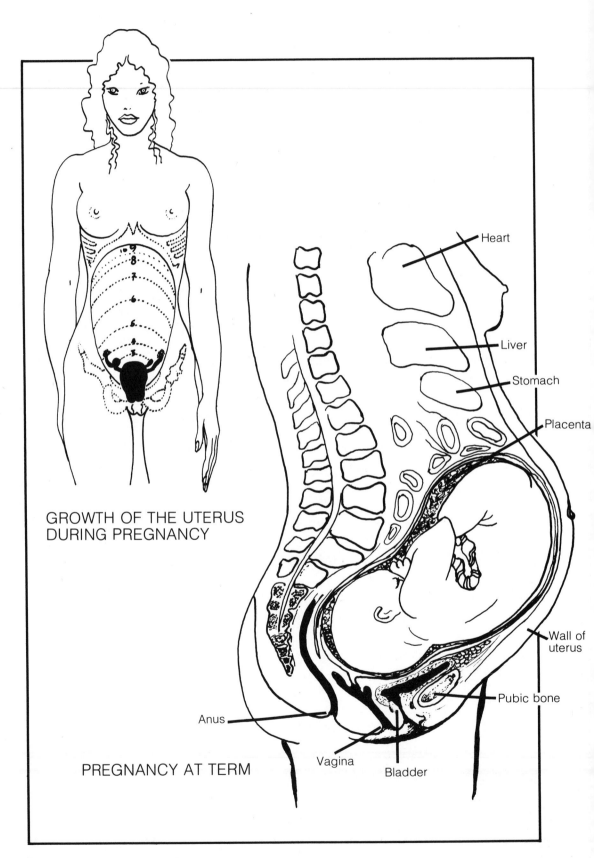

GROWTH OF THE UTERUS
DURING PREGNANCY

PREGNANCY AT TERM

Heart

Liver

Stomach

Placenta

Wall of
uterus

Pubic bone

Anus

Vagina

Bladder

shorter than the arms; the hands now have distinctive little nails. The breasts of both baby boy or baby girl may be protruding as it receives the same substance (estrogen) that makes the mother's breasts enlarge in preparation for the milk. In the last month, the baby has also been receiving special combatting proteins: the antibodies. They will keep it immune to most diseases during the early part of babyhood. Born now, the chances of survival are almost equal to full term birth.

## TENTH LUNAR MONTH

(Forty weeks) The meeting of the two cells blended into one has produced some hundred million cells in the short time span of ten lunar months. Full term is reached approximately in the middle of this month. The child has gathered all it needs to live outside the mother's womb. It can not grow or move much anymore. Growth stops about a week before birth as the cramped placenta's feeding efficiency lessens. This brings about a change in the hormone balance which sets in motion the actual birth process. Soon the uterine muscles will start contracting. The uterus, expanded to maximum size, drops down a few inches from last month's position. The child at term usually weighs seven to seven and a half pounds (3½ kg) and measures an average of nineteen inches (45 cm). The head, or bottom, becomes further engaged in the tight pelvic bone passage. It moves through the slowly dilating cervix and the expanding vagina. It is ready for the big journey out . . . . . . . . . . . . . . . . . . . . . . . . . . . . . . . . . . . . . . . . . .

Barbara Nessim Nov. 1969

20

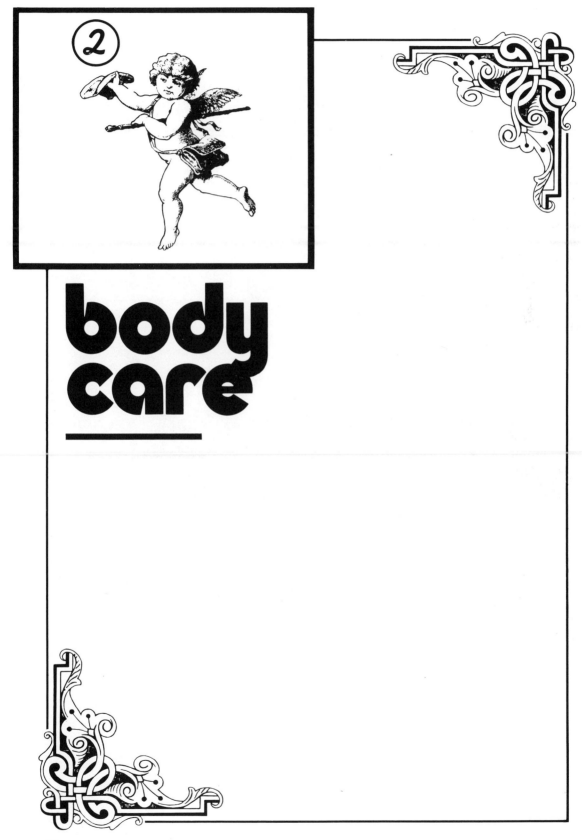

# body care

# PREGNANCY ... PREPARATION

SO LONG AS ONE FEELS
THAT ONE IS THE DOER
ONE CANNOT ESCAPE
FROM THE WHEELS OF BIRTH
—BUDDHA

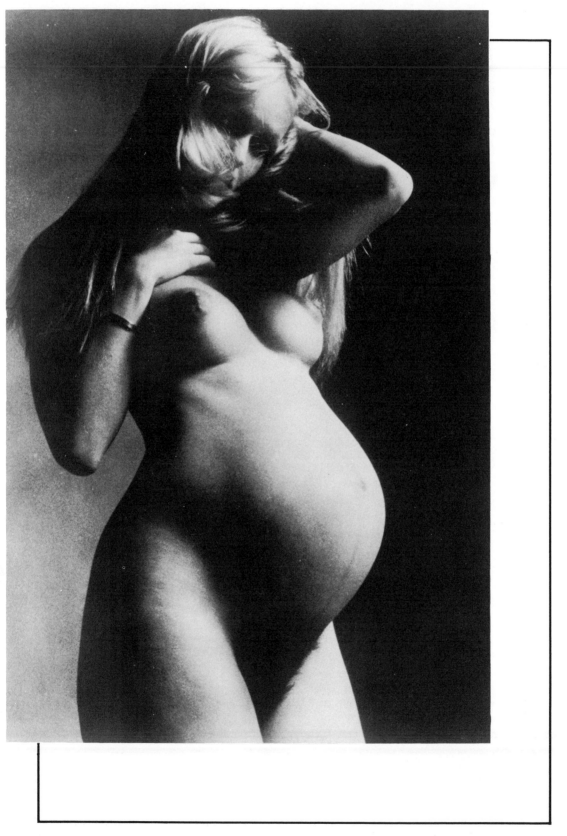

ince you are going to have this child with a positive attitude and in a relaxed manner it makes sense—during this unique period —to give a lot of attention to the body that is producing a new person.

# HARMONY IS THE STATE
# TO ACHIEVE
# AND MAINTAIN

**Harmony Inside** By knowing the details of the baby's development, by eating healthy foods, by understanding the process of reproduction with clarity.

**Harmony Outside** By keeping the body supple, strong, alert, clean, by wearing easy and pleasant clothes, by getting involved in activities outside of your emotions.

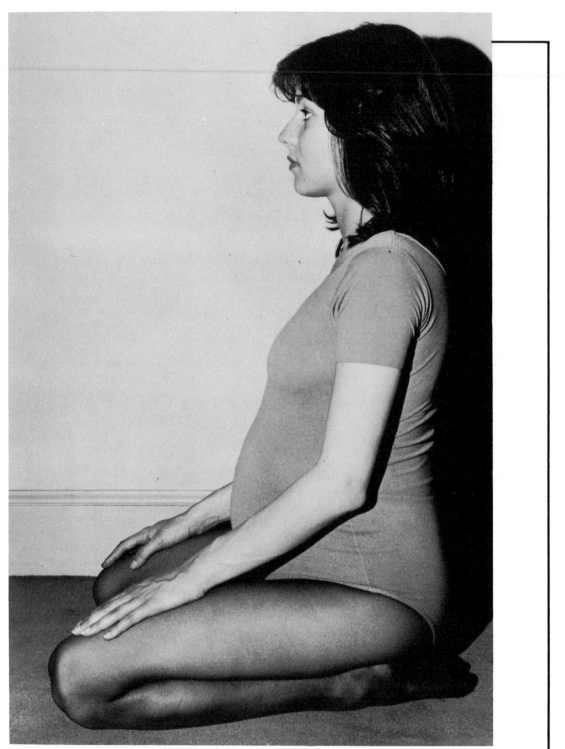

**SITTING:** AS AN ALTERNATIVE TO SITTING ON A CHAIR, SIT AT FLOOR LEVEL, CROSS-LEGGED IN TAILOR POSITION (SEE PAGE 22) OR AS ABOVE: WITH A STRAIGHT BACK, FEET TUCKED UNDER YOUR BOTTOM, THIGHS SLIGHTLY APART.

# limbering exercises

**Total Relaxation.** Before doing any exercises, it's best to give the body a layback period to relax: unwinding, decontracting the muscles, breathing.

**When to Start.** Most childbirth exercise classes begin towards the middle of the seventh month. But, it takes time to become aware of the body, to learn to control muscles and respiration, to know how to distribute energies. It is really a good idea to start doing gymnastics around the fifth month. Muscles are not strengthened in a few days. Fifteen minutes a day (before breakfast or dinner) is preferable to one a hour a week in a rush. If you find it boring to do the same exercises daily, then add gentle variations, stretching movements of your own invention that feel good. In giving birth, a woman needs strength and endurance and this is where gymnastic training can be helpful.

**Clothing for Exercises.** Best is naked in a warm environment. In cooler places, wear leotards or body suits that will stretch to any size. A t-shirt and bikini pants are also okay. Manuella (the woman in the photographs) chose a leotard and tights because these pictures were taken in England where central heating is rather rare. At that time she was seven months pregnant with her and Gilles' first baby.

**Begin by Lying Flat on Your Back.** Fold a blanket lengthwise in two if the floor feels too hard. A cushion can support your head if that feels more comfortable to you. A folded towel placed under the thighs near the knees makes some people feel even more relaxed.

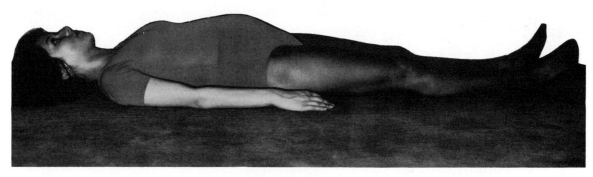

**1** Lie at ease . . . . . . Breath slowly . . . . . . In . . . . Out . . .
Let the whole body go loose from head to toe . . . Let the hands open up and find an easy position . . . . Roll the legs a little . . .

The feet will most probably point outwards when settling . . . Stay loose a few minutes . . .

**2** Once the body is at rest, the mind relieved of daily hassles, and a few deep breaths inhaled and released, you are ready to start the limbering exercises.

From the lying flat position bring both legs up as in the above photograph.

. . . . . . Bend your knees and bring the right leg up to the side of your abdomen, hold for thirty seconds and put the leg down. This helps to stretch the pelvic floor muscles.

Repeat 5 to 10 times. End this set of exercises by bringing up both knees at the same time.

Return to total relaxation position . . . . Breathe slowly and deeply.

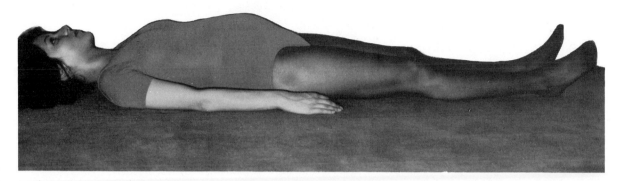

**3** Let your head roll from side to side, untangle the neck.
Then, stop moving your head.
Close your eyes.
Erase the lines on the forehead.
Unclench your teeth.
Breathe regularly.

**4** Bend left leg. (Note the position of the arm and open hand.)
Lift the right leg, keeping it straight and pointed in an outward right position,
hold for a few seconds.
Repeat the movement with left leg, keeping the right leg bent.
Repeat 5 to 10 times.

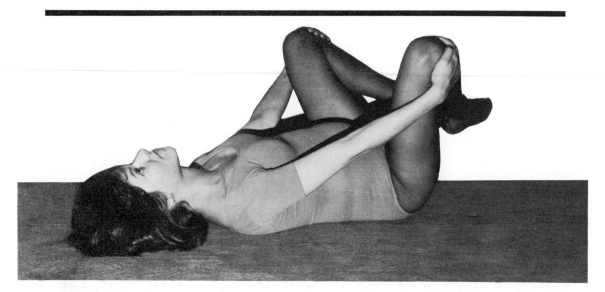

**5** This exercise will be useful during the expulsion phase — the second stage of labor — when you push the baby out.
(For more comfort, place a pillow or two at shoulder level.)
Starting from the total relaxation position, draw your legs up against your abdomen, grab the knees or thighs,
take a deep breath . . . . .

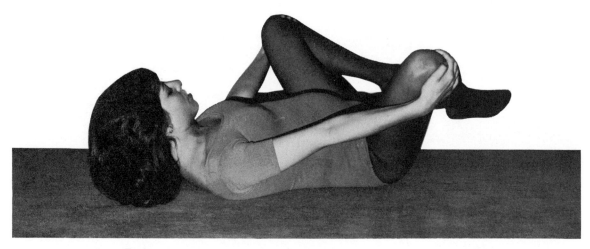

. . . . . . Raise your head, blow out.
Take another deep breath and hold (or pant).
This will be the stage during which you push at birth. DON'T PUSH NOW!
Exhale and let your head go back.
Take another deep breath, hold it, head forward. (Ready for another push as if a contraction had come.)
Rest.

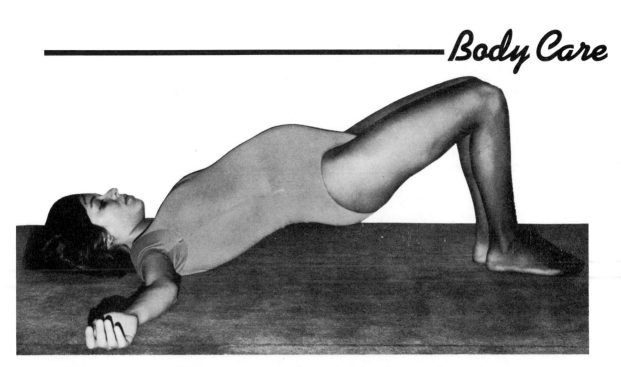

**6** This exercise will help to strengthen the back muscles. Lie on your back, and bend your legs. Gently pressing down on the feet and stretched out arms, raise up your bottom and arch your back in the shape of a bridge. Inhale as you go up, exhale slowly on the way down . . . Repeat . . . Relax.

**7** DISASSOCIATION EXERCISES: Usually, we use our muscles in a coordinated way, one muscle reacting in direct response to the other. Although this works fine for everyday activities, this coordinated response wastes energy during labor. For example, if your body can remain relaxed while the uterus is contracting, you can channel the saved energy into a form of deep breathing which will relieve the strain.

Check yourself on disassociation at exercise time or while lying on your bed before or after sleep. Concentrate on special areas of your body. For instance, make a tight fist with your right hand and then tighten the muscles in your left leg. Now, check the rest of your body. Is the back of your neck loose? Is the left arm at rest? Check it, or better still, have someone else see if it is really relaxed . . . . Let go . . . Repeat, this time tightening other parts of your body.

**8** RELIEVING ABDOMINAL PRESSURE: Stand on hands and knees, breathe in, pull the abdomen inwards, round the back, tighten up the bottom, lower the head slightly.

Breathe out, let the belly go slowly, decontract the abdominal muscles, let the back curve in gently, relax the bottom.

**9** TONING THE MUSCLES OF THE BACK AND ABDOMEN: Starting from the hand and knee position, straighten out the right leg, hold a few seconds and kneel again. Do the same with the left leg. Repeat both exercises 5 to 10 times, taking great care not to strain yourself.

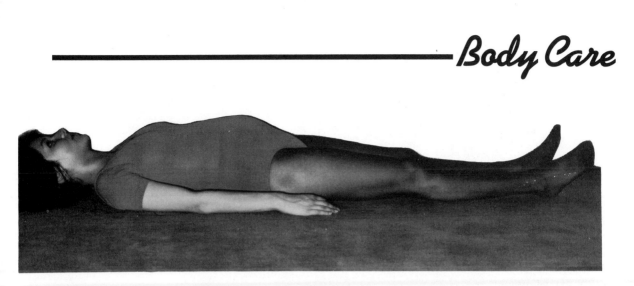

**10** TOTAL RELAXATION: Concentrate on decontracting every muscle in your body: starting with the scalp, then the forehead, the brows, the eyelids, the cheeks, the nostrils, the jawbone, the neck, the nape of the neck, the spine, the shoulders, the right arm and hand, the left arm and hand (all the way down to the fingers), the solar plexus, the torso, the stomach, the abdomen, the hips, the buttocks, the thighs, the calves and the feet, all the way down to the smallest toenail.

**11** KEGEL EXERCISE: The muscles surrounding the vaginal opening and the perineal area used to be strong when we squatted to relieve ourselves instead of sitting on toilets. These muscles need to be — and can be — strengthened with a simple exercise that can be done anytime and anywhere, waiting for a bus, after brushing your teeth, at the post office. . . .

Contract the muscles around the vagina as if you were trying to stop or hold from urinating. (These are the muscles to work on!) Hold them tight for a few seconds and release slowly.

This is an excellent exercise to do before, during and after birth. During labor, the pressure is on the pelvic floor and the opening needs to be relaxed in order to let the baby through. You can help if you learn to control these muscles. This same little exercise can be useful in toning up and firming the whole area starting a week or two after the baby is born.

If you have been practicing yoga, many of the exercises will be familiar to you. You can continue enjoying yoga, in particular the padmasan or lotus position. But remember, whether you are doing yoga or any of the limbering exercises already mentioned, always exercise slowly without forcing or straining your body.

## Recommendations:
☐ Do not exercise on a mattress or soft ground. This will disturb your equilibrium.

☐ Do not wear anything stiff or hard while exercising. Glasses, tight clothing, jewelry, etc. would be constricting.

☐ Empty yourself of waste matter before exercising.

☐ Do not exercise during digestion.

☐ Do not force yourself to exercise when you are in a hurry, feverish or have breathing problems.

☐ You may find it easier to relax and exercise after a warm bath.

☐ Try to allow for a rest period at the end of the session, wrapping yourself in a blanket to keep warm.

## ASTRINGENT BATH RECIPE

If your muscles are aching and/or your skin is in need of tissue strengthening, try the following soothing bath which is recommended by a French doctor and botanist. Allow at least an hour for preparation and bathing.

**Utensils**

A muslin or cheesecloth bag, the size of a small pillow.
A large cooking pot that can hold a gallon of water.
A piece of string.
Rubber gloves.

**Ingredients**

A quarter pound of bran.
A pound of walnut tree leaves (or heather).
Two to four pounds of rock sea salt.

Place the bran and walnut leaves in the cloth bag, fasten it tightly and place in the pot. Cover the bag completely with hot water. Let it boil for fifteen minutes.

Meanwhile, draw a hot bath and dissolve the rock salt in the tub.

Wearing rubber gloves, lift the hot bag out of the water and squeeze all of the juice out of it into the pot before throwing the bag away. Pour the scented liquid from the pot into the hot salty bath, distributing it evenly.

# NOW YOU CAN RELAX IN IT.

You can make this a dip bath — not one in which you necessarily wash with soap — so that it can also profit another person when you are finished.

It gives you so much energy that the effort of getting everything together is well spent.

# breathing: the rhythm of life

Notice the way you are breathing now as you read this. In a quiet regular rhythm? Is there a tense muscle in your body? Shoulder muscles perhaps? Concentrate on relaxing them by breathing slowly. Breathe in through the nose . . .Exhale through the mouth. Again. The tension will soon be gone, replaced by a warm mellow feeling.

Conscious breathing can be the magic key to an easier childbirth. It will help you through times of stress without wasting precious energy. Also, conscious breathing will make it easier for you to handle tension and excitement without the use of drugs. It is a good idea to learn how to relax through breathing as early as possible in pregnancy so that you will be well prepared when labor begins; and you will be able to participate full time in the birth of your baby.

There are many organized classes given to teach breathing and preparation for childbirth. Six lessons usually cost between $25.00 and $60.00 and will prove to be very useful to you. (Find the location of a class near you listed under "Addresses" in the Appendix.) But you don't have to wait for the classes to begin. Start practicing now. There are three basic kinds of breathing: deep breathing, shallow breathing and pant breathing. Guide lines for each will be found on the following pages.

**To Begin.** Sit in a tailor position. Focus your attention on one specific point or object. You can tear out and pin up the left-page image on the wall opposite you. It represents the female element in the meditative illustration of the tantric tradition. At birth-time, place it in your room at home or in the hospital. It will remind you to open up.

# DEEP BREATHING

(As recommended at the beginning and end of each set of exercises.)

# CLOSE YOUR EYES. FREE YOUR MIND OF ALL THOUGHTS.

# BREATHE IN DEEPLY THROUGH THE NOSE. THE AIR (OXYGEN) WILL GO DOWN THE BACK OF YOUR THROAT, SWELL THE LUNGS, AND EXPAND THE ABDOMEN (SEE IT RISE).

# RELEASE THE BREATH (CARBON DIOXIDE) VERY SLOWLY.

A good cleaning of the respiratory tract takes place.

When the first abdominal contractions occur (which may be at labor time or just as a warning, tuning-up days before D-Day), you can override them smoothly with deep breathing. Each breathing exercise can be conveniently timed to last one minute, assuming it is a contraction. However, contractions do not necessarily last exactly one minute. Sometimes they are longer, sometimes shorter. The same holds true for labor, which varies in intensity and length for each person.

## SHALLOW BREATHING

As labor advances and the contractions get stronger, you need to relieve the pressure on the abdominal walls. Deep breathing will only be used at the beginning and end of the stronger contractions. To alleviate the more intense contractions, you can practice shallow breathing.

# START WITH DEEP BREATHING.

# RELAX THE WHOLE BODY. BREATHE SHALLOW, FROM THE CHEST ONLY. PUT YOUR HANDS ON THE RIB CAGE. SEE AND FEEL IT RISE.

# BREATHE NOT TOO FAST, LIGHTLY,EFFORTLESSLY, IN THROUGH THE NOSE, OUT THROUGH THE MOUTH, LETTING OUT A FAINT SIGH.

# GRADUALLY BREATHE SLOWER. END WITH DEEP BREATHING.

You will notice that if you do this exercise too fast it will make you high. Don't let yourself get dizzy or you will lose the beneficial rhythm and you may even faint. If you get dizzy, take a short deep breath and hold it for ten seconds. Vertigo should disappear. Start shallow breathing again at a slower pace.

During the first week of practicing shallow breathing ask someone to time you. When your friend gives you the signal to start, go through the motions described above until the minute is over. Take a deep breath. You are in total relaxation, as you will be between every contraction during this phase of labor.

## PANT BREATHING

When delivery is near, you may have to hold your urge to push until the time is really ripe. To prevent the diaphragm from pressing on the abdomen you will breathe in small blows.

# BREATHE IN AND OUT THROUGH YOUR MOUTH.

# BREATHE-PANT IN A REGULAR RHYTHM, QUITE QUICKLY TO MAKE IT EFFECTIVE, BUT NOT TOO FAST OR YOU MAY BECOME DRY-MOUTHED AND DIZZY.

# REST WHEN THE CONTRACTION IS OVER.

It takes a while to find out the correct way of panting. In the course of practicing you will find your own comfortable rhythm.

A variation to this panting exercise, which you may find easier, is to pant and then blow out the air (as if blowing out a candle).

# BREATHE QUICKLY WITH MOUTH OPENED.

# A FEW FAST PANTS (1, 2, 3, 4, 5, ) AND BLOW OUT.

# REPEAT, LIKE THE REFRAIN TO AN INSIDE TUNE, NOT TOO FAST.

STOP A MINUTE LATER (OR WHEN THE DESIRE TO PUSH IS GONE).

DEEP SIGH, AHHHHH...
RELAX.

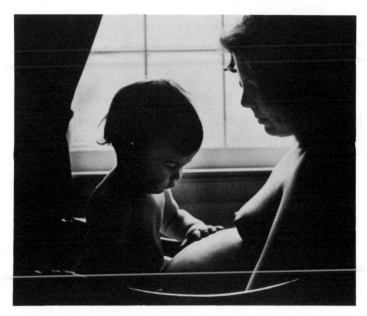

# activities

Unless you have a special condition and your doctor has advised against certain activities, anything that you used to do before you were pregnant is fine now too.

If dancing feels all right then do it. The same goes for sports. But, there is no need for competitions which accelerate the heart and circulation unnecessarily. Obviously, riding a motorcycle is uncomfortable and not recommended. Snow or water skiing is dangerous because of the alteration in the balance of your weight and the possibility of falling. Swimming and bicycling feel the best during pregnancy and walking at least an hour a day is a must. Traveling by train is the safest and most restful means of transportation. Many women take jet airplanes up to the last weeks of pregnancy without any problems, but others say that the pressure and lack of oxygen interferes with their breathing. Also, the restricted amount of space on long flights can be most uncomfortable and claustrophobic. Even though stewardesses have training in emergency childbirth, it's better to delay a trip if a few contractions have already occurred or if it's really close to due date. Moving by car is the unavoidable way of everyday life for many women. Remember that going at an easy speed may reduce sudden stopping which is a real danger for women prone to miscarriages.

## PHYSICAL LOVING

It begins with loving your own body. As your body grows into this extraordinary shape, you get flashes of established attitudes from past and present fashion-conscious people who believe that a pregnant woman is unattractive! But these are only superficial fashion cramps. What could be more fantastic than to see and feel this miraculous transformation which will happen only a very few times in your life. Examine your preconceived prejudices, open your mind and then take a long look at the full rounded shape of a pregnant woman with all its beauty and wonderment. There are many women who feel sexier when they become pregnant. Others are scared that sex will hurt the baby, which it cannot if love is a harmonious exchange. You can use different positions so that the man's weight does not make you uncomfortable. If you feel timid, just touch each other. Show him how to caress your belly with the round soft strokes (called "effleurage") that you will do while in labor to relax your abdominal muscles. Feel free to love and to be loved.

However, it would be dangerous to have sexual relations if there is any bleeding, if the waters have already broken or if you have an irritation. In these instances, see your physician. Also, it is best to abstain in the early months if you have had a previous miscarriage.

## MASSAGE

A good way to relieve the fatigue that will sometimes come from carrying a baby inside of you is with a gentle sensual massage. Also, your companion, in helping you, may feel closer to and more familiar with the unborn child. If he does not feel like doing it, try asking a good friend.

After a warm bath or shower (in the same manner as for the exercises) lie on a surface that is not too soft. Place a towel or a washable cloth under you. Put on some music. Make sure you are in a warm place and that you won't be disturbed. The person massaging you must have clean hands. She/he could start with the head; running her/his fingers through the hair, softly pulling on it by the handful. Then, with the thumbs pressing lightly on the forehead and temple, massage in a rotating motion . . . . With flat hands move down the neck and chin . . . . With both hands massage the back of the neck and head . . . . Up in the hair, down to the shoulders, where all the tension gathers. All the tight muscles of that area should be worked over until your facial expression is truly relaxed. Then massage the shoulders and arms all the way to the tips of each finger. Smooth the flesh with warm oil or a good cream. Slide along the muscles of the upper arm, press the palms around the shoulders. Brush-caress towards the chest. The looser you are when being massaged, the better it feels. With flat hands press down to the breast and around. Come back with both hands between the breast to the base of the neck and reverse the movement, pressing with the tip of the fingers.

Go easy on the abdomen. Spread on some warm oil. Use soft circular strokes round and round with cupped hands from the base of the belly to the top, and down again with a brushing of the fingertips. Next come the legs. Knead the thighs and calves strongly to stimulate the circulation. They have been supporting the weight of the whole body and need to feel relieved. Press down on the thighs with both hands from the hip to the knee and in a downsweep to the foot, up and down making a halt at the knee. Work on the kneecap with the thumbs. Give special attention to the calf as it can get quite tense from walking. Massage the feet with both hands all the way to each individual toe.

Turn to the side for a back massage. The lower back may need extra care because of the abdominal pull. Repeat firm strokes from the spine to the hips with the flat of the hands, and press with the palms. Vibrate the buttocks with a shivery hand, then rotate each well-oiled buttock with separate hands, fast or slow, in the same or different direction, as desired. Finger press the base of the spine then work up the spine, over all the dorsal muscles. Long strokes for long muscles, running each index finger along the sides of the spine. Knead the short muscles running from shoulder to neck. Turn over to the other side for a repeat performance. At the end, use your fingertips to play piano all over the back of the person you have been massaging — this will feel great. Terminate with a soft brushing

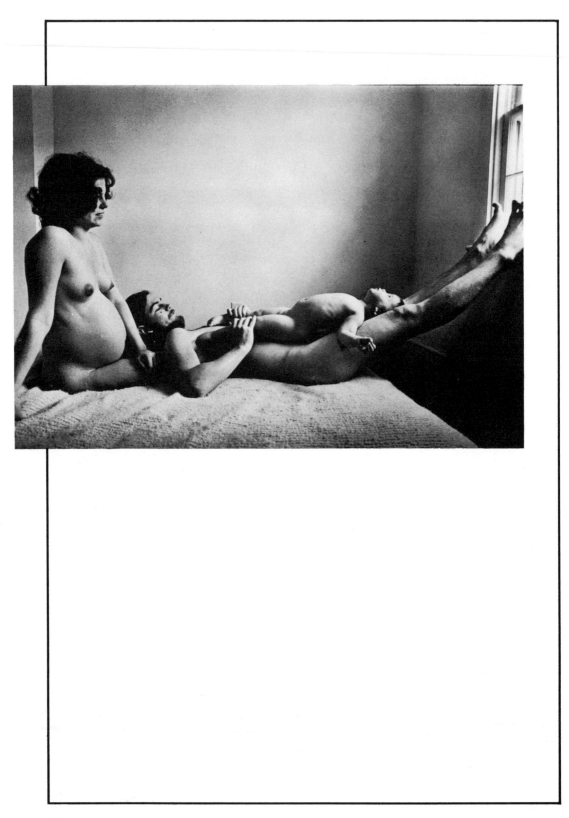

before you wrap her up in a blanket to keep her warm.

**Ointments.** The most ancient skin-care secret is refined olive oil. It was treasured by people all around the Mediterranean long before the year one as a complete body massage ointment. If you are in a cold place, warm the oil to body temperature. One of the ways to keep it warm during a massage is in a container surrounded with very hot water. Midwives in many parts of the world anoint the perineum with warm olive oil to ease the stretching just before the baby's head is about to pop out. Coconut and almond oil smell delicious if they have been refined the natural way. Apricot kernel is also very good for the skin. A health-food store will usually stock any of these oils or can order one for you. If you do not have such a store near you, check the local pharmacy. Vegetable oils can also be used for massaging. Sesame and safflower are excellent, but corn, peanut and walnut are too thick and sticky. You could use lanolin oil, scentless or with a few drops of your favorite perfume or essence extract. Spread the oil first on your hands in small quantity and then spread it on your body. You can also break up a pearl of vitamin E and lubricate your skin with the contents. However, this will be more expensive and quite messy.

The liquid creams—almost of a milky consistency—spread better than the ones you usually use on your face. Most popular brand-name firms manufacture body liquid-creams.

**Recommendations:** Remember to care regularly for your breasts, hips, buttocks and abdomen. Massage once a day with oil or a fluid cream to help the elasticity, as the skin will stretch during the progression of the pregnancy.

This is a good time to learn some songs or practice an instrument; recorder, guitar. Tunes to cool you, your companion or the baby when the going gets rough.

# preparation for breast-feeding

For some women, breast-feeding is inconvenient, unpleasant and, considering the available commercial substitutes, may even seem "backwards." However, there are a great number of women who feel it is part of the continuous process of growing and nurturing the seed. Feeding and watering the growing baby from their own well. It doesn't take a special kind of woman to breast-feed. Anyone who feels like it can do it. However, it is true that living in a city and working at a job is not conducive to nursing. This doesn't mean that all city mothers wanting to breast-feed their babies should move to the country, but they should allow themselves time after the birth to enjoy it in an unhurried manner. You will need time to discover what works best between mother and baby concerning supply and demand and time for the breasts to adjust.

From the beginning of pregnancy, the breasts become more tender and enlarged. The areola around the nipple gets darker and tiny little fleshy protuberances sometimes appear. You could start gentle massages in the early months to keep the skin supple and avoid stretch marks. This should be done regularly in the last months. Further along in the pregnancy there may even be slight leaks from the nipples as the mammary glands are preparing to produce milk. Breasts swell the most during the first and last months of pregnancy and you may feel the need for the support of a bra if they become very enlarged.

If the nipples are protruding it will be easier to breast-feed. Try producing a little liquid to get the feel of it. If the nipples are inverted, flat or small it is essential to prepare them by drawing them out between the thumb and index finger during the last months of pregnancy. Do it for a short time after the exercise period. The nipples should become more elastic and better prepared for the baby to suck.

# medication

Any kind of medicines that you do take — aspirin, tranquilizers, antacids, sleeping pills (these are the most frequently used drugs) — have their drawbacks. They affect your own ability to re-establish a natural balance. Most drugs contain elements that may not be beneficial to a growing embryo. Few drugs have definitely been linked with birth defects, but all are considered hazardous during pregnancy. To absorb unnecessary or unproven medication is to take a serious risk. Remember thalidomide?

Pregnancy is not an illness, but as the body's metabolism changes, certain transformations may (or may not) bring some discomfort. The most common ailments are nausea, indigestion, constipation, and/or swelling of the hands, ankles and feet. These could be caused by the enlarged uterus squeezing the digestive system and blood vessels or by an imbalance in nutrition. Before taking any medication, you should see if these minor ailments can be corrected through your daily food intake. You can also try the basic medicinal herbs (see page 55), nature's own curatives. To counteract nausea, a daily intake of 5 mg. each of B1 and B6 is recommended, as well as Brewer's yeast and other natural sources of B vitamins such as yogurt.

Of course if a problem persists, your doctor may prescribe a drug. Discuss with him/her what the medication contains and any possible side effects that may occur. Prenatal vitamins are always a good idea because women often change their eating habits as pregnancy advances. The baby takes from the mother everything it needs to grow, and this may cause the mother to feel certain cravings, a need for certain foods. It is not the baby that suffers; it is usually the mother who will be weakened if she does not take proper care of herself. The baby, being a parasite, will draw as much as it needs. Your need for iron, calcium and vitamins is increased and should be supplemented with proper amounts prescribed by a competent medical authority.

There has been a lot of controversy over the need for folic acid. Some physicians feel that if there is a folic acid deficiency, premature labor may occur. However, even in women with marked folic anemia the baby is not affected.

Do not exaggerate the taking of vitamins. If you are eating good, wholesome, unprocessed food in enough quantity, chances are you will not need to take extra vitamins. A lot of people around the world are giving birth to healthy children every day without ingesting anything besides their regular meals.

## DRUGS

Most substances absorbed by a pregnant woman seep through the placenta and reach the baby. This includes harmful chemicals, soda pops, alcohol or puffing on any kind of smoke as a daily habit!

Most of the damage that occurs because of drugs happens during the first four months of pregnancy. At that time some damage can occur to the baby's growth because the cells are being formed and the structure of the new person is developing. In the later months, drugs could cause minor complications. The problem is that most women, even though they may know of their pregnancy during the early months, do not realize the extent of damage that can be caused by drugs. This is especially true at this early stage since you do not really feel or look pregnant. Yet, it cannot be over-emphasized that these are the most crucial months in the formation of the new being.

Grass can be relaxing, but if smoked as a habit, it can increase a latent paranoia. Strong weed can sap your energy besides attacking your vitamin C supply. If marijuana gets you high, you should know better than to impose a continuous lethargy on your baby.

People taking narcotics are not only harming the baby but they are weakening themselves. It's one thing to wreck yourself, but why impose it on the baby? It's mean, cruel and vicious. If you want to have a healthy baby then give it a clean start. Heroin addiction tends to cause small, lightweight babies. The smaller the weight at birth, the greater the hazards to the baby. In addition, the newborn babe has to go through withdrawal of whatever drug its mother was addicted to (i.e., morphine, heroin, methadone, de-merol, etc.). It is a violent, sickening and often deadly process.

People who abuse barbiturates (Nembutal, Seconal) are putting their babies in extreme danger. Instead of withdrawal symptoms starting right away, they take seven to nine days to begin. This means that if the baby was born in a hospital, it will no longer be under the care of the medical staff in the nursery. There is nothing to counteract barbiturates. A baby withdrawing from heroin can at least be given phenobarbital as a cure. Cocaine, amphetamine, laughing gas, downs . . . . Pass them all up.

L.S.D. has been observed to be the cause of chromosome breakup in the mother but not in the child. It is a very powerful chemical. If you want to take acid, whether you are familiar with the chemical or not, why don't you wait until after you have had your baby? It is such a strong experience that it is bound to reflect on the baby in some way. You would not want it forced on you, so don't force it on your child!

# cleanliness

Each person has a different idea of what it means to keep clean. To some, it means showering morning and night; to others it is a daily bath or a bath every two days. It depends on what your body demands and how your skin reacts to being washed.

During pregnancy it is important to keep clean as naturally as possible. Avoid being influenced by chemical companies trying to sell their products. In reality you need very little to keep you clean: a good mild soap, castille shampoo, a bristle toothbrush, toothpowder or ordinary toothpaste, a natural bristle hairbrush and scissors.

The external genital area particularly should be washed daily with soap and water. Gently cleanse over and inside all the folds, as it is a sensitive area. Avoid douches and all chemicals around the vagina as it may upset the delicate mechanism that cleanses it automatically. When wiping yourself after a bowel movement, the most hygienic method is front to back.

Being fresh and clean really makes you feel alert.

WATER MINT

# herbs

Plants have the property to attract from the earth nutritive matter, vitamins, and minerals that are essential to living. A small percentage of these plants contain curative properties which, if chosen knowingly and prepared with care, can be fully effective.

Herbal medicines had been forgotten for a while. Phytotherapy, or the art of healing with plants, appears to many people today as a very esoteric science, but curing minor illness with plants can be simple and beneficial.

Our grandparents knew all these remedies without ever having studied botany or medicine. The recipes were passed down from generation to generation. Herbal medicine in fact goes as far back as the refined Greek and Egyptian civilizations.

Herbs, roots and bark can help us. This does not mean you should not consult a doctor when in pain. Chemically based medication can be a blessing when the need to find a remedy in an emergency and in quantity is imperative. However, there is no one miracle drug and a chemical that cures one part of the body may cause side effects in other parts. For mild disturbances such as digestion difficulties, sleeplessness, constipation, tension, etc., herbal teas can be as effective as chemicals and less taxing on the organism. And, you may really appreciate a basic herbal remedy in place of sitting for hours in a doctor's office waiting for advice on curing mild nausea.

**Preparation.** Herbal tea is best prepared in an enamel pan. If elements (seeds, roots, bark) have to be simmered, use a pan with a lid to avoid the loss of volatile essences and precious oils. Otherwise, proceed as for regular tea. Pour boiling water on the dried plant and let it sit for five to ten minutes. Drink from an earthenware cup to keep the flavor and the warmth.

Avoid adding white sugar. If the herb tea tastes bitter, sweeten it with untreated honey. If the smell needs to be altered, squeeze in a few lemon drops. Drink it very hot in little gulps. Take it three times a day, once in the morning on an empty stomach, another full cup in the early afternoon and the last one before going to sleep. Use these remedies when needed at a particular time or daily as a prolonged treatment.

Latin names of herbs are given along with the English name so that when acquiring the herb from a botanical garden or a shop in any country (see Addresses) there will be no confusion. These plants have been classified under Latin names for centuries.

## HERBS TO REMEDY NAUSEA

**Peppermint** (Mentha piperita) Mint and spearmint have been popular plants throughout Europe, North Africa, the Middle East, and North America for a long time. They grow everywhere and are easily recognizable by their strong menthol smell. In the form of tea or alcohol they have many

HOPS

uses. One is the treatment of nervous vomiting. A warm cup of mint tea will settle the stomach. In cases of vertigo, a handkerchief or a piece of sugar imbibed with a few drops of alcohol will help a person see straight again. It is also taken as a digestive and a stimulant but may keep a sensitive person awake at night.

**Hop** *(Humulus lupulus)* The same plant which gives beer its bitter flavor is also a tranquilizer or sedative. The plant itself is very ephemeral. Prepared as a concentrated extract, the fresh female hop cones have been recommended for centuries to cure nausea. A few drops of the tincture in a cup of hot water acts as a calming agent.

**Camomile** *(Matricaria or anthemis nobilis)* Camomile, also known in English as scented mayhew, is a tiny yellow flower that has a strong fragrance. It has the power to relieve many ailments, especially those generated in the womb and the stomach. If you are prone to vomiting, brew a tea of the dried flowers in the morning. It will also relieve intestinal gas.

**Balm** *(Melissa officinalis)* Balm is characterized by its lemony smell. It contains powerful ingredients with the same properties as the above herbs.

Other plants that can help in the relief of nausea are **Marjoram** (a cooking herb), **Peach tree leaves,** and **Anise seeds.**

## HERBS THAT AID DIGESTION

**Garden Thyme** *( Thymus vulgaris )* A cup of tea made with a teaspoonful of this sweet smelling cooking herb is a great stomach settler. Get it by the half-pound bag, as you will want to drink it often, even if your digestion is not a problem. Use it in place of Indian or Chinese tea, which have a tendency to over-stimulate the heart.

**Tilleul (small leaf lime)** *(Tilia cordata)* Use the leaves and flower. Tilleul must be the most popular infusion today, as for the past few centuries, all over Europe. The tree that bears these leaves is fairly scarce in the United States. Lime-tilleul is taken after the evening meal to settle the stomach and to induce a restful night of sleep. If taken in heavy doses, it will make you perspire (as will sage and camomile). It activates the production of bile and is highly recommended in cases of indigestion, heartburn and liver problems.

**Rosemary, Vervain, Camomile,** and **Mint** are also good for digestion. They are easily obtainable by the bagful from an herbalist, natural food-store or in the spice rack at the nearest supermarket. The only difference is that the supermarket herbs may not be as carefully dried and picked from chemically free gardens as those fresh from a herbalist or natural food store.

**Cumin, Coriander, Fennel,** and **Anise** are seeds that can be used for the

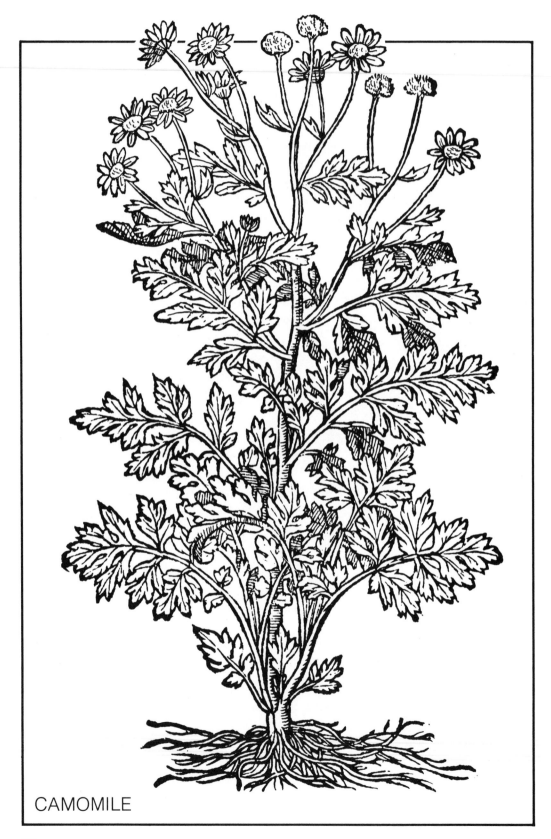

CAMOMILE

same effect. They each have a particularly fine aroma and are also used to flavor various types of food.

For immediate relief of a heartburn chew on a lemon peel, on a fresh mint leaf or drink a glass of milk. But most of all, consider the foods you have been eating! Watch out for the starches (pastry, white bread, cookies), over-refined sugar, and grease in fried foods. These can really be treacherous during pregnancy.

## HERBS TO INVITE SLEEP

**Valerian** *(Valeriana officinalis)* The valerian root is the most powerful herb to induce sleep, but the smell is really foul. You can add mint or lemon. But, be careful with valerian because, in large doses, it can cause headaches.

**Camomile, Vervain, Hop, Tilleul, Marjoram** and **Balm,** already mentioned, are also used effectively to induce sleep.

## HERBS TO EASE BIRTH

**Red Raspberry** *(Rubus stringosus)* The leaves of this plant are best known to promote a relaxed delivery and as an astringent.

**Spikenard** *(Aralia racemosa)* The spikenard root is known as a blood purifier. It is very effective if taken daily in combination with red raspberry leaves during the last six weeks of pregnancy.

**Lobelia** *(Lobelia inflata)* Lobelia, also called Indian Tobacco or pukeweed, is a very powerful seed and plant. It is used by the American Indians. Place one level teaspoon in a cup of boiling water and allow to stand for 15 minutes. Take one to three teaspoonfuls a day at the onset of contractions. It has the unique ability of acting both as a relaxant and as a stimulant. This tea should only be handled by people who are familiar with herbs and dosages as an excess may induce strong vomiting. Use with great caution.

There are many other plants taken by women during childbirth, but being less popular they are more difficult to obtain.

## HERBS TO HELP HEALING AFTER GIVING BIRTH

**Comfrey** *(Symphytum officinale)* The root and foliage of this plant is very helpful in healing wounds. A poultice made of fresh crushed leaves laid on a cut or tear will help the edges to blend together and heal faster. A great tonic is a daily drink of comfrey and alfalfa mixed with any fruit juice.

**Goat's Rue** *(Galega officinalis)* Flower and seed.

**Juniper** *(Juniperus communis)* Fruit and bark. A gentle stimulant.

**Shepherd's Purse** *(Capsella bursa-pastoris)* Plant. Excellent if you are prone to hemmorhage.

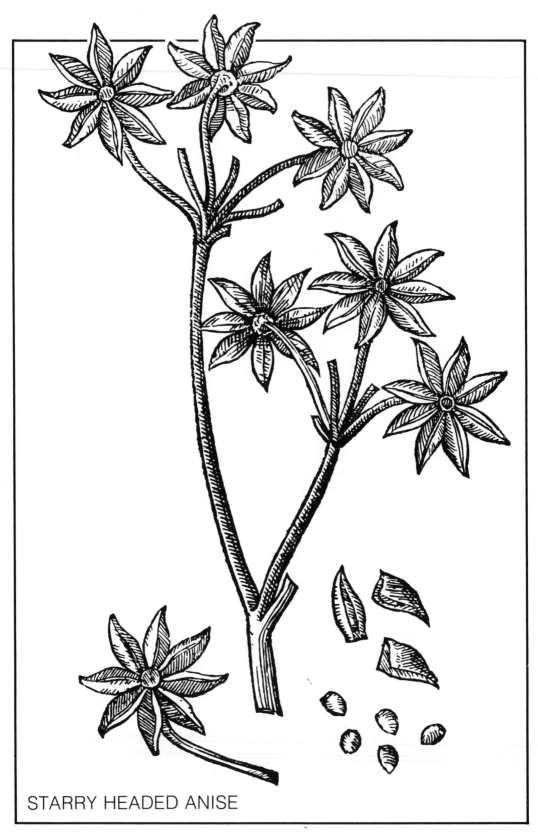

STARRY HEADED ANISE

**Squaw Vine** *(Mitchella repens)* Plant. Similar to blue cohosh.

**Recommendation:** Remember that one person's treat is often another person's poison, so we strongly advise caution in the use of the more powerful herbs.

## HERBS TO FACILITATE LACTATION

**Borage** *(Borago officinalis)* The seeds and leaves of borage are rich in potassium and calcium which influence the glandular system. A tea made with the seeds and leaves should help to increase the mother's milk. If picked fresh from the garden, the leaves can be steamed and eaten like spinach.

**Fennel** *(Foeniculum officinalis)* Brewing the seeds and leaves of fennel can be traced all the way back to ancient Egyptian. The seeds boiled with barley is a helpful and stimulating drink for nursing mothers.

**Anise** *(Pimpinella anisum)* An oil is extracted from the seeds of anise and, because of the high concentration of anethol, it acts as a gland stimulator. It should always be highly diluted, a few drops in hot water blended with a little lemon. Besides helping the milk flow, it is very refreshing. Anise is commonly drunk as a liquor and used to flavor pastries.

**Basil** and **Cumin,** common spices for food, also possess elements to help increase maternal milk.

## HERBS OF VARIOUS VIRTUES

**Sage** *(Salvia officinalis)* Brew the leaves. In antiquity, Egyptian women drank sage tea to become fertile, but it became better known in later days for women who wanted to wean a baby. One to three cups a day will eventually terminate lactation.

**Aloe Vera** *(Aloe vera)* Aloe vera leaves are very effective in the treatment of cracked nipples. Cut a piece of the cactus leaf and apply the moist part to the damaged nipple. Repeat a few minutes later after it has dried. At the next nursing period, feed with the other breast only. Before you feed again with the aloe veraed nipple, be sure to wash it carefully. Repeat the application after each feeding until healed. Aloe vera, incidentally, was used extensively as one of the few elements that could bring relief in the treatment of radiation burns and lacerations caused by atomic explosions.

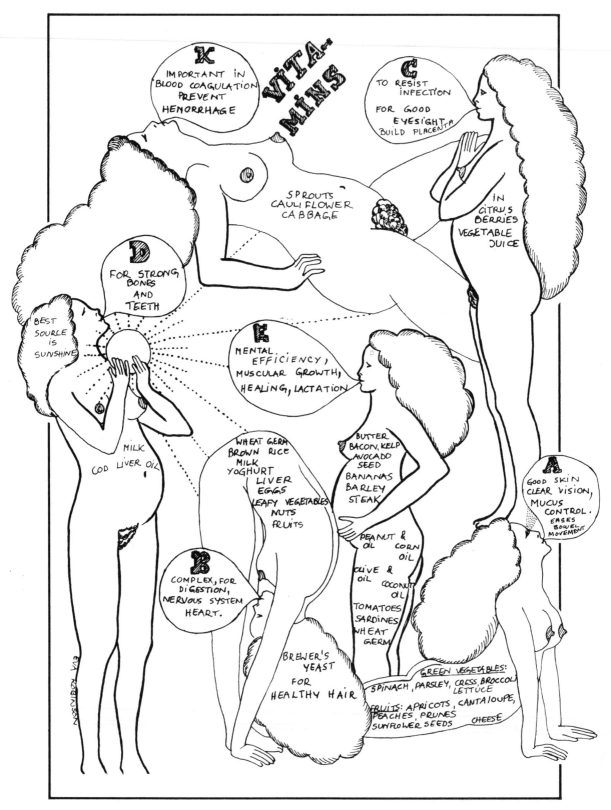

# foods

You are what you eat! And your baby will grow from the foods that you eat. Being healthy is a lifelong process. However, it is never too late to start eating with care and discrimination. The sooner a person begins to understand their real basic needs, the kinds of food that suit their personality, activities and climate, the easier all aspects of life become.

In all probability, healthy mothers and fathers will procreate healthy children. A pregnant woman who takes it upon herself to see to her dietary, physical and emotional needs will have an easier delivery than one who does not.

How do we know which are the best foods to eat during pregnancy? Everyone has different tastes and eating habits but the basic ingredients are the same for all of us.

Your body will tell you if you are choosing the right foods by the way it reacts. If the food agrees with you, you will feel alert, energetic and your bowel movement will come easily. Conversely, the body will rid itself of incompatible foods through diarrhea or vomiting. Discomforts are often caused because the stomach or intestines are being slightly squashed by the expanding uterus; but, they are also due to a disagreement with the foods you are consuming. Heartburn may be caused by indulging in greasy, fried food or too much starch and pastry. Gas is the result of poor food combinations or improper cooking preparation. If pimples appear, your system may be telling you it needs a rest. It is eliminating undesirables in all directions other than the proper channels.

Cleanse yourself, fast for a day, eat a yogurt, drink a large glass of fresh squeezed lemonade.

Pregnancy puts additional demands on your body and it is up to you to establish a proper balance with good quality food and fresh products. Choose the right combination for your metabolism amongst the dairy products, fruits and vegetables, fish, meats, nuts, and liquids. You do not need to be an expert to figure out how to get the needed proteins, minerals, fats, vitamins and carbohydrates in your daily food intake. All you need is curiosity.

To remind you of all the good foods available, we have provided a hint list and a few "happy body" basic food recipes on the following pages.

# PROTEINS

The most important element for the mother and growing baby is protein. Proteins are essential to growth, maintenance and repair of body tissue, smooth skin, elastic muscles, healthy blood and shiny hair.

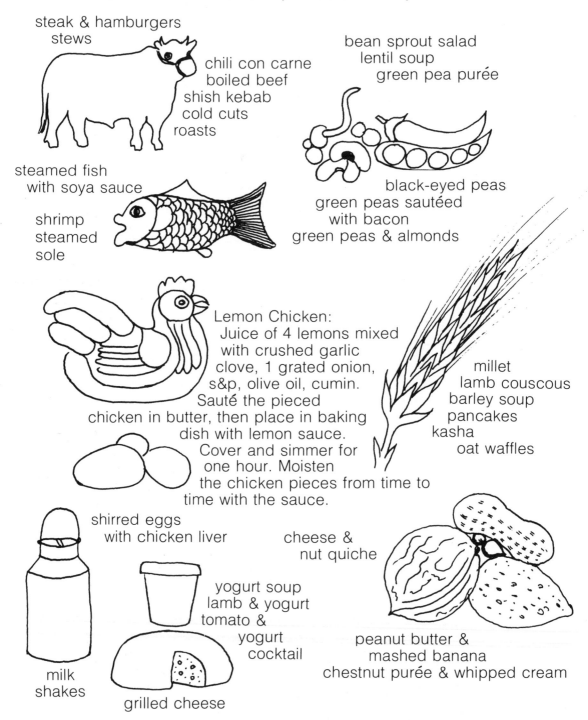

steak & hamburgers
stews
chili con carne
boiled beef
shish kebab
cold cuts
roasts

bean sprout salad
lentil soup
green pea purée

steamed fish
with soya sauce

shrimp
steamed
sole

black-eyed peas
green peas sautéed
with bacon
green peas & almonds

Lemon Chicken:
Juice of 4 lemons mixed
with crushed garlic
clove, 1 grated onion,
s&p, olive oil, cumin.
Sauté the pieced
chicken in butter, then place in baking
dish with lemon sauce.
Cover and simmer for
one hour. Moisten
the chicken pieces from time to
time with the sauce.

millet
lamb couscous
barley soup
pancakes
kasha
oat waffles

shirred eggs
with chicken liver

cheese &
nut quiche

yogurt soup
lamb & yogurt
tomato &
yogurt
cocktail

peanut butter &
mashed banana
chestnut purée & whipped cream

milk
shakes

grilled cheese

# CARBOHYDRATES

Carbohydrates help sustain and invigorate the body, providing heat and vitality.

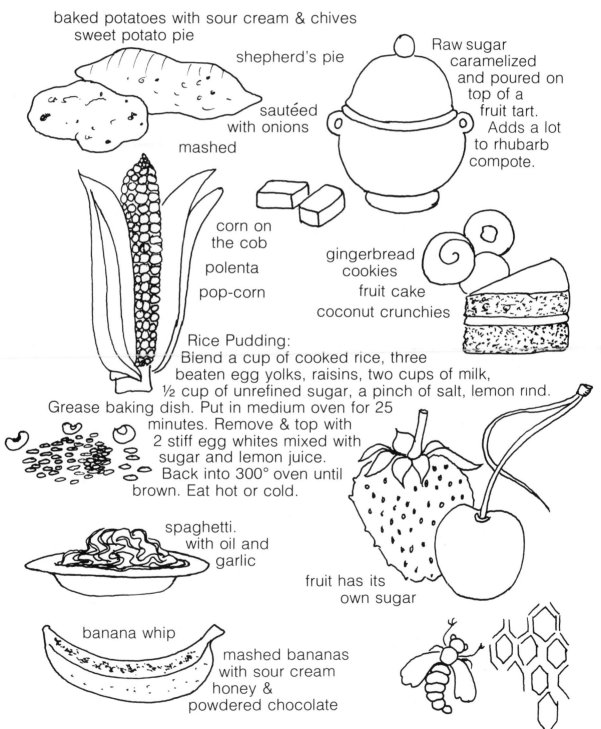

baked potatoes with sour cream & chives
sweet potato pie

shepherd's pie

Raw sugar caramelized and poured on top of a fruit tart. Adds a lot to rhubarb compote.

sautéed with onions

mashed

corn on the cob

polenta

pop-corn

gingerbread cookies

fruit cake

coconut crunchies

Rice Pudding:
Blend a cup of cooked rice, three beaten egg yolks, raisins, two cups of milk, ½ cup of unrefined sugar, a pinch of salt, lemon rind. Grease baking dish. Put in medium oven for 25 minutes. Remove & top with 2 stiff egg whites mixed with sugar and lemon juice. Back into 300° oven until brown. Eat hot or cold.

spaghetti. with oil and garlic

fruit has its own sugar

banana whip

mashed bananas with sour cream honey & powdered chocolate

# FATS

Fats supply energy in a concentrated form. They should not be consumed in excess as they are heavy to digest.

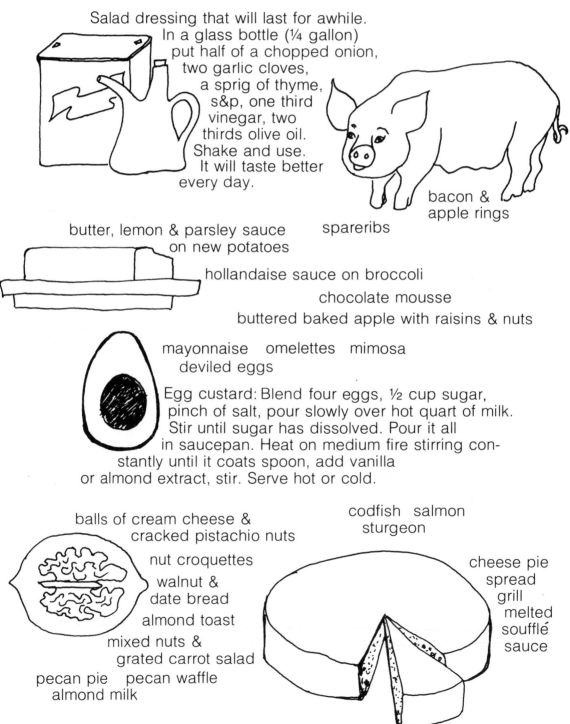

Salad dressing that will last for awhile. In a glass bottle (¼ gallon) put half of a chopped onion, two garlic cloves, a sprig of thyme, s&p, one third vinegar, two thirds olive oil. Shake and use. It will taste better every day.

bacon & apple rings

spareribs

butter, lemon & parsley sauce on new potatoes

hollandaise sauce on broccoli

chocolate mousse

buttered baked apple with raisins & nuts

mayonnaise   omelettes   mimosa
deviled eggs

Egg custard: Blend four eggs, ½ cup sugar, pinch of salt, pour slowly over hot quart of milk. Stir until sugar has dissolved. Pour it all in saucepan. Heat on medium fire stirring constantly until it coats spoon, add vanilla or almond extract, stir. Serve hot or cold.

balls of cream cheese & cracked pistachio nuts

codfish   salmon
sturgeon

nut croquettes

walnut & date bread

almond toast

mixed nuts & grated carrot salad

pecan pie   pecan waffle
almond milk

cheese pie
spread
grill
melted
soufflé
sauce

## MINERALS

Calcium (milk, cheese), iron, iodine, phosphorus, sulfur, and other minerals build and repair bones and teeth and maintain the body's liquid balance.

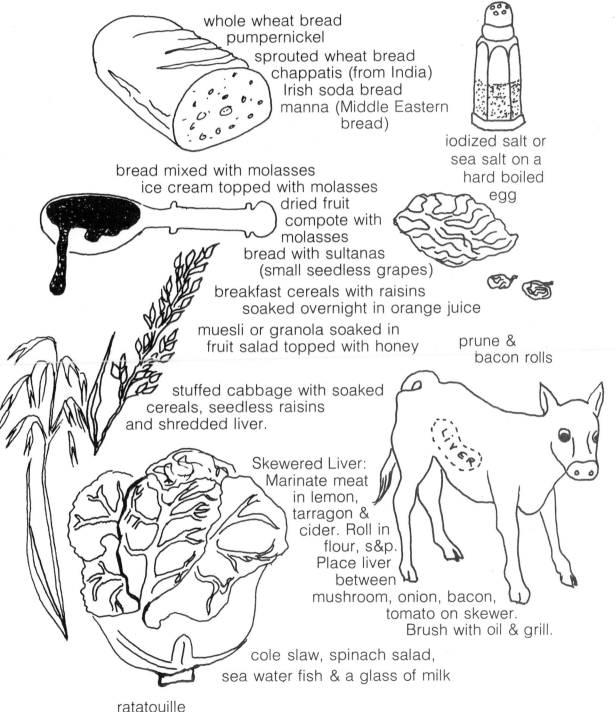

whole wheat bread
pumpernickel
sprouted wheat bread
chappatis (from India)
Irish soda bread
manna (Middle Eastern
bread)

iodized salt or
sea salt on a
hard boiled
egg

bread mixed with molasses
ice cream topped with molasses
dried fruit
compote with
molasses
bread with sultanas
(small seedless grapes)
breakfast cereals with raisins
soaked overnight in orange juice
muesli or granola soaked in
fruit salad topped with honey

prune &
bacon rolls

stuffed cabbage with soaked
cereals, seedless raisins
and shredded liver.

Skewered Liver:
Marinate meat
in lemon,
tarragon &
cider. Roll in
flour, s&p.
Place liver
between
mushroom, onion, bacon,
tomato on skewer.
Brush with oil & grill.

cole slaw, spinach salad,
sea water fish & a glass of milk

ratatouille

EVA ROBINSON

# clothing

Everyone has a different remedy for those times when they are feeling out of sorts. For some it is to do yoga, others eat a lot, go to the movies or go out shopping for new clothes. Pleasant clothes certainly make you feel better and they can help change your mood and put you in a better frame of mind.

As pregnancy advances, your moods change from one moment to the next. This is partly due to the change in metabolism and partly because your shape is also changing. By the fifth month, your choice of clothing narrows considerably. This doesn't mean that you have to buy maternity clothes! Use your imagination! Look in your closet. Chances are that you have quite a few pieces of clothing you haven't worn in a long time which will now be perfect.

If you have time and enjoy making clothes, we have drawn a few suggestions on the opposite page. Or, you can inspire yourself from these basic suggestions when you are shopping.

Please yourself first when getting dressed and it will make all the difference in the way you will carry yourself.

**Shoes.** Flat shoes or low heels make much more sense than high heels or platform shoes which put an extra strain on the legs and back.

**Stockings.** Support stockings can help if your job includes standing for long hours. According to medical studies, they are supposed to relieve the compression on the veins and ease the circulation. Many find the wearing of stockings a nuisance, especially during pregnancy, as the apparatus to hold them up is so uncomfortable. Pantyhose make much more sense.

**Underwear.** As the breasts enlarge, you may need to wear a bra to help the muscles carry the new weight. On the other hand, without the pull of a bra, the skin breathes better, and the pectoral muscles will get stronger with a little bit of exercise.

The most comfortable panties are the stretch or cotton bikini type as they fit right under the belly. The waist-high underpants tend to put pressure on the middle of the abdomen due to the elastic. Best is to not wear any underwear. It feels much more comfortable, particularly under long dresses, skirts and loose pants.

Girdles, or maternity corsets, except in very rare cases, are more cumbersome than helpful.

**Pants.** The jeans you have been wearing all along will do fine. Remove the zipper or buttons when you cannot fasten the pants anymore and replace with criss-cross lacing or a wide piece of elastic cut as a pointed triangle (see drawings). You can sew your own easy pajamas with draw strings that can adjust as you grow. Another comfortable pair of pants is the

low-slung long bloomer type. It comes off well in nylon tricot, silk jersey, or thin wool knit. Insert a two inch elastic strip at the belt (the type used for underwear that stretches easily) and in the ankle seams. Adjust the elastics loosely and wear low (under the belly) in front and higher (above the bottom) in the back.

**Tops.** For all seasons a regular shirt is usually loose enough to leave room for a growing baby. When the abdomen starts to bulge, choose the kind of shirt that is slightly shirred at the top, a smock. An oversized t-shirt feels good against the skin.

**Dresses.** The Bedouin women of Palestine wear one kind of dress all year round. When they are expecting, they let out two seams tucked in front underneath the embroidery panel and, after the child is born, they stitch them back as before. The dress has a classic shape, the same as the popular cotton Indian shirt worn by men and women alike. Any blouse shape in the drawings can be made long, to the knee or to the ankles to fashion a dress.

**Skirts.** These can be the folding types or on the same principal as the draw-string pants. In the skirt shape it tends to exaggerate the prominence of the womb which can be beautiful.

**Coats.** Jackets and coats are usually wide enough to wear in any condition. If it gets too tight towards the end of the pregnancy just don't fasten it. Best is to wrap yourself in a woolen cape that can also be used as a blanket to take a nap anywhere at anytime.

# common and out-rageous fears

Basically, we are all the same. We may appear strong, indifferent or confident but we all have a certain amount of apprehension when confronted with an unknown situation. This is particularly true if the change involves physical alteration of our usual state. We all have fears concerning childbirth. It's neither abnormal nor weird to be fearful. Throughout history pregnancy has been termed "confinement," which is disagreeably synonymous with detention and seclusion. As for birth, it is often associated with pain and a hard time. For centuries, women have been told horrifying stories of unbearable pain and suffering. These fears may have been instilled in us from our own families—from our mothers, grandmothers, aunts and relatives—in hushed conversations not meant for children's ears. And later on, we are told more stories until our imagination begins to overcome our reason. No wonder many women are scared to have a baby! But, we know better today. Modern research and inquiry show that the majority of births occur without problems.

It is better to face and talk about our fears rather than avoiding, ignoring or keeping them locked up inside. Talking to other mothers, midwives and physicians is always helpful. Not being in the same high emotional frequency, they can rationalize and clarify some of your fears. Childbirth education centers are familiar with the intricacies of pregnancy and motherhood and may be able to offer you different points of view. Women's centers, now springing up in most cities, are also valuable places to go, talk and inquire.

Fear stops us from functioning well physically. A positive attitude makes for better health.

## PREGNANCY = GROWING
## BIRTH = CHANGE

The first and foremost fear is of physical pain and mental suffering.

It is now well established that if you have prepared carefully and are in good health, there is rarely any suffering involved in pregnancy and childbirth. There is no denying that everyday life brings its daily share of disappointments but the interesting part is to overcome them with one's own resources rather than sinking deeper into despair. If giving birth does become painful because of various physical incompatibilities, and they cannot be overcome mentally, medical science has devised fast ways to relieve suffering.

Equally strong is the fear that the baby will be born with some form of handicap or deformity.

It's a universal thought: possibly every pregnant woman has recurring visions of giving birth to a handicapped child. Often this is associated with a feeling of guilt: "It will happen to me because I have done a bad deed in my life and this is my punishment." So little is known concerning the causes of birth deformities. It is absurd to blame oneself if all good care has been taken. Statistics show that 95% of all babies are normal, 4% are born with diseases and only 1% with deformity. We are taking certain risks when we become pregnant but there is no use torturing ourselves mentally during nine months. We know it is a slight possibility, a matter of fate to be dealt with if and when it happens. We are not alone in this world. There are other people who have had such experiences and, along with specialists, have formed groups, centers and magazines to help each other.

Women who have had a miscarriage will naturally fear having another one. There is no wrong-doing in losing a baby. Most of the time it cannot be prevented. It is a particularly trying time if it has taken the woman a long time to get pregnant. It is sad and frustrating to be so suddenly without the expected child. But there will be new cycles, new seeds, new eggs to come. Besides, procreation doesn't have to come from your body exclusively. There are many children waiting to be adopted.

The fear of death — mother's death, baby's death — is another common fear. Mother's death in childbirth is so rare nowadays that it has become a remote possibility. Our time to die can come at any moment and there is nothing one can do to change fate. However, it is incredibly difficult to deal with the death of a baby one has been carrying intimately for so long. It is a shock. Knowing in advance that it can happen may help prepare for such an eventuality, although it's not a comforting thought. Talking to women to whom this has happened gives a better understanding that there can be subsequent children born and raised without repeated trauma. (See pg. 159)

The fear of raising a child presents a problem to many women. It is a twenty-year responsibility to raise a child and, since we now have a choice, we should consider this carefully before we get pregnant. The responsibility is to provide for the child, possibly entirely, if we decide to live apart from the father or if we become widowed or divorced. It's nothing fearful; it means loving, working, playing and finding out what help is available to do it best.

Other common fears include:

Fear of looking fat, of not getting back in shape afterwards; fearing that the man in your life will lose interest and patience; fear of not being able to get hold of the doctor or midwife or not getting to the hospital in time; fear of not knowing enough, not having practiced enough for an undrugged childbirth.

Fear of changes; fear of being out of control; fear of isolation, of not being part of the dancing crowd anymore; fear of losing friends.

Fear of being pushed, rushed, crushed if living in a big city. Fear of environment.

Oh! so many fears, and there are so many more kept hidden, hurting whoever is suppressing them. Make it lighter for yourself.

Air out those gnawing feelings and find the positive mental attitude to balance out the negative input.

We each have the choice to take it easy or make it difficult.

**3**

# choices

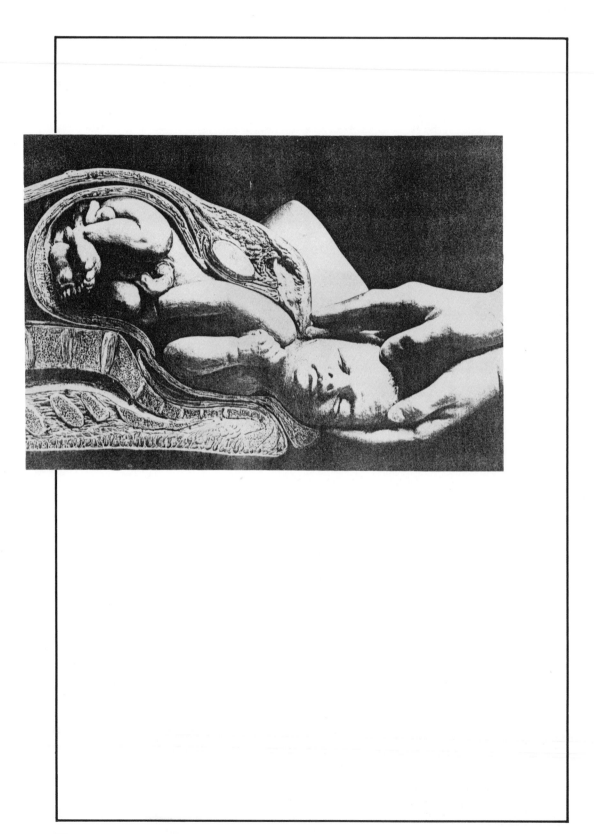

# BIRTH IS NOT ONE ACT
# IT IS A PROCESS
# —ERICH FROMM

hen a child is expected, a great deal of thinking goes into "the idea" of having a baby: health, food, air, rest, love, clothes, preparations for the day of birth. Equally important is your choice of method, locations, and the amount of medical help you will use to give birth. This chapter will outline the methods and choices available to you. Also, we have briefly described possible complications that you should be aware of both during pregnancy and labor. This chapter includes the following:

CHOICES: Medical help, Location, Cost.

METHODS: As It Comes, Prepared Childbirth, Breathing and Exercise, Tranquilizers, Hypnosis, Partial Anaesthesia, Induced, General Anaesthesia, Caesarean, Acupuncture, and various other less frequently used methods.

POSSIBLE COMPLICATIONS DURING PREGNANCY: Anemia, Toxemia, Preeclampsia, Edema, Bleeding, Abortion, Infection, Rh Factor, Ectopic Pregnancy, Placenta Previa.

POSSIBLE COMPLICATIONS AT BIRTH: Premature Labor, False and Slow Labor, Breech Presentation.

LABOR: Progression, Symptoms, Rhythms, and descriptions.

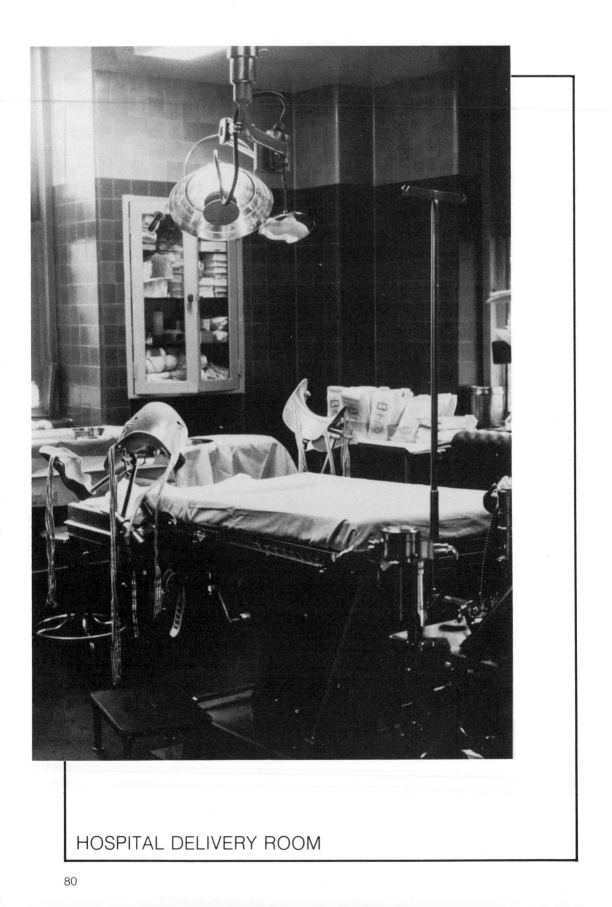

HOSPITAL DELIVERY ROOM

# choices

**Doctors.** Once your pregnancy test is positively confirmed, find out whether or not your regular doctor delivers babies. If not ask him/her to recommend someone who does do maternity work. Or, call the medical society in your county for a listing of obstetricians or doctors who deliver babies in your neighborhood. Also ask for recommendations from your friends who have recently given birth.

**Medical Help.** There should be no hesitation, at any stage during pregnancy, to try another doctor or midwife if the parents feel ill at ease with their first choice. There are many kind and competent medical people who believe that birth-time is a very special experience for the mother and father. These are the people who will answer the plainest or weirdest of questions in detail, with patience, knowledge, experience and compassion. These are also the ones who do not keep you stupidly waiting in a sterile room. Of course there are always unexpected delays, but to wait over half-an-hour without previous warning is really an abuse.

The more informed a person is about internal development during pregnancy, the more fascinating the whole adventure becomes. Ask questions without fear, look at films, photos and diagrams until the mechanism is clearly understood. Remember, you are paying for these services.

**Location.** Basically, the place to have a baby is either at the hospital or at home. (Birth sometimes occurs in between the two places, but that's hardly a choice!)

**Hospital or Maternity Ward.** These places have a high concentration of trained medical help, drugs, and equipment which may be needed in case of difficulty or an emergency.

It is essential that you visit beforehand the hospital where the delivering doctor is affiliated in order to become familiar with the unusual environment.

☐ Know the location of the entrance and the registration formalities.
☐ Know the labor room: individual or to be shared?
☐ Think of what will feel good to wear, to smell (flowers), to read, knit or doodle.
☐ Think of something special to look at, to concentrate on in long labor.
☐ Know the delivery room: look around, ask for the lights to be turned on as they will be on D-Day, as if for a rehearsal. It is not practical to try out the delivery table since it has to be kept ready and sterile for a potential birth, but know what to expect.
☐ See the maternity ward: they are either rooms with several beds and a glass booth room for the babies in their transparent cribs or individual rooms (according to the money situation, unfortunately). Talk to the registering office and nurses about timetables, food, visiting hours.

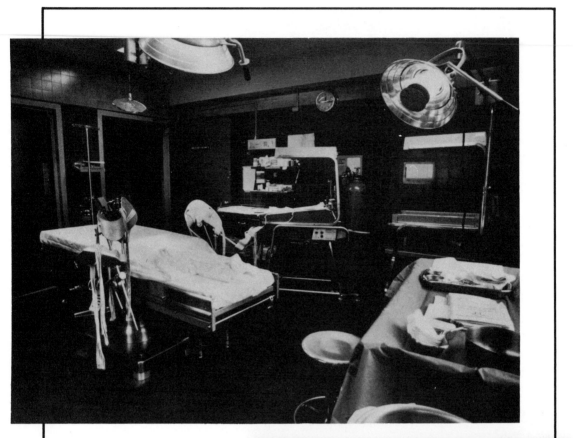

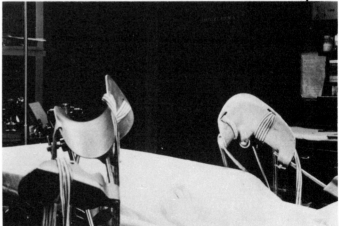

HOSPITAL DELIVERY ROOM

The more information gathered beforehand about the hospital procedure, the more one can relax and concentrate, knowing without apprehension what is to be expected.

Many people are working towards passing laws for a more socialized form of medicine in the United States as it already exists in many European countries. Great Britain's "National Health" services and the Swedish system are among the most understanding concerning people's physical, material and emotional needs. In Great Britain, if you prefer to have your child at home, a mobile intensive care unit can be ordered in advance to come to your house in case of an emergency.

**Cost.** There are several steep fees involved. The hospital cost, even if one chooses to go through the clinic (where a resident doctor is in charge of deliveries) will add up: the room, food, and any emergency services for you and/or the baby start at $600.00 and can go up much higher. Part of this cost can be reimbursed if you have a medical insurance program. However, there are still many difficulties for unmarried mothers in collecting money from insurance companies. (Women should make sure to include a special clause in their medical insurance plan covering childbirth fees without the formality of marriage, if that is their preference.) Remember that some hospitals will ask for as much as $1500.00 advance deposit if you have no insurance coverage. Also, fees for private doctors vary widely, starting at approximately $350.00 and skyrocketing all the way up to $1,000.00 and over, in the northeastern United States.

**Home Delivery.** In the bedroom, bathroom, or special place where the mother feels most comfortable, home can be the most pleasant place to give birth. This is true only, however, if you are 100% positive about this decision. The parents should inform themselves thoroughly on how to prepare for the birth, physically, mentally, and accessory-wise. There should be a midwife or doctor who likes to deliver babies at home and who, after examining the mother and fetus' development closely in the last few months, has declared them probably fit for home delivery.

*What You Will Need:*

A well aired room, warm 68° F or 19° C.

A bed, not too soft, cushions.

A dependable light just in case the baby is born at night.

A little crib or basket.

A special clean area for instruments.

Receptacles for antiseptic and hand washing.

Disposal bags for soiled dressings.

Large pieces of plastic for under the sheet and the floor.

A pan for boiling water.

Antiseptic soap.

Sanitary napkins.

Sterile gauze pads.

Absorbent cotton.

Cotton swabs.

Scissors.

Diapers.

The doctor or midwife usually brings the rest. His/her fee for prenatal care and delivery varies greatly and can be anything from $200.00 to $500.00.

Giving birth at home means you and the ones close to you are in charge of the ceremony. There are no routines, no formalities, no set codes of behavior to observe. Your calmness sets the tone.

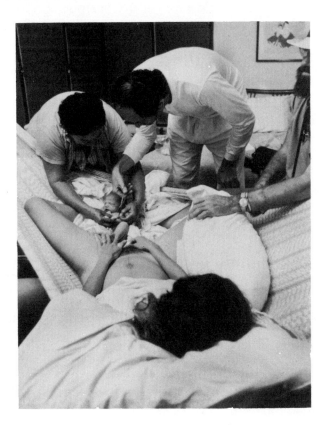

# methods

Childbirth is a natural event that has the same basic elements for everyone. What makes the difference in birth experiences is the way one approaches and prepares for the adventure and what happens along the journey.

It's a good idea to find out, well before mid-pregnancy, what kinds of help for self-training and medical techniques are available. Then you can choose the right method for yourself. Once you have chosen a method of giving birth that suits your character, continue researching it from different books, by having conversations at women's centers, and by talking with friends and doctors. Remember that there are no rules saying you cannot change your decision at any time.

The following information concerning the use of drugs and surgical techniques is not meant to frighten. We only want to help you familiarize yourself with the different possibilities available. There are many variations for each of the techniques mentioned. We will outline the most widely practiced methods and make notes of less popular ones.

## INITIALLY WITHOUT MEDICINE

To begin with, you could simply "let it happen!" and, in most cases, the baby would be born by itself. About 95% of all births happen without complications. However, for the first child at least, it's safer and easier with professional assistance.

**Breathing and Exercises.** These are the basic elements involved in what is termed "natural childbirth" or "painless childbirth" (which should more aptly be defined as *prepared childbirth*). Conducted mostly by a professional physiotherapist (teacher), the classes draw from the findings of humanist Doctor Grantly Dick-Read (who wrote *Natural Childbirth* and *Childbirth Without Fear*) and the psychoprophylactic (meaning mind-health preventive) teachings developed by the Russians Pavlov and Nicoläiev, in the forties. It concentrates on physical and mental relaxation and on conditioning reflexes with self-induced signals. These signals are applied during uterine contractions from the beginning of labor through birth until the expulsion of the placenta. Variations such as the popular "Lamaze Method" can be practiced either at the hospital's antenatal classes or in private institutions. They usually start six weeks before the baby's due date, but for full benefit, exercises should really start around the fifth month. Changes in the anatomy are also clearly explained with colorful diagrams during the course. Some yoga professors also teach prenatal relaxation through deep breathing and stretching exercises that have proven to be very effective for easing labor and childbirth. Trying any of these methods does not rule out the use of medicine if the mother finds she eventually needs it.

**Hypnosis.** It is not a widely used method anymore but since Franz Mesmer made it popular in the eighteenth century, way before the invention of anaesthesia, a few thousand childbirths have been directed under hypnosis. Any willing person can be hypnotized. It is best to practice and be under the influence of a hypnotist with whom one feels completely at ease. Hypnosis is based on gradually bringing out from subconsious levels a psychic strength to overcome built-in fears that have been acquired through the years. This is done through the power of repeated suggestion. Subconscious fears are replaced with the knowledge that the body can be commanded at will by either an expert or, subsequently, by oneself.

It takes quite a while to achieve the complete state of hypnosis. Myths have been perpetrated that hypnosis is not recommended to pregnant women with psychiatric problems and that once a hypnotic trance has been entered it may take a while to come out of it. However, an experienced hypnotist assures us that it is not so.

## PARTIAL USE OF DRUGS

One of the main reasons for preparing thoroughly for birth is to enjoy the experience instead of fearing it and to be able to utilize the body's full potential instead of numbing it with drugs. But, birth is not an endurance contest and there are times when sedation is comforting and partial anaesthetics are really helpful.

During labor, a woman may find the going too rough and she can ask for a medication to take the edge off the pain. There are various drugs that will help without knocking a person out altogether. The problem with relying on drugs is that none are really free of drawbacks either to the mother or to the infant (sometimes to both) which should be considered when accepting or asking for medication. If you are giving birth at home, remember that many of these drugs cannot be administered in your bedroom.

**Tranquilizers** are the mildest medication. In moderate doses, the drawbacks from tranquilizers are nominal and they can help relax the tension brought on by the strangeness of contractions. Some well-known tranquilizers are Librium, Valium, Equanil, and Miltown.

**Barbiturates** such as Seconal and Nembutal do not alleviate pain. They can relieve anxiety and bring on sleep but in excess may be harmful to the fetus. Barbiturates slow down the breathing and reactions of the mother as well as the fetus once they have crossed the placental barrier. The effect can be long lasting (sometimes up to a week) in the newborn.

**Regional Anaesthesia** is the numbing of a particular area of the body. There are various ways to anaesthetize an isolated section where tension concentrates.

**Epidural** is the name for a drip-injection of Xylocaine given in the lower part of the back. The needle doesn't go into the spine. Rather, it goes into a thin layer of fibrous tissues through which passes a network of nerves. If the injection is successful, which it is most of the time, the pelvic area will be numbed and there should be none of the sensation brought on by contraction and expansion. It is an expensive service and can only be performed by a skilled professional team in the hospital.

The mother can still participate, but only as instructed by the doctor because she cannot feel anything when the time comes for pushing. The side effects are said to be minimal for the mother. On occasion, this procedure has been known to cause a mild transitory slowing of the fetal heart.

**A Low Spinal** (also known as "saddle block") is an injection that directly reaches the spinal canal. It is done mostly at delivery time as an effective method of stopping sensations from the waist to the knee when the need for obstetrical intervention arises. Its use is limited as some women may complain of violent headaches during the week following the injection.

**Twilight Sleep** is a combination of drugs used to induce sleep. It can be Demerol (painkiller) and Sparine (tranquilizer) or morphine (painkiller) and Scopolamine (an amnesiac). Such an injection will knock someone out completely. Recovering from the drugs, the patient will not recall what she was doing previous to the injection, even though she may have been screaming and violently thrashing about in all directions.

In addition to the drugs already mentioned, general anaesthesia often has to be administered to stop the wildness if the woman cannot control her movements of her own free will. Many women demand this without realizing that while they are seemingly asleep they can get excited and violent to the point of hurting themselves if they are not constantly observed (which they are), and that's not the only problem. Many physicians believe that a woman spared the recollection of her labor may be psychologically harmed. As for the fetus, its breathing may be slowed down if a high dose of Demerol has been injected into the mother.

**Gas and Oxygen** are relatively simple means to relieve painful second stage contractions. Gas is inhaled from a mask; usually it is nitrous oxide (laughing gas) mixed with oxygen, or Trilene by itself which comes through a tube from a compression tank. It is quite safe for a mother and infant. In certain hospitals, the laboring woman can choose to use the mask at her convenience, putting it over mouth and nose to inhale the gas. The effect it produces temporarily is a certain euphoria which erases pain. If too much is drawn (nitrous oxide & oxygen) it can make the person laugh uncontrollably and feel pretty high.

Ether and chloroform are not used much any more as they often cause vomiting and aspiration, leading to further complications. Gas is an essential element in emergencies when there is no time to wait for the delicate task of locating the correct injection area, and in the delivery of twins. The

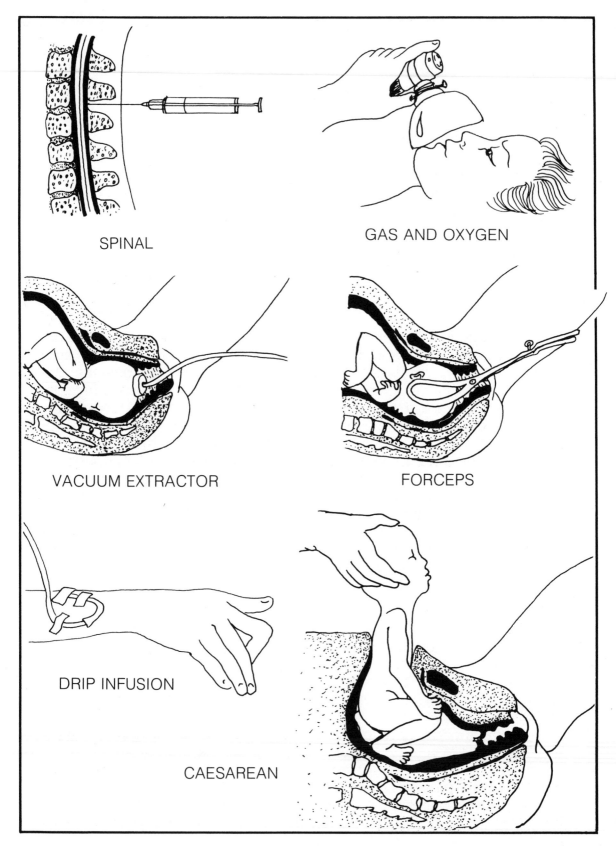

SPINAL

GAS AND OXYGEN

VACUUM EXTRACTOR

FORCEPS

DRIP INFUSION

CAESAREAN

uterus will sometimes begin to contract after the first baby is born, and gas is then used for uterine relaxation, facilitating delivery of the second child.

## GENERAL ANAESTHESIA

As women begin to understand the birth process and seek to participate fully in its every phase, there are fewer demands for complete anaesthetization. General anaesthesia, or the medical way of suspending sensation and consciousness, is brought on by gas inhalation (cyclopropane) and/or injections (Pentothal and curare). It is used for cases of Caesarean section or other complications. It has to be administered by an anaesthetist and is used only when really justified.

## INDUCTION

Induction is an artificial means of starting and speeding up the process of labor at a chosen time around the due date, rather than letting the body begin by itself when it is fully ready. The physician can do it by breaking the bag of waters, which in many cases will start labor. The baby should be delivered approximately twelve hours from the time the membranes have ruptured. Labor should never last much over twenty-four hours from the rupture or an infection might set in. Induction can also be started by an injection of Pitocin, an extract of the pituitary gland. It is injected into the vein and labor is continued by a constant drip through a little tube (an intravenous catheter ) into the middle of the arm or at the hand. The medication causes the womb to contract strongly and in a more regular pattern than it normally would. The injection will induce labor only if the whole system is ready to give birth. A woman can be conscious or put out during the procedure depending on the individual case. Induction is done for various reasons besides personal convenience. A woman may be induced if she has diabetes or toxemia, if the baby is two weeks overdue or if tests show that the baby's growth is affected by anemia.

## FORCEPS

Forceps is a metal instrument resembling two hollowed spoons joined together in the middle. This instrument is placed on the side of the baby's head, like iron hands, to help out in a difficult situation such as exhaustion on the part of the mother or eclampsia or malpresentation. The forceps are usually used for those purposes, after general or regional anaesthesia and an episiotomy.

Forceps can be used to protect the baby from excess pressure on its head, especially in the case of uncontrollable pushing by the mother. Or, they may be used to speed delivery if the infant has a low heartbeat; if the umbilical cord comes out before the head and endangers the baby's oxygen supply; if there is a premature separation of the placenta, or if a breech extraction is necessary.

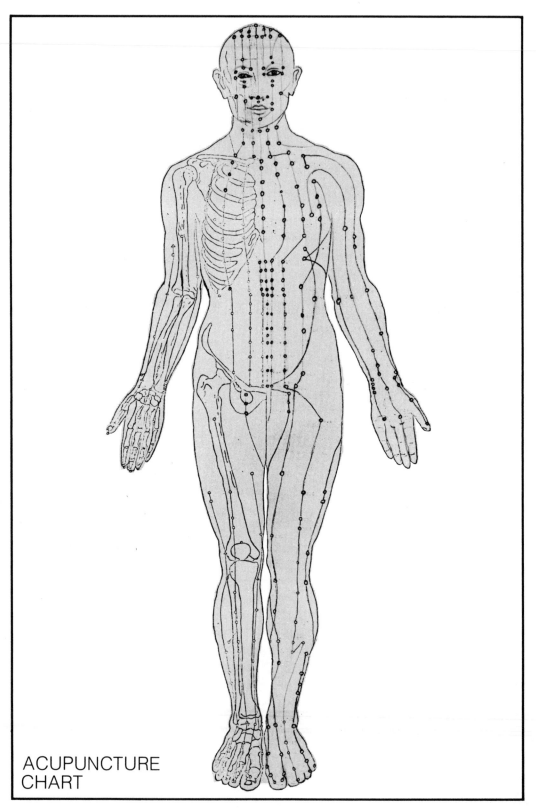

ACUPUNCTURE
CHART

The name forceps rings a mean bell in most women's minds because, up until a few decades ago, they were used to reach way up, where the baby's head was still in a very tight place, and they often caused pain and damage. However, since those days, smaller and lighter instruments have been devised and forceps are now mostly used only in the lower parts when the head is showing. They sometimes leave traces on the baby's cheeks which should disappear in a day or two.

Anaesthetics (general, spinal, and epidural) and analgesics often interfere with the mother's desire to push and this may account for the necessity of using forceps.

Forceps have been used in the delivery of babies for many centuries. They were invented by Guillaume Chamberlain in the seventeenth century. Chamberlain passed his invention on to his sons who kept it a well guarded family secret until the eighteenth century.

**Vacuum Extraction** is used for the same purpose as the forceps. But, instead of inserting instruments, suction and traction are applied via a metal cup on the head of the baby. It is a very unpleasant procedure for the mother, often quite traumatic, without any real advantages over forceps, and used only infrequently in the United States.

## CAESAREAN SECTION

Caesarean section is an obstetrical operation which delivers the infant through incisions in the abdominal and uterine walls. Legend has it that the name Caesarean came from a law passed by the Emperor Julius Caesar ordering the operation upon dying women during the last few weeks of pregnancy in the hopes of saving the child. In those days, in fact up until the sixteenth century, no woman was known to have survived the operation. Now, a Caesarean is a much safer operation, thanks to modern obstetrics, performed almost always with success.

There are various conditions which require a Caesarean. It is necessary for a difficult breech presentation (when the baby's position is unusual); when the pelvic bones are too narrow; if the uterine contractions are too weak; if the child is too large; when there is little progress in the dilatation over a long period of time, or in the case of preeclampsia.

Once the need for the operation has been established by the obstetrician, the mother undergoes a general anaesthesia. If she feels strong enough, she can ask to have only spinal anaesthesia.

## ACUPUNCTURE

For women who cannot tolerate and/or have a dangerous reaction to the drugs necessary for a general anaesthesia, another possibility is slowly emerging and that is the centuries old art and science of acupuncture. This ancient Chinese method, dating back as far as 2500 B.C., is used for curing and for therapeutic anaesthesia. Specific areas of the body are treated by inserting very fine needles in some of the 365 defined spots situated on the skin surface along the meridians (channels) which are mapped out from head to toe. In ancient times, the needles were made of gold or silver but today they are made mainly from steel.

The insertion of needles have a stimulating or equalizing effect. They reestablish a harmonious balance within the nerves (or of yin and yang), according to the fundamental Chinese law of evolution and the eternal permutation of nature.

Lately, the practice of acupuncture has resurfaced with increasing intensity. Western doctors have a new found interest in its application for various operations and as an anaesthetic in various fields such as obstetrics.

In May of 1973, a thirty-year-old woman from Washington, D.C., gave birth to a healthy infant boy through Caesarean section using acupuncture as the only painkiller during the operation. She had had two previous Caesareans, which had left her feeling doped up for days from the anaesthetics. This time she didn't need a medicinal painkiller during and for two days after surgery. For acupuncture to succeed, there has to be an appreciation and proper attitude on the part of the patient. This Caesarean, performed by Dr. Oscar I. Dodek, Jr., with acupuncture administered by Dr. Shalom A. Albert, is believed to be the first one in the U.S.

In Europe, acupuncture has been performed by two anaesthetist-acupuncturists for three Caesarean operations. The French team of doctors was headed by Professor Roccia and Dr. Marcel Niboyet; the operation was performed once in Turin, Italy, and twice in Saint Joseph's Hospital in Marseille, France. In China, this method has been used extensively for thousands of deliveries. Acupuncture can also be used for normal deliveries to relax certain areas of the body.

Since western medicine guarantees safe results through anaesthetics and there have not been extensive studies done in the West concerning the advantages of acupuncture, the widespread general use of the procedure is not likely to occur very soon. However, this does not mean that the art of acupuncture should be regarded as remote or frightening. Acupuncture could become a precious tool, in the hands of specialists, to prevent pain for people who have adverse reactions to synthetic painkillers.

# possible complications during pregnancy

As children, one of the most fascinating things to do was to peek into the forbidden medical books high on the shelf in our parents' library. We read about all the weird diseases, getting quite frightened by the accompanying color photographs. Holding our breath, we would quickly close the book three or four pages later, feeling all those strange conditions creeping up on us all at once. It feels a little similar reading specialized medical books during pregnancy. Suddenly, the exceptions, the rare cases, almost become the rule. It is quite an absurd way of thinking if we bear in mind that 95% of all pregnancies in the United States terminate with normal birth.

To be prepared for the most common problems, we have outlined the possible complications of pregnancy: **Anemia - Toxemia (Preeclampsia, Edema) - Bleeding - Abortion - Infection - Rh Factor - Ectopic Pregnancy - Placenta Previa - Breech Presentation.** There are many in-depth books covering the medical explanations. For further information see the bibliography at the end of this book.

With your help, the doctor or midwife will be able to diagnose and treat these conditions early enough so that they will not be a problem at birth. However, a home birth is not recommended in cases of bleeding, toxemia, infection and placenta previa.

## ANEMIA

Anemia may develop during pregnancy in women who are not prone to the disease at other times in their lives. This is because of the additional volume of blood being circulated through the body and the increased demand of iron from the baby.

Anemia can be reversed simply by eating the right foods and taking iron tablets. If you are taking extra iron and are not really in an anemic state, your body will establish a block to stop the absorption, and the most inconvenience it can cause, if such is the case, is constipation.

## TOXEMIA

In the early days of obstetrics, toxemia was thought to be a condition caused by an intoxication running through the whole body. Hence, the name *toxemia* was given to the condition. It may occur after the 24th week of pregnancy (except in the cases of twins and abnormal developments). It is detected by three main symptoms: the blood pressure goes up, there are proteins in the urine, and there is an increase in the reflexes.

For a first pregnancy it is also called preeclampsia which, at its worst and in very rare cases, can turn into eclampsia or coma and result in death. The incidences of death have been greatly reduced in the last 15 years, but preeclampsia is still with us. It is common in first pregnancies that are unattended and unwanted, and for women with diabetes and heart disease.

What are the symptoms?

Rapid weight gain, accumulation of fluid.

## EDEMA

Puffiness around the eyes, swelling of the fingers and of the legs (especially upon arising in the morning, not after a long day of standing or walking, when such a manifestation of tiredness may show itself), are symptoms of edema. With these signs may come severe headaches, dizziness, epigastric pains, persistent nausea.

How do you avoid it?

Follow a healthy and varied diet, low in salt intake (limit to pinches of iodized salt), low in carbohydrates and free of carbonated beverages which have a high content of sodium, the fluid retentive mineral. If you eat enough proteins, you will need little salt. And remember that the desire for salt is increased if you are eating a lot of carbohydrates. Avoid eating too much. You may think you have to eat for two, but this is not true. Remember that the tiny little one inside of you is infinitely smaller than you are. Edema is still one of the causes of premature birth. If you suspect edema, get in touch with your doctor.

## BLEEDING

Bleeding during pregnancy has different meanings according to which term of pregnancy you are in when it occurs:

1.  First trimester bleeding is due to implantation (usually it is more like spotting) or to threatened abortion. A natural abortion or miscarriage (which is the rejection of the fetus by the body for a variety of causes) can be due to illness, shock, malformation, etc.

2.  Second trimester vaginal bleeding can also be caused by the rejection of the fetus due to blood problems.

3.  Third trimester bleeding is a more serious problem. It can mean the separation of the placenta before the onset of labor. This is something that happens in 1/85 to 1/200 pregnancies, known as abruptio placenta.

Bleeding may also be caused by toxemia. Usually the woman will go into labor prematurely. The real danger is to the baby, particularly if it is an internal hemorrage. It is characterized by sharp pains in the abdominal regions and should be reported to your doctor as soon as possible.

**Placenta Previa.** Another cause of bleeding in the last months may be due to the abnormal site of placental implantation. Instead of being anchored high in the uterus near the fundus, it lies low near the cervix or even worse, over it. Heavy spotting in the seventh month may be a warning. It could be followed by a hemorrhage of serious consequences.

**Ectopic Pregnancy** (first trimester). Another uncommon but less frequently discussed abnormality is the ectopic pregnancy. It is called this when the embryo implants itself somewhere other than in the uterus such as in a fallopian tube or in the abdominal cavity. It is difficult to detect in the first six weeks of what appears to be a normal pregnancy with all its regular symptoms. Vaginal bleeding may be the result of this ailment. Other symptoms include: rapid pulse, signs of fainting, piercing pains in the lower part of the abdomen and right shoulder pain. Consult with your doctor immediately as ectopic pregnancy usually requires prompt hospitalization and surgery.

**Detection and Prevention.** Today thermogram sonar wave tests are used to detect the position of the placenta. Also called the ultra-sound machine, it is used in the same way as an X-ray machine except that there is no risk involved. The pregnant woman's abdomen is rubbed with oil while she lies on her back. The machine's eye scans back and forth over the belly, monitoring sound waves from within and projecting them onto a tiny tv screen. These sound waves become a visual outline of the baby and the placenta within. This amazing machine can also register the size of the baby's head, the fetal heartbeat and can show if there is more than one baby within. It's an extra expenditure, of course, to be tested on the thermogram, but well worth it in cases of doubt. And, it's nothing to be afraid of as it's just a big machine that doesn't hurt the patient at all. It is recommended that the patient not have had an internal examination before the test.

# Rh FACTOR

Among the various tests conducted in early pregnancy, one is done to determine the Rh (rhesus) factor of the blood. If it is present, as a substance coating the blood cells, the blood is Rh Positive, which is the case for most people.

If both you and the father are Rh Negative none of your pregnancies will be affected. If his blood group is Rh Positive and yours is Rh Negative, it is possible that the baby will turn out to be an Rh Positive. In this case your system may develop antibodies against the foreign blood spilling over in the bloodstream. During the next pregnancy these now permanent antibodies would be present and would break down some of the unborn baby's red blood cells, causing anemia. It is the reason, very often, for jaundiced infants, as the tiny liver is not yet ready to handle all the required processing and filtering. There are also certain nuclei in the brain that get jaundice and are the cause of permanent brain damage.

With an Rh Positive mother, pregnancies will not be affected. If the mother is Rh Negative it will usually not cause any trouble in the first pregnancy. But, an injection of Rhogam medicine within seventy-two hours following the birth of an Rh Positive baby is given to protect an Rh Negative mother.

If you have had an Rh conflict in your last pregnancy and no Rhogam (gamma globulin) shot, an amniocentesis test can be performed during the new pregnancy to determine to what extent, if at all, the baby is affected. Sometimes labor may be induced as early as the thirty-fourth week of gestation if the fetus shows rapid anemic progression. A transfusion can be given to the baby while it is still in the womb. If the baby is born at term, a test is performed to find out its degree of anemia and, if needed, the baby's blood is exchanged with a donor's.

One Rhogam injection is also recommended in cases of pregnancy termination for the woman who is Rh Negative.

# INFECTION

Basically, infections are the same during pregnancy as at any other time. They used to be a major cause of death before delivery, but this is no longer true since the advent of antibiotics.

There is an infection of the kidneys which is common during pregnancy. It is located in the portion of the kidney where the urine is collected before it is excreted. Whether it is caused by pressure from the enlarged uterus or another reason, is not known. Besides the burning irritation when emptying the bladder, this infection may induce a premature birth.

**Phlebitis.** An inflamation of the veins, phlebitis, is also a possibility. Any repeated pains in the calves is a forewarning. It may mean a blood clot. Check with your doctor.

# labor

"*Fear is in some way the chief pain producing agent in otherwise normal labor*"– Grantly Dick-Read, M.D.

Many months of physical and mental transformation have taken place and now the much awaited baby is going to be born. Mysterious signals are being sent through your body and mind. Is this labor?

Scholars have debated for centuries over the correct interpretation of the Hebrew word in the Old Testament:

# בְּעֶצֶב - BE-ETZEV - IN SADNESS

from the fifteenth century adaptation of the King James version of the bible. Still being read today, the passage reads ". . . Woman shall give birth in sadness." That is our heritage perpetrated through the centuries. Thanks a lot to the men who wrote it! In fact, however, the actual translation of the word can also mean "hard work". Birth is certainly one of the most strenuous physical efforts a woman may have to do in her lifetime but then there are some people who get excitement and pleasure from hard work. This conflict between fact and legend makes it difficult to describe the period of time before the actual birth — termed labor — to a woman who is having her first child.

No two people experience labor in exactly the same way, with the same intensity or duration. However, for women who are venturing into the unknown and having their first baby, we are going to attempt to describe the baby's motions, the rites of passage, the birthday of the new being. For the woman having another child we hope to add new insights into this fascinating phase of life.

We deal with the progression of a normal, prepared delivery. It will be brief because the next chapter is a series of interviews with mothers and fathers describing personal experiences and perceptions about pregnancy, labor and birth.

How do we know when labor begins?

It becomes a silent haunting question from the middle of pregnancy. But, in truth, the start of labor cannot be missed.

Towards the end of the ninth month (or ten lunar months) there will probably be warning signs. Contractions will sometimes be felt as strong menstrual cramps. It is only when contractions occur at regular intervals, with the rest period in between gradually getting shorter, that one can be sure it is real labor.

There are other signs which do not necessarily happen in sequence. One of these is that the baby's head settles in the pelvis. The mother may feel she can breathe easier as the pressure of the diaphram is relieved as the baby moves down. Known as "lightening", this may happen weeks before D-Day. Also she may urinate more frequently since now the pres-

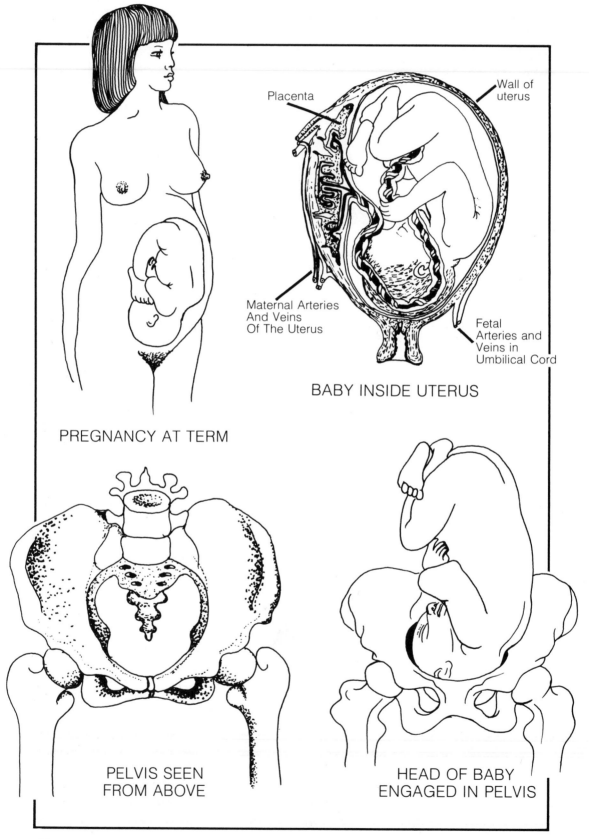

Placenta

Wall of uterus

Maternal Arteries And Veins Of The Uterus

Fetal Arteries and Veins in Umbilical Cord

BABY INSIDE UTERUS

PREGNANCY AT TERM

PELVIS SEEN FROM ABOVE

HEAD OF BABY ENGAGED IN PELVIS

sure is increased on the bladder. Another sign is an uncontrollable rapid flow of liquid from the vagina. This means the membrane of the sac surrounding the baby has ruptured and the amniotic fluid is running out. A late sign is "the show" or a thick mucous discharge tinged with blood from little broken vessels of the cervix as it begins to dilate.

It may take a few hours to a few days from "the show," or "bloody show," as it is sometimes termed, for rhythmic labor to start.

If you are having the baby at home, there is still plenty of time left to prepare a nest where you will give birth and to center your mind on what's happening to your body.

If you are going to have your baby in the hospital don't forget to take things that comfort you. Any of the following SUGGESTIONS may brighten up a sterile environment.

Smell: cologne, perfume, incense, flowers or dried petals.
Sight: images, statues, mobiles, colors.
Touch: colorful scarf, sweater, socks, body cream, smooth stone.
Entertainments for the labor room and the days following birth: illustrated books, cards, notebooks, markers, small tape recorder and music cassettes or a small radio with earphones.

FOR THE BABY (they can always be brought by someone later):
Infant cotton tee shirt, receiving blankets, soft and light blanket (preferably wool or brushed cotton) or a tightly knit shawl. Bonnet, sweater, slippers, almond oil.

## RHYTHMS

During labor the body has a rhythm all its own. The woman and infant should dance along with it rather than resist. It is more powerful than painful. Birth is a different kind of sexual act, also done through the vagina. Oxytocin, the hormone released in the act of lovemaking, is also secreted while giving birth and nursing. The mind should direct the body so that it doesn't get tense when birth-pangs occur. It can really be fascinating to witness one's own body being taken over by BIRTH-FORCE. It is another dimension of sensations. Faced without fears, birth can be one of the highest moments in a woman's life. If you need warmth, reassurance, or feel out of sorts, don't feel shy about cuddling with your companion, husband or a friend.

When a pattern is established with regular contractions every ten minutes, the first stage of labor has begun. It is time to call the doctor or midwife and let them know.

Upon arrival at the hospital, you will be directed to the preparation room after having registered at the admission desk. The mother and father will be comfortable now if they have previously visited the hospital and are familiar with the building and the procedures.

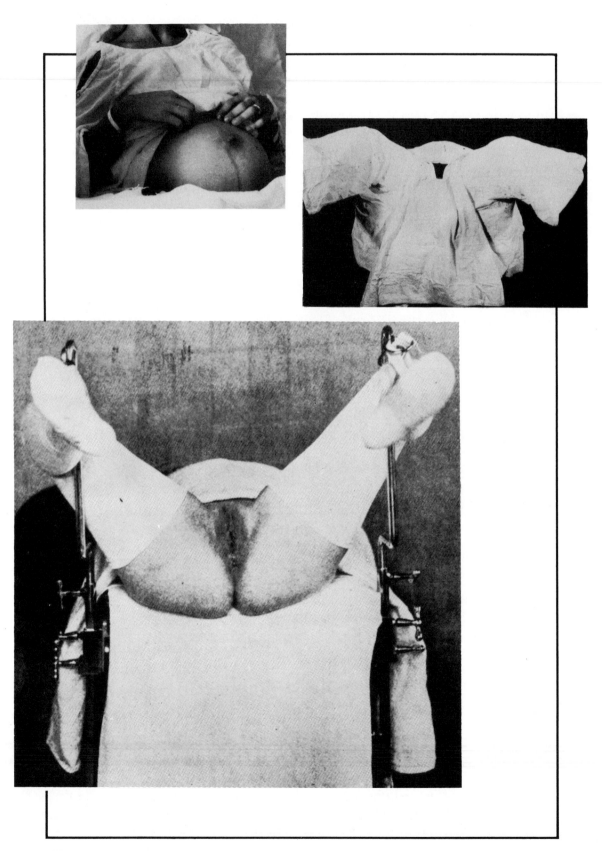

The medical staff will make a chart, noticing the mother's temperature, pulse, blood pressure and the fetal heart rate. The frequency of the contractions will be timed and a vaginal examination will be given. The routine varies with each establishment, but it is usually part of the preparation to shave and clean the pubic area and to give an enema. These are unpleasant procedures but they do not hurt if done early in labor. Some hospitals are eliminating the shaving. In home birth, most women do not have their pubic hair shaven as they find it unnecessary. However, the area is kept very clean. Also, enemas are not usually given in home births unless the woman is constipated. In most instances the body will empty itself during the course of labor. The pregnant woman is then taken to the labor room.

The contractions come and go . . . . . Breathe deeply . . . . . Walk around or rest . . . . . Empty your bladder and bowels . . . . . Doodle or doze in between contractions . . . . . You may have hot flushes with perspiration. Ask for quietude or retreat to a calm area if too much is happening around you and you feel the need to concentrate.

The first stage of labor lasts from four to twelve hours. It varies with each person.

The cervix passage has been closed tight for nine months holding the child in the uterus. It will take a great deal of uterine contraction to open it up completely. The cervix flattens, stretches, begins to dilate (5 cm ). The contractions are short. In early labor, they are often felt from low down in the back, slowly gaining ground through the body to the abdominal area. The rhythm gets tighter over the hours. By late labor, each contraction lasts 45 seconds with an interval of three to five minutes in between.

No straining or pushing . . . . No hanging on to a clock for the exact timing . . . . . Let your body be guided by its own rhythm and by your intuition . . . . . Mother strength . . . . . Have confidence in yourself and trust the natural flow . . . . . Let it happen . . . . . Breathe slowly and deeply.

**Deep Breathing** (see pg. 38). The contractions can hurt if you tense up. They become pains if you forget that most of the time your mind can cooperate with your body. It's an intense sensation to bring forth a child. Keep your mind on it. Calmness can help the muscles to relax. Lie down the way it feels best. Many women feel constricted by the narrow beds in the hospital labor room and say they should have brought along their own thin foam rubber exercise mattress to be able to sit or lie on the floor and have more room to move and stretch. Focus your eyes on an image inside or outside your head.

Along the way the contractions have become longer and sharper, each lasting 45 seconds or longer with an interval of two or three minutes in between. The rhythm is not always that regular, it does not follow the hands of a watch. The contractions may even appear to override each

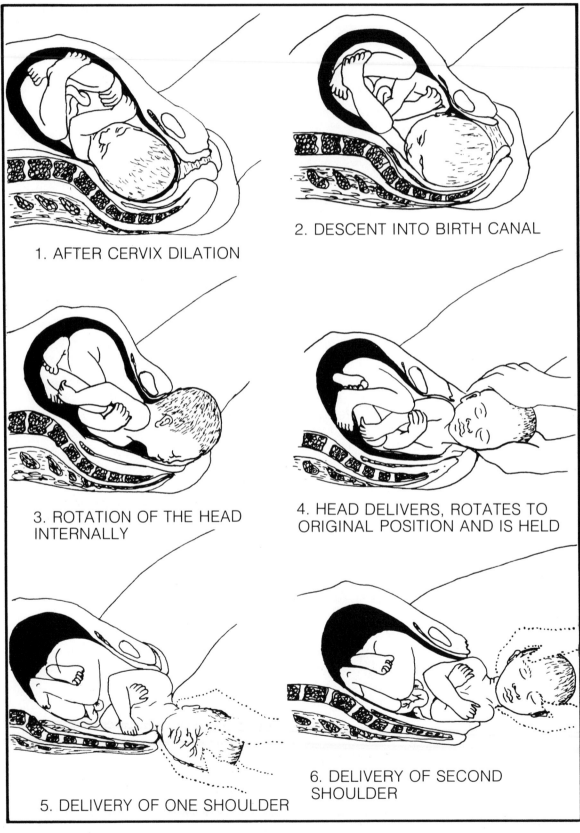

1. AFTER CERVIX DILATION

2. DESCENT INTO BIRTH CANAL

3. ROTATION OF THE HEAD INTERNALLY

4. HEAD DELIVERS, ROTATES TO ORIGINAL POSITION AND IS HELD

5. DELIVERY OF ONE SHOULDER

6. DELIVERY OF SECOND SHOULDER

other and breathing has to be adjusted accordingly. If the membranes have not ruptured yet, it may well happen at this stage. By now the cervix is about eight centimeters dilated and the baby's head is pushing through. The head could have become engaged a few weeks ago or it can happen after full dilatation. The intensity of the rumble as the head comes through the cervix can be overwhelming.

It may leave you a little shaky. In the hospital, medicine will be offered time and again; we have noted the benefits and drawbacks. Take it or leave it.

The end of the first stage is quite an effort. You may be perspiring and shivering at the same time. It may even feel as if imaginary plugs have been pulled out of your body. The nose and the eyes may run. Some women vomit and others spend a lot of time on the toilet. It feels like a thunderstorm. It's draining but interesting to observe. As the contractions become more powerful it can get uncomfortable. Relieve your abdomen of the pressure with the breathing method you have learned or try shallow breathing.

**Shallow Breathing** (see page 39). Rest when the contraction is over. You probably will not feel like talking. Make yourself as comfortable as possible. Tuck pillows here and there. Wipe yourself cool with a wet handkerchief. If your mouth gets dry, suck on a wet cloth, sponge or ice chips. Kneel on all fours if it helps. Women from the Santa Cruz birth center in California have had wonderful experiences giving birth that way. Try a squatting position for a while. Don't feel inhibited . . . leave that for another day.

Your companion could massage your back if it's pulling. Tell him/her where to apply the hands. He/she can help make the passage smoother.

In the hospital the father, coach or a friend can be in the labor room with you, but not all hospitals allow another person in the delivery room. Find out beforehand the rules and regulations of the establishment.

The baby's head is advancing through the tight pelvic bones. There is a certain resistance and the little head flexes, the chin touches the chest. As the head passes through the bones, it rotates a bit to accommodate the oblong shape of the pelvis and straightens up afterwards. The baby is in a transition stage between the uterus and the outside world. It is making its way through the vagina to the perineum. The first phase of labor has ended with full dilatation.

After being examined you are wheeled to the delivery room. In your home environment you are probably finding the most suitable position. If you are lying down, have your back propped up, either held by your husband or with big cushions. It is considerably more difficult to give birth lying flat on your back. The doctor will examine you to see how tight the skin is around the perineum, and to establish the need for an episiotomy. You strain and feel the need to push. Sometimes, instead of breathing,

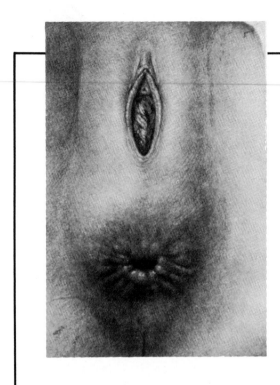

(LEFT) TOP OF HEAD BEGINNING TO SHOW AT VULVA

(CENTER)HEAD OF BABY CROWNING

(BELOW) DELIVERY OF BABY'S HEAD AFTER EXTERNAL ROTATION

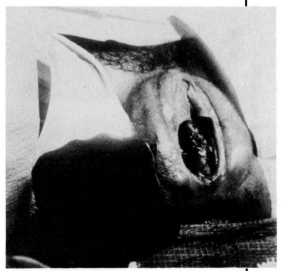

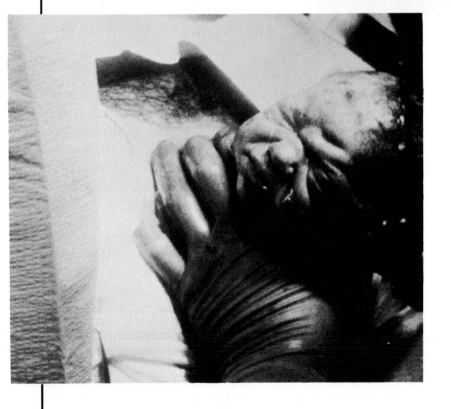

voice expression, chanting, singing, sounds not necessarily words can be really satisfying. However, shallow or pant breathing relieves the pressure best in the long run.

The second stage of labor is beginning. It lasts about 50 minutes and should not exceed 2 hours. The baby's head begins to appear through the vulvar opening as it is pushed out by each successive contraction. When the contraction is over, the vulva closes a little and the head recedes less and less. The same process recurs, stretching the expanded vaginal muscles a little more with each new push. The skin becomes very taut, forming a mound around the shape of the head. When the vulva has encircled the largest diameter of the fetal head, it is known as "crowning".

A calmer period follows after this storm, and you can gather up your strength. At this point you probably feel tired but elated, finding the whole procedure weird. It's been quite a journey and there is still some way to go. The urge to push the baby out is strongly felt. When the contraction comes, you will breathe deeply and hold the last in-breath while bearing down. With all your strength, you grab your knees or the straps on the side of the table and press your feet on the leg holder.

The fetal heartbeat will be listened to in order to verify its regularity. During the second stage women often have cramps in the legs and feet due to alteration in the blood circulation. If it happens to you, move your legs around, ask a friend or the nurse to massage the area, strongly, for relief.

As the baby's head pushes on the perineum, concentrate on that area, remember the Kegel exercise and then try to relax those muscles. As the head struggles to emerge, the doctor may perform an episiotomy (a small incision of the perineum which will later be sewn up). The episiotomy prevents tearing which would cause a ragged edge, very hard to sew together. The head is held in place and you may be asked to stop pushing just as the baby is ready to come out. This is to prevent the head from bursting out. PANT BREATHE in a fast manner; it will help to stop the pushing urge. Later, the labia separate and the head of the baby is born with its eyes and nose facing downward.

There is a slow external rotation of the head towards the thigh. The doctor holds the baby. The next contraction helps deliver the shoulders gently, and the rest of the body slides out, tugging along with it the umbilical cord. The baby gives a good cry. Mucus is drawn out of the nose and mouth if necessary and a drop of silver nitrate is put into each eye in order to prevent gonorrheal infection of the eyes which may have been picked up during the passage through the birth canal. She/he is still attached to the uterus and the placenta. When the blood has stopped pulsating through the cord, it is clamped or tied in two places, one close to the baby's abdomen and the other a little bit further up. It is severed with a sterile surgical scissors in between the two knots.

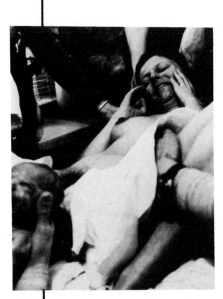

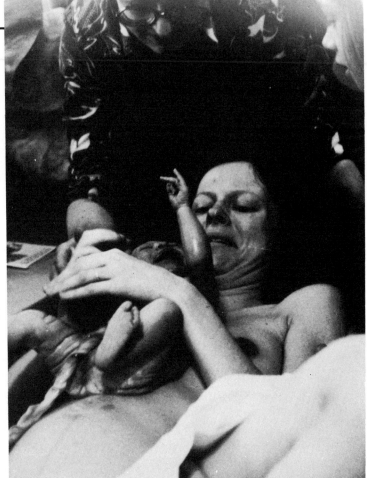

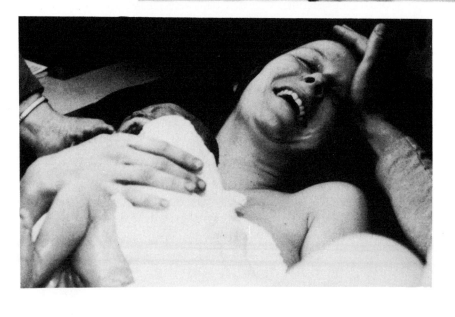

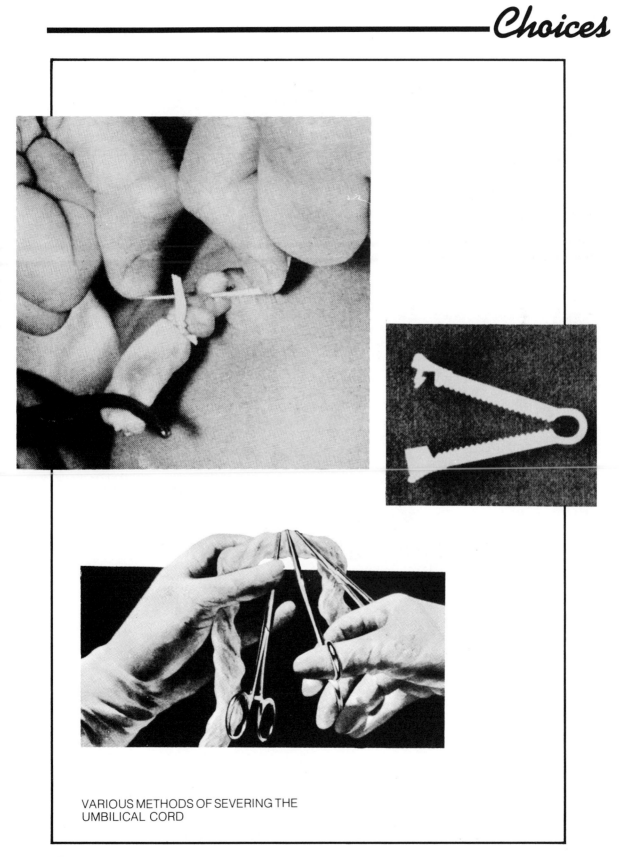

VARIOUS METHODS OF SEVERING THE
UMBILICAL CORD

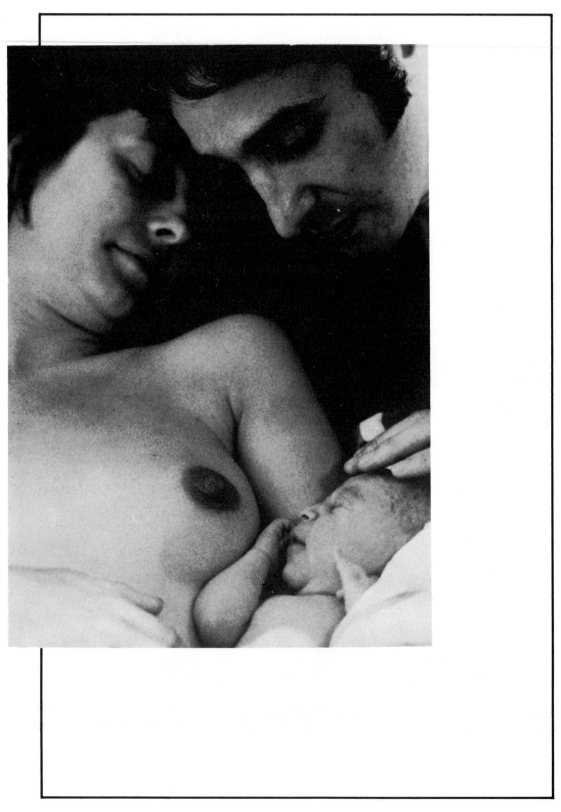

This is truly the most incredible moment! Suddenly, you see the person you have been carrying within you all this time. It is more than a surprise, it's a shock to find that there really is a new individual in the room and in your arms!!!

There is a tremendous feeling of boundless power in giving birth, but also of entire helplessness when you realize that without the father, midwife, doctor and friends, this moment of life could have been very different.

The child is born! There remains the placenta to be delivered which is the third stage of labor. Spontaneous mild contractions will bring out the remainder of the cord. The placenta is attached to the cord. No tugging or pulling. Most of the time, the placenta will slip out easily, anywhere from five to thirty minutes after the birth. The doctor will make sure that it is all in one piece as there should not be any part of it left within the uterus. Once the placenta is delivered, labor is over. If there has been an episiotomy, it is then sewn up.

This last stage requires minimal effort on your part: patience and pushing when the contractions come along, resting in between. There will be some bleeding from the rupture of the blood vessels as the placenta separates from the uterus. You may have held the little baby from the minute the shoulder was out or the baby may be given to you now. If the infant has a desire to suck from your breast, all the better as she/he will take in some of the colostrum. The milk will not come through yet, it takes a day or two, maybe three. The colostrum contains antibodies, vitamins and proteins that are meant for the newborn and can only be beneficial.

In the hospital, the infant gets cleaned, weighed, measured and foot printed. Its reflexes are tested and an identification bracelet is put around its wrist. After the father, mother and baby have gotten acquainted and rejoiced, the baby is taken to the nursery for the next eight hours so that the mother can rest. It can be frustrating if the mother doesn't really feel tired. However, if the hospital has a rooming-in system, the baby can be with the mother all the time. The mother will be wheeled or walked back to her room and can lie back.

At home the baby is cleansed, but often the vernix, the buttery substance covering parts of the skin, is not removed. Instead, it is spread around the tiny little body with the hands. The vernix sinks into the skin within the next twenty-four hours. It is believed to guard the skin against heat loss. The navel is well covered, the body is warmly wrapped and diapered. If the newborn cries hard a little warm water in a teaspoon may soothe. The crying may stop as soon as she/he is lying on the mother's abdomen, close to the beat of the heart, a familiar fetus-days sound. Once asleep, the baby can be gently moved if you want to change position or get up. The infant will rest best in an area where the light is not bright. The mother may do likewise. Rest. Take a shower with someone's help, have a light meal or just celebrate and rejoice.

# possible complications at birth

## PREMATURE LABOR

The fetus can be expelled by the body at any time during pregnancy. If expelled before the embryo reaches one pound (500 grams) it is considered a miscarriage. By the time it weighs three pounds, it is already a premature infant. Born with a weight over five and a half pounds, it is considered a full term baby. Most of the time the exact cause of prematurity is not known. In certain cases it can be traced to toxemia infection, twins, or the separation of the placenta. The administration of analgesic drugs in such premature labor is restricted as much as possible in order to give the infant the maximum chance for survival. The two days following the birth will determine the development. If the infant survives the first week, chances are good that he/she will be strong enough to carry on. Premature babies always have to be kept under special observation until they reach their full maturity potential.

## FALSE AND SLOW LABOR

Sometimes it appears as if labor is starting; there are contractions here and there, odd sensations in the back and lower abdomen. If they do not recur at regular intervals it is probably only a prelude for the real labor which will come in a few days or possibly weeks. If these sensations continue over a period of a day or more, it may be a case of slow labor due to the weakness of uterine contractions. If the labor is progressing, all that is needed is a lot of patience; but, if nothing much is happening, the doctor may recommend drip-infusion of Pitocin to stimulate the strength and regularity of the contractions. Another cause for slow labor might be the disproportion in size between the mother's pelvis (either an odd shape or a small diameter) and the baby's head. If the head is large, it can take quite some time to go through the birth canal. In extreme cases of incompetent contractions or halt in the descent of the head, a Caesarean section may have to be performed before any maternal or fetal complications set in.

## BREECH PRESENTATION

Another birth complication, called breech presentation, occurs if the baby's head does not come out before the rest of its body. For every one hundred deliveries, about three present with the bottom or the feet first. If the pelvis is wide enough to accommodate then there should be no problem, but the baby may have to be helped out.

If the doctor notices a breech presentation in the last month's examination she/he may attempt to externally manipulate the baby in order to turn it around. Often, however, the head has moved back up right before delivery. Further tests can be carried out to determine the size of the pelvis and the possible need for a Caesarean if the bone spacing cannot allow passage. If this situation is diagnosed, the baby should not be born at home.

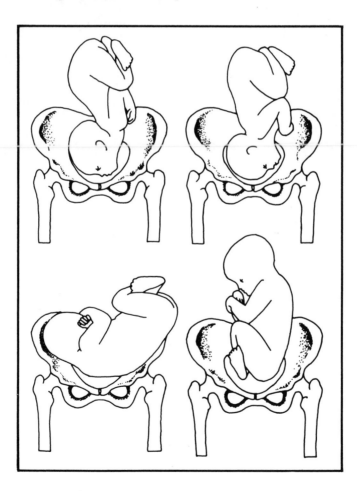

# 4

# birth experi- ences

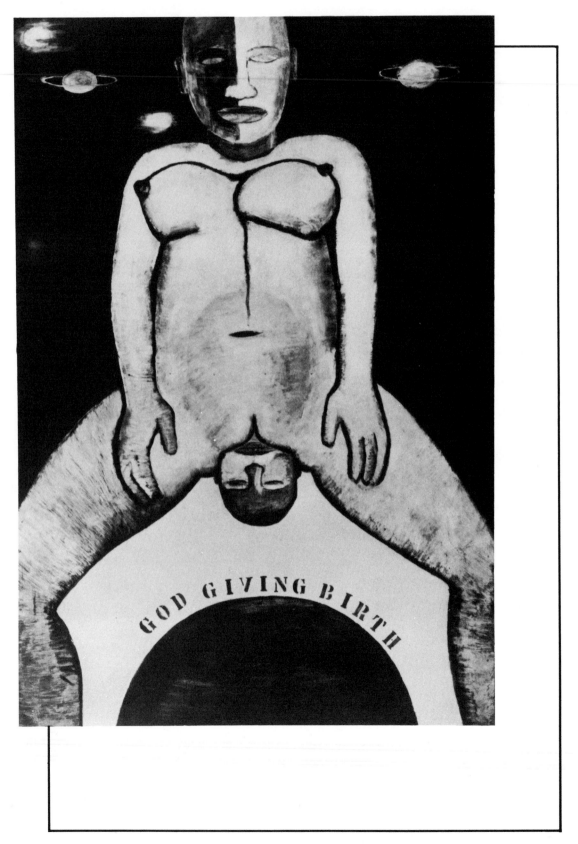

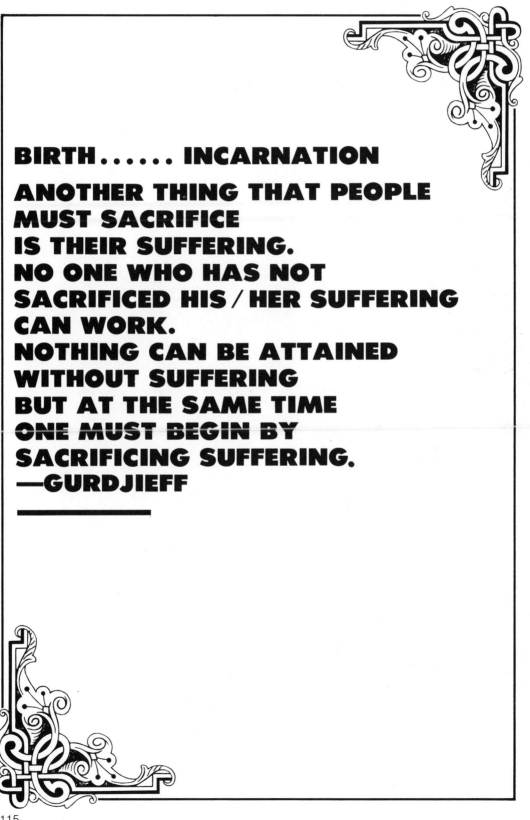

BIRTH......INCARNATION

ANOTHER THING THAT PEOPLE
MUST SACRIFICE
IS THEIR SUFFERING.
NO ONE WHO HAS NOT
SACRIFICED HIS / HER SUFFERING
CAN WORK.
NOTHING CAN BE ATTAINED
WITHOUT SUFFERING
BUT AT THE SAME TIME
ONE MUST BEGIN BY
SACRIFICING SUFFERING.
—GURDJIEFF

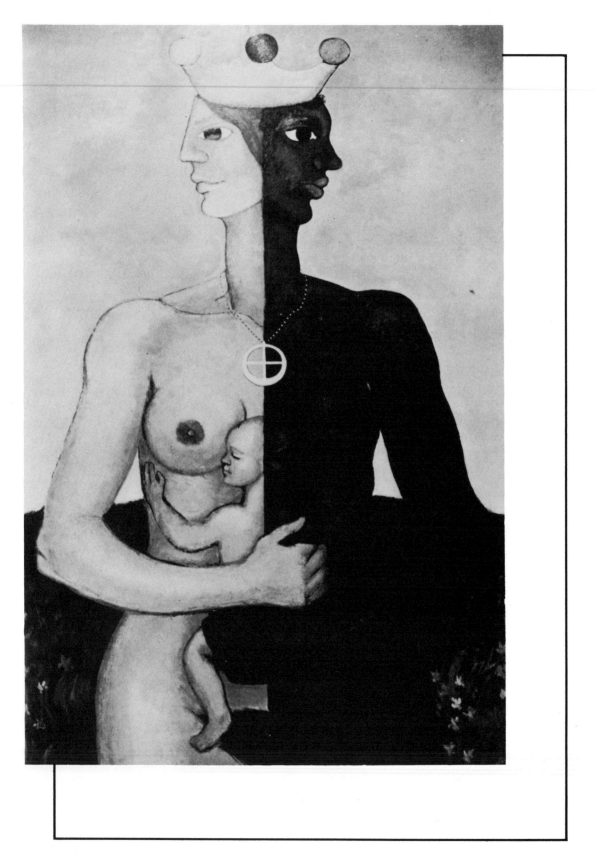

**t**his chapter is a collection of birth stories as told by the mothers and fathers of newborn infants, in the form of conversations, interviews, poems, and letters. They tell which methods they chose for delivery and why, about their expectations, the development of labor, the description of birth events, their moments of disappointments, joys and surprises.

Contributors to this chapter are:

Deedee Brigewater: New York, Prepared breathing, Hospital.
Caterine Milinaire: New Mexico, Prepared childbirth, Home.
Les Structures Elémentaires de la Parente.
Camilla Hoover: New York, Induced labor, Hospital.
Jill Williamson: New York, Prepared childbirth with complications, Hospital.
Joel Block: Switzerland, Assisted in wife's delivery, Hospital.
The Story of Kelly.
Lisa Law: New Mexico, Prepared childbirth, Home.
Joan Weiner: New York, Prepared childbirth, Stillborn, Home.
Iara Scudera: New York, Prenatal courses, Caesarean, Hospital.
Brigitte Mars: Missouri, Self-taught preparation, Home.
Lilian Bron: England, Hypnosis, Hospital.
Barbara Margetts: England, Prepared childbirth, Home and Hospital.
Maxime De La Falaise McKendry: England, Prepared childbirth, Home.
Minium Cayemite: Haiti, Yoga professor who assisted delivery of his nine children, Home.
Zilina Luc: Haiti, As it comes, Childbirth in the fields.
Gladys St. Louis: Haiti, Yoga exercises and breathing, Hospital.
Ann Simon: Ohio, A Personal View of Nurse-Midwifery.
Barbara Johns: New York, Breathing and exercise course, Hospital.
Frederick Le Boyer: Paris, Welcoming the Newborn.

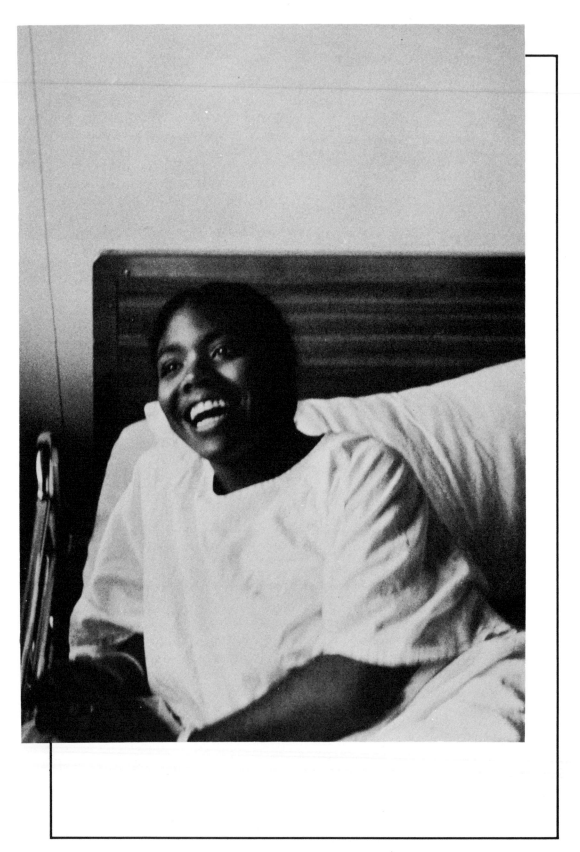

# DEEDEE BRIGEWATER
# A Singing Birth

**Caterine:** When did you have your baby?

**Deedee:** Tulani, a girl, was born at 7:43 yesterday morning.

**C:** When did labor start?

**D:** The day before, at 3:00 in the afternoon, but it had started very gently in the morning around 8:00. But the last two hours before birth needed sheer hard concentration to stay on top of the contractions.

**C:** What sort of preparation did you follow before giving birth?

**D:** I went to prenatal classes. In a way, I feel I was not prepared enough or told enough about the enormous physical strength required to bring your child about in this world in the natural way. It's definitely the most colossal physical effort a woman will come across at one single moment during her lifetime. I kept on thinking, "Will I have enough strength to complete natural childbirth without drugs? Because I really want to see this baby, awake, from the first moment the head is out." I really concentrated on what was happening without panic and I knew that everything would be all right.

**C:** Was the father of the child with you?

**D:** No, Cecil is a musician and he was on tour. He arrived today and, let me tell you, I was only half myself during this birth episode. The father's presence is essential when it comes to emotional support. I know I would have been more relaxed had he been there, and also the energy circulated between him and me and the baby would have smoothed out a lot of tension. You see, in that hospital where I went I was placed in the labor room with another woman who was screaming and obviously did not know how to channel her fears. So it's kind of hard on you to hear these screams when you know you can avoid it and concentrate on breathing instead. My breathing turned to singing and that seemed to help us both.

It was a good thing I braided my hair before going to the hospital, I kept on having this compulsion to pull on it. It feels good to pull, squash, hug something, better someone . . . and I am sure it's meant to be the father of the child. You know, counter-strength . . . the alchemic vases . . . the strong partnership all the way.

**C:** What do you remember most about your visual surroundings as you were going through labor?

**D:** Blank walls, nurses, blank walls, blank ceiling! It was a very limited visual journey. It would be so great if they had flowers around and patterns on the ceilings and designs on the walls. It would be good to have a choice of either a blank room or a room like our world, you know, filled with images.

**C:** How was the delivery?

**D:** I followed the doctor's instructions. I concentrated hard because pushing the head out is really a big effort but it felt good. I was given an

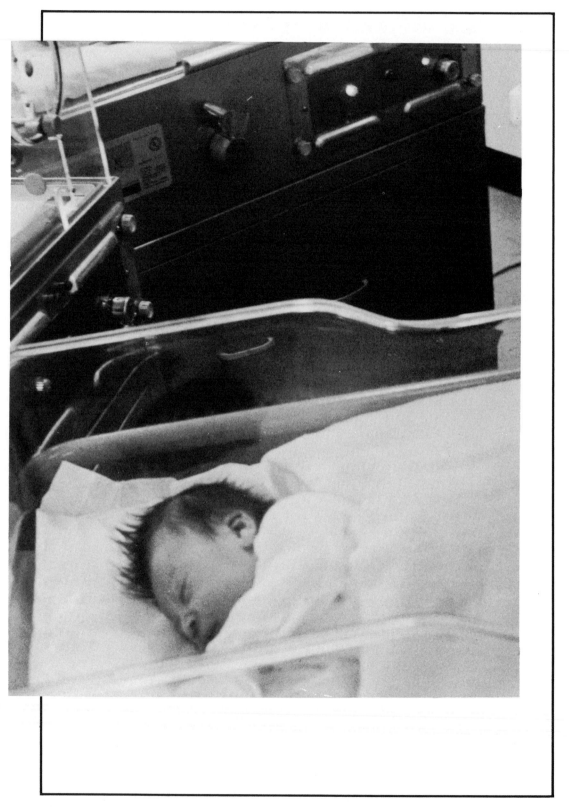

episiotomy. After the baby's head slipped out, it was sheer relief. And to see a baby being born from me was the most incredible event of my life! And then I got to hold the baby, but only for two minutes and it was taken away and only given to me today. That's a drag. The baby was taken to the nursery which is located directly across from the abortion rooms at Hillcrest General Hospital in Flushing, Queens. How much more insensitive can hospital planning get?

My next child I want to have at home with all my family there. I felt like cuddling up with my baby and was left exhilarated but in tears and frustrated from not being able to get to know my own child straight away. I know it's being done for your own good and rest, but two minutes after nine months of waiting is absurd.

**C:** Are there any special discoveries that you would like to tell a sister or remember particularly about giving birth?

**D:** The miraculous moment was when I started singing as a continuation of the breathing. I sing to earn my living and I sang to bring about this baby like I have never sung before. Imagine a labor room with singing women, what a chorus it would be! Singing was a great outlet for my emotions during pregnancy and at birth. It took the place of self-pity. So, when you are in doubt, keep on singing.

Photo by Irving Penn

# CATERINE MILINAIRE
## Home Birth*

*"May the magic of our baby's birth keep the smile eternally shining within us and around us."*

What a strange fate humans have inflicted upon themselves: the fear of birth and the wish to be desensitized before witnessing the incredible bodyquake happening.

If one has been so traumatized through youth as to think childbirth is a painful experience, nature has provided nine full months of preparation. Time to think deeply about the new life. It's not too long. Time to adjust to body changes, time to breathe and stretch, time to get into healthy nutrition, time to erase antiquated concepts and figure out a personal code through intuition and common sense.

A NEW LIFE IS COMING. Children don't need us; we need them more than they need us. A child, the irresistible magic gift, the real bond, the total blend of two souls. The zero population growth movement is making us desperately aware of earth's critical overpopulation threat. It's time, more than ever, to be fully conscious of every phase of childing: conception in total ecstasy, pregnancy wished by both parents and carried through with thoughtful health care and the climax is birth! Birth is the greatest feast of joy, to be shared and helped with celebration by anyone who wishes to participate.

A slow evolution occurred in my mind from the time I decided to have a child until the sixth month of pregnancy. The more I went to see doctors and looked over hospitals, the more I became convinced that a home should be the place where the baby would be born. It became an obsession.

New York couldn't be the place. No air, no space, no peace, no rest. New York is a great playground but never a nest.

One day a friend talked about sunny Santa Fé in New Mexico. The same day another friend passed by telling us about the beautiful adobe house he bought in Santa Fé and about another one which was for rent. Everything began to fit. Oxygen for the baby, quiet rest, more time to be together in this sweet life meant to be enjoyed.

Once in Santa Fé I called the ASPO (American Society for Psychoprophylaxis in Obstetrics) who recommended two doctors. The first one I telephoned turned out to be extremely kind and calm. He and I convinced Mati, the baby's father, of the positiveness of home delivery. This new baby won't need liberating. It will be born free.

THE NINTH MONTH. Everyone is so impatient. The house is full of friends. Every day there is a new invention to induce the baby to show up. Syncopated chants, walks to the top of the mountain, painting the crib with

good prospect symbols, long mineral baths at warm springs under the falling snow, drinking raw milk, reading the police emergency childbirth manual.

I am in no rush. I walk around proudly, tuning in to that other life moving along with mine. I laugh when we both feel so good I can run, dance and swim, knowing that the baby is enjoying all this from inside.

In the middle of the night the baby pressures me to get up, move around and get rid of the liquid squashing it. As if it were a TEACHER OF LIFE, the baby tells me: "Enough routine, get rid of your time habits, sleep at different hours, hear the night, see the dawn, feel yourself grow with me." I sleepwalk and sleeptalk with my baby.

Looking at me, self-declared fortune tellers announce without hesitation — a boy. Tarot card experts draw out "Male." And, when I am asked for a preference, "A boy? A girl?" I honestly don't care! Often at the end of my daily breathing exercises I would try very hard to center on sensing the sex of the baby but nothing was revealed. Instead, I would go off into the flames of the fire I had lit or the clouds behind the window. During the seventh month I had a dream of giving birth to a girl. She was lying next to me, a newborn. The next dream image was her at seven playing with angel Eleonore. Then she was my age, a twin sister sitting on a cloud. Last image was a mother figure, fading, while I was still in my 1971 present state, experiencing my daughter for the flash of half a century.

I AM READY — NO PANIC. I know the baby has to come out and will do so in its own time. Curious? Yes, extremely since I really can't figure out what the coming forth of this new life will do to me. Friends, experts, books, films, nothing is descriptive enough. It's *the* personal mind-body experience. Apprehension? No, I know it must be a joyous event, otherwise why would women keep on having more than one child? The Morrocan woman who mixed the henna for my hair last summer had thirteen children all around her and all were born at home. She was shining health and strength.

When is delivery day going to surprise me? One night on the road from Taos back to Santa Fé my body starts shaking, rumbles of an internal storm at the same moment that the car stalls, in the middle of a mountain climb. I lie down on the back seat preparing to have the baby in the car. Three or four contractions over the last half hour. The body was only tuning up.

A week later. I went to bed late, fluids start running down my legs, a little, no more. I fall asleep but awake in the middle of the night. A dream? Reality? Am I swimming in a warm pool? The rest of the liquid has been expulsed. Mild muscle contractions. A pull-let go motion. Of course nothing the way I had imagined. I feel an incredible urge to empty my body of all waste material; to be completely alone and figure out the strange spasms overtaking, with strength, my insides. Even though I had not planned consciously to confine myself, I lock myself in the bathroom. Everything was ready, at hand's reach, for the easiest development possible. The

mandala Mati painted for me to focus on while out-breathing the contractions (Mati is a painter of intricate dreamscapes); a candle (it was still dark
and I felt the bathroom light would be too bright); my favorite purple cotton
t-shirt; two pillows and a foam mattress covered with batik.

As I am quickly gathering all of these essentials, Mati wakes up,
moaning something about picking another night. He is tired and not ready
for birth labor. My head is dazed but my body feels very strong. "Mati,
please sleep. I don't need any help yet."

It's odd. I know it must be "the day" and I can't help feeling it's all a
dream. Is it time already? So suddenly? Contractions come like waves,
sometimes a gentle roll and at other times an enormous rush of energy
bursting at the body's boundaries. The vibrant colors of Mati's painting in
front of me open up into rotating depth dimensions in space. Doors of a
mental-physical harmonious team, letting through a new force. Brightness
forever on the baby's consciousness!

As I try to breathe the way I was taught, in the psychoprophylactic
method, I slowly discover my own rhythm with each contraction: deeper,
slower, inhaling and exhaling. In between I doze off, resting, dreaming,
shaking loose.

THE DEEP SPRING CLEANING OF MY BODY IS OVER. Rid of food
and liquid through every body orifice. As after an extended fast, there is a
great feeling of lightness and I know instinctively nothing will be in the way
at birth time. Once again the natural body processing proves to take care of
itself, with the benefit of faith.

Between deep breaths, I draw a hot bath, sending sandlewood fumes
over the whole house. Doors are opening, hush, murmurs, dawn is on,
daylight brings relief of night's dark corners. Brightness everywhere on a
birthday. Little knocks on the bathroom door. My friend Barbara with an
offering of camomile tea and Mati softly smiling, coming to hold my hand.
They want to call the doctor. I think it's too early. They telephone him
anyway. Mati is massaging my back. I don't have to tell him where, he
senses it. Hand strokes, riding over inside tensions with their strength and
warmth. The doctor, gentle and friendly, steps into the bathroom. "How is
it?" "Good, crazy, shaky, incredible!"

The baby is slowly entering the labyrinth. The bathroom is getting too
small. It's cool in the house. I put on the purple cotton t-shirt barely covering
my bottom (perfect for delivery) and it is loose and smooth against the skin.
So important, the feel and touch of familiar clothes, if there have to be any
during a major body mutation. In the large room I have to walk through, on
the way to the bedroom, the friends, Barbara, Reno, Michael, Ramona and
the doctor are all sitting close around the big table, speaking low. The
preparation is over, I feel the baby coming.

BIRTH — WHAT A CEREMONY. I probably would have turned pale
grey, having the baby at home in New York; but here in the space and

clearness of Santa Fé it is a joyous feast. Encouraging friends all around, completely in tune with each of my explosions. They are coming quickly now. I am either sitting or kneeling on the bed which is a mattress on the floor. Mati grips me, vibrating, shaking the baby out from the back. Like a chant, my voice turns to music, inhaling, breathing out faster, to a pitch. Sounds of birth-raga. Barbara sits beside me, breathing to a concentrated rhythm, bringing me back to it whenever I go too fast. Michael is taking photographs, Ramona is holding Noah (Barbara's baby). I ask Reno to get the movie camera and the gun light. With one hand the doctor's wife fixes his sterilized mask and with the other holds her own baby. The doctor is sitting on the floor and I am opposite him at the edge of the bed, held tight by Mati's legs. The rumble inside me is so strong, I jump up a few times and start walking out of the door; not pain, but bursts of emotion. Incredibly intense sensation of the body being turned inside out. How sweet to see warm, friendly, surprised faces and colors all around the room rather than starched hospital white. Instead of anaesthetics: music, sun and air. Instead of nurses: friends who have experienced a similar adventure. Barbara (twenty years old) who also had her baby at home three months ago, has tears in her eyes.

ALL INHIBITIONS ABOUT MY BODY ARE GONE. There is no shame, only an overwhelming openness. Being totally at ease with myself, becoming easy, as never before. I ask the doctor if I can put my feet up on his shoulders. How he was able to perform this way remains a mystery.

"Hold it, hold it, hold . . . Okay, now push that little baby out of you!"

Pushing, laughing, puffing, waiting, panting, squashing and pulling on Mati's hands with unknown force. My whole being impatiently expels the new life.

10:54 A.M. THE SUN IS FLOWING INSIDE THE BEDROOM, BLASTING WITH VITAL RAYS A NEW HEAD. Push . . . episiotomy incision with my consent. Totally painless, the perineum is numbed by the baby's pressure. Push . . . the top of the head is out to the mouth and already screams. A reality sound, voice rendering concrete a long-awaited child. What a blessing to be a woman! What a magical gift! I cannot remember a more extraordinary burst of happiness in my life. Rapidly, the rest of the tiny body slips out. Alive in front of us, a long and thin little person, moonstone color, kicking and yelling, still circuited to me by a pale blue umbilical cord. Thank you!

"How is it?"

"Good, forceful, supernatural!"

After removing the mucus from the baby's mouth and nose, David, the doctor, places the child on my stomach; still covered with vernix and sucking on my breast avidly. He then asks Mati to cut the cord.

"Please do it David," I ask. I have visions of falling into bottomless depth if Mati moves one inch away from me. One more push, the placenta,

like a glorious piece of food, exists in one large mound. Reno, after filming every moment of the actual birth, takes the placenta to bury it in the garden, planting a tree on top of it. Local anaesthetic injection. Three stitches.

Mati, totally exhilarated, still holding me from the back, asks after a while: "What sex is it?" I had completely forgotten to look. "A girl!" He beams, Mati loves to be surrounded by women.

David tells me to get up. I glide around the house with Baby Serafine in my arms. I can see my smile reflected on everyone. It goes from head to toe. They are wordless but not soundless. Wows and phews. Tears and laughter. We have all witnessed the most real and sacred of ceremonies — the rites of life.

I HAVE WHAT I HAVE GIVEN.

It's time we realize we don't have to perpetuate the fears and rules of our ancestors. Time for the individual to open up and be as it goes: lifefully.

# LES STRUCTURES ELEMENTAIRES DE LA PARENTE

Spread her legs, showing
Scenic, piscean, piñon-sided thighs
Near a mouth of the wilderness
at the lip of a watershed

In between: little holy faith creek coming down the cañon.

Grandmother water and her daughter Acequia Madre
Cloaca Mater and her mother
offering a tributary and a good example

I lived on fat hill
They lived across the canyon on Mother Ditch street
In between: the same red finches, blue jays
        the same black raven

Who is she to me?
What's our relation celebrating here?
We been on this road before?
      —what might have been—
      —lives of friends—

Doing the things we do, so often
for wrong, Horrible reasons,
And by grace of god's gift
Having them come out all right

Gestures begun in accident or vanity
Becoming examples, blazes, models
because become sincerity
    in spite of us
Become an event in the history of goodness
    fragile promise of what could be

Pathfinder, pathbreaker, build us a road that we can take for granted
    lucky that it came out so well

Paid my respects, thought that would be it
Got called to spread manure in a friends garden
Shovelling hard turning holy shit
The thought of her stayed in my mind all day
    If she ever wanted immortality amongst the shit shovellers
    She got it and me too

Made the great contact
Consciously

We married in secret
What went down between us was for us alone
spread the dung and got you fertile
Made you pregnant with seeds
Harvesting with your own hands
       from your own fields
       in your own house

Raised your own seed bearing fruit
my child

**D.P.**
*Santa Fé, New Mexico*
*March, 1971*

Birth Experiences

# CAMILLA HOOVER
# Induced Labor

**Katerine:** Your new baby boy is two weeks old now, how did the birth go?

**Camilla:** Quickly, I had it induced.

**K:** Were you aware of the different choices that you had?

**C:** Yes, I know about natural childbirth and exercises. I heard about having babies induced eight years ago when I first came to America from Sweden. I thought it was a fabulous idea. My girlfriends all did it that way. For Herbert, my first baby, I was going to do it that way, but he came one month early so I didn't get a chance.

**K:** Induced means that you choose the time of birth?

**C:** Yes, you choose the time to bring on the labor with certain drugs. Usually, the doctor waits until your due date. Mine was February 5th, my doctor came back the 29th of January. I went to see him and said, "I can't stand this anymore. I am getting fat and I am really impatient for this baby to be born." He said, "Let's examine you." I had had a few contractions already. They didn't mean anything, it was just the baby turning around and he said I was a little bit dilated. So I was really ready despite the fact that it was a week early. He said, "Do you want to have it this afternoon?" and I said, "No, I have a party tonight, but tomorrow will be fine." I went and had my hair done first and I went to Doctor's Hospital at five the next day. They wrote down all the information like age, address and then, up in the bedroom, I filled out another form. Then they took a blood test, blood pressure, listened to my heart and the nurses asked me what I was doing there! I guess they did not know I was going to have it induced. They asked my husband Bunker to leave and they started preparing me: an enema and a shave, but only half way, just between the legs.

**K:** How did you feel about that?

**C:** It's embarassing, but I am very ticklish so I was actually giggling.

**K:** How did you feel about being administered an enema?

**C:** That's nothing. It goes very fast and they are very professional. I was talking on the phone to a friend at the time. It didn't bother me the second time. Once you've had it done you know how it goes. They took me downstairs to a preparation room. I took my book along because I figured it would take awhile as the doctor hadn't arrived yet. A little while later they inserted a needle in my hand. It must have had different tiny little exits, like a hollow fork, because they kept on adding different solutions at the same time without ever removing anything. My hand was taped flat on a wooden plaque. They gave me glucose drops, it makes you stronger and helps you come around faster afterwards. My husband was allowed in again. The doctor arrived a few minutes after him and straight away they added the stimulator of labor: Pitocin. And I tell you, within minutes, the whole process

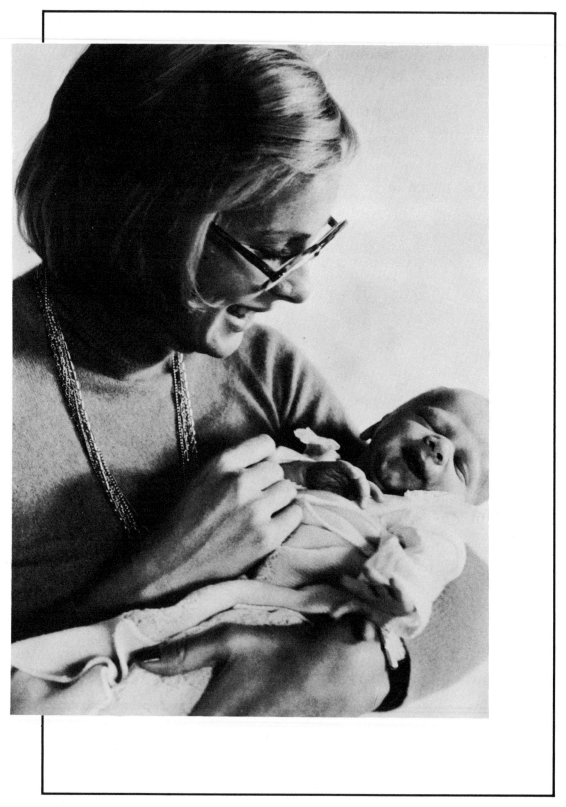

started. The whole grapefruit stood up!

**K:** What grapefruit?

**C:** Well, I guess the bottom of the baby when it starts to get into position. It looked funny, that grapefruit shape. Bunker had his eyes wide open watching it.

**K:** What did the medicine feel like?

**C:** It didn't hurt. It was the first contraction. They listened to the heartbeat. They have this special machine that amplifies the sound. It was pounding through the whole room! Tsch . . . schut . . . tsch . . . schut! Within ten minutes it started hurting because the drug brings it on so fast. Instead of dragging on for hours, it's within minutes. Like very bad period pains down in the back and I said, "All right Doc, I don't want to be around anymore!" Bunker had to leave and the doctor said, "All right, this is going to take thirty seconds and you will be out. It's going to burn first." It burns in your veins. It's the Demerol to put you to sleep and Sparine. They never had to give me another shot or anything. It all goes through that needle. From different bottles, into the needle, out into the veins through various exits, peculiar! I thought, "Surely it can't take thirty seconds." And then this thing started burning and I said, "It really burns!" They told me to close my eyes and I did. I promise you that within fifteen seconds I was floating. It's a great feeling and I wanted to tell them I could still hear them talk, my mind was still working. I could not actually make any sense out of what they were saying. I wanted to tell the doctor he had been fooling me because it didn't really take thirty seconds, but I couldn't form the words. It came out like a blur. I imagined or maybe heard the nurse saying, "Mrs. Hoover you are just drunk, you are an old drunkard." And then I was out. I remember waking up a little bit when they moved that table to the delivery room.

**K:** How about the breaking of the waters?

**C:** Oh, I have forgotten to tell you. The doctor broke my water before. I had asked him if he had to do it while I was still awake, usually they do it after you are out. But he had to examine me anyway to see if the medicine was really working, if I had dilated enough. He put a couple of fingers in, I guess, and said it was dilated a lot. He was examining me and it was hurting a lot. You know how it is to get touched at that point. He put in a small instrument and caught the membrane surrounding the waters and broke open the bag. Fluid came rushing out and I said, "Jesus Christ, that hurts!" And then it was finished, it took a second.

**K:** Back in the delivery room . . .

**C:** I was completely out. Apparently, they wait until the baby starts to come down the birth canal to wheel you into the delivery room and they give you gas and oxygen as the delivery happens.

**K:** Now the contractions are going on and the baby is on its way out but, since you are not pushing, do they have to deliver the baby with forceps?

**C:** No, they had to with my first baby because he was all twisted, but since

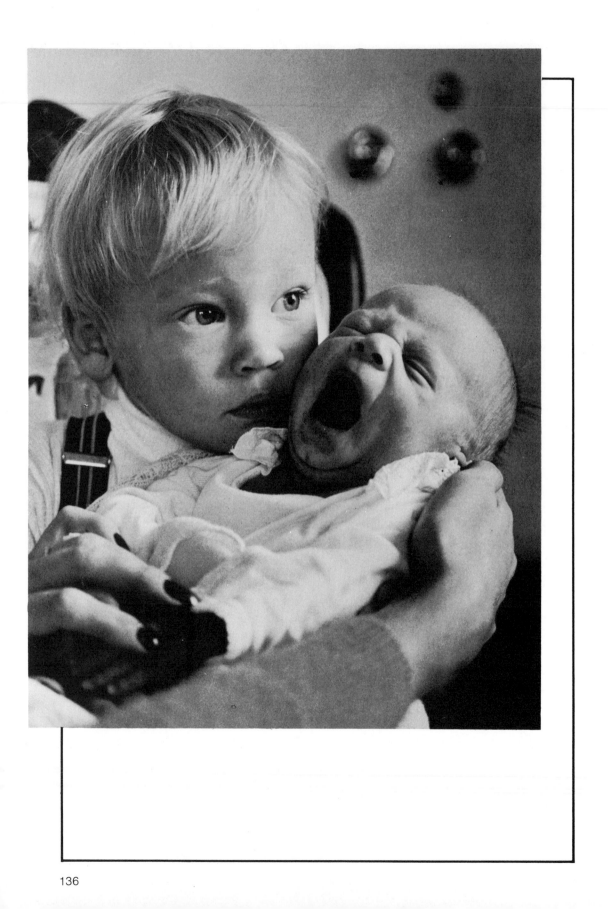

the muscles are still working, they can expel the baby. It's your mind that is asleep.

**K:** How long did it take?

**C:** The doctor came at seven at night. A few minutes later he gave me the drug to stimulate labor. The baby was born at ten. Three hours. I woke up in the recovery room. I had been there an hour. The first thing I remembered was being wheeled out of that place into the corridor. It was around eleven at night. They took me by the nursery and pointed through the glass separation saying, "Look, there is your baby." Bunker was there and some other people. I remember someone saying, in a cute tone, "Isn't this a happy moment?" I was completely groggy. Bunker was holding up my head and I kept saying to him, "I can't see without my glasses." He went to get them. I felt very much as if I was very drunk and all I could say was "Oh! It's a little boy, how nice! Bunker, are you disappointed?" I knew he wanted a girl. His answer came back but I forgot it the minute he said it and I would ask again. I was taken to my room and slept all night. I did not see my baby until the evening of the next day. You know, I had cramps after this second baby for two days afterwards. They had to give me a lot of codeine and it also hurt from the episiotomy. While I was out I was also given a shot to dry up the milk.

**K:** So, for two days you were loaded with medicines?

**C:** I loved it. I felt good. People would come with flowers and I'd welcome them happily. I didn't feel any pain. I really don't like pain.

**K:** How do you know you are going to be in pain?

**C:** Because it was painful enough before I got the shot. I didn't want to hang around, really. Bunker was very disappointed. He wanted to see the birth. I could watch you having a baby but I couldn't watch me having a baby!

**K:** You thought about having natural childbirth?

**C:** I thought about it for a very short time, like two seconds. You know the only trouble when you are put out is that you cannot connect the baby with yourself. It's like going to a place, you go to sleep and the next day are given a present of the baby. I could not put the womb and baby as part of each other because I did not see it happen, I suppose. That's the only thing I sort of regret. But I would much rather endure that than worrying about being around. I am a different kind a person than you.

It was very difficult for me. I kept on looking at that baby and saying, "I cannot believe it, I cannot believe he came from me." It was not a big thing but I thought about that for awhile after I had been put to sleep to have my first baby.

| DATE (MO., DY., YR.) | LOCATION | SERVICE | Williamson |
|---|---|---|---|

| AGE | DOCTOR | | IF NO PLATE, PRINT NAME, SEX, AND HISTORY NO. |
|---|---|---|---|

Parents Copy

TAPE No.             SEX

DATE OF BIRTH           RACE

PRINTS TAKEN BY

DATE

BABY'S LEFT FOOTPRINT      MOTHER'S RIGHT INDEX FINGERPRINT      BABY'S RIGHT FOOTPRINT

**THE NEW YORK HOSPITAL**      **NEWBORN IDENTIFICATION**

# JILL WILLIAMSON
# Prepared Childbirth

*Jill Williamson took breathing and exercise classes in England. She hap-
pened to be in America during her last months of pregnancy and decided
to give birth in the hospital. In the middle of labor it became obvious that the
baby was presenting the back of its head rather than its face. Jill breathed
right through the cross-cut incisions that became necessary in order for the
baby to be born without ripping her.*

**Caterine:** Your baby took a long time before it decided to come out?

**Jill:** It was right on time. He was born three weeks before due date but the
doctors thought that it would be more premature so it made the wait a little
longer. In the true Williamson tradition he had to do it his own way. The
whole development was so extraordinary. Friday night we were supposed
to go out (the baby was born on Saturday). I felt very heavy and I did not feel
like moving, so I stayed at my parent's apartment and my husband went to
the theater and to dinner after the show. My mother was making me
something to eat but I felt I had better not eat anything. I couldn't. And then
my husband came in at about two in the morning and offered to prepare
cereals for me, but I did not feel like eating at all.

In the morning, at about a quarter to eight, I got up and went to the loo. I
felt a pain, a contraction I suppose. I looked at my watch but I didn't have a
second hand on it and I thought, "Well, at the beginning of labor the pains
are supposed to take place every fifteen minutes or half-an-hour apart or
something." I went to the bedroom and then got another contraction almost
straight away. Also, I started to bleed. I took my husband's watch, it was
phosphorescent with a hand for seconds and I timed them. The contractions were three minutes apart. I remembered that the doctor said I should
get to the hospital when they were five minutes apart! I woke up my
husband and I said, "Darling, I have started labor." He said, "Well, just
relax, do your breathing and relax between contractions." I said, "I don't
think that's possible, they are three minutes apart!" He jumped out of bed,
went to get my mother and then went to take a shower. Meanwhile, I was
sick, sick to my stomach, vomiting. I called the doctor and told him. He said,
"Are you sure you don't have the flu?" "No," I said, "I am sick with every
contraction and they are coming every two and a half minutes now!" He
said, "Get your ass in here fast!" And Nicol is singing in the shower!

We arrived at the hospital and, for openers, you have to fill out all sorts
of forms while you are doubling over with contractions. They ask you for a
$600.00 deposit before you can get any further! It's insane! They could ask
for any amount and you would say yes because you want so much to go
and lie down somewhere! Luckily, my mother had a hospital credit card.

Can you imagine that? It's like going to shop for a very expensive toy in a big department store.

I was put in a little room and the nurses started preparing me. When they saw how advanced I was they immediately called the doctor. Nicol was marvelous, he kept reminding me to take the contractions on, to relax and breathe and I kept on being sick all over him and everything else. The doctor arrived and examined me. The water hadn't broken yet but there was a lot of blood. The baby had turned the wrong way. He was facing upwards instead of down and the contractions were coming on so fast that they had to slow them down with medicine and monitor the heartbeat. Something was slipped inside of me to attach to the baby's head and register the rhythm. I was huffing and puffing but there is really no description for it all. It seems to happen in another dimension. The first time I looked at the watch it was a quarter to eight and the baby was actually born at four minutes past four in the afternoon and that was the next time I looked at the clock! I thought, "Where did the time go?"

Finally, they could not turn the baby around. He was blocking off my bladder. They broke the water bag and took me up to the delivery room. Meanwhile, the baby turned sideways, presenting the broader side of himself. The doctor had to cut me lengthwise and sideways, all the way into the muscle of the leg. That is the only pain that I feel now, the stitches.

It was the most incredible feeling when the baby came out. I had to pant and hold it as they were making the incisions. It didn't hurt because somehow the pressure of the baby had numbed the area. I was given a paper bag to breathe into because of hyperventilation and they told me to push.

**C:** And Nicol was with you the whole time?

**J:** No, he had a matinee performance scheduled at the theater and the doctor told him that it would be a difficult birth. So, around one o' clock, they suggested that he go to the theater to perform and come back afterwards. The moment the curtain came down, at the end of the play, Luc was born.

I hadn't realized that anything was wrong. I was so much in my own little world. Nicol knew and he was so fantastic all the way through. It was so good having him there. At one point, he hugged me really strongly as the contraction was shaking me and that felt really good.

When the baby was actually being born, there were five people in attendance: the doctor, a young Chinese doctor, an English midwife, and two nurses. They were all helping me with the breathing. It was like a group of friends around me. But at one point, when the baby was actually being born, someone pressed and pushed hard on my abdomen and that really hurt. I would take a very deep breath and then scream it out and, oh!, the ecstasy when the baby came out!

**C:** At the time you were in pain, did they give you any painkillers?

**J:** They tried to give me an epidural but it didn't work. It must have been too late in the labor. It was all right in a way because I wanted to feel the pushes my body demanded. I was so busy concentrating on what I was doing that eventually nothing mattered. I didn't want to do anything else but get the baby out. It was painful but when he came out, it was the most incredible feeling and the tummy popped right down again. The cord was very short. When it was cut, they gave me the baby. It was fantastic! Nothing else like it! And I said, "Oh, what a beautiful boy, isn't he? What a pleasure and I would really love a cup of tea."

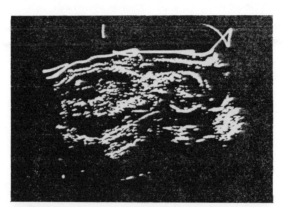

SONAR WAVES, PROJECTED ONTO A SCREEN, DETECTING POSITION OF BABY IN MOTHER'S WOMB.

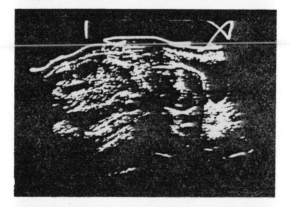

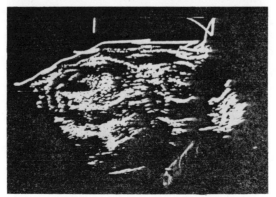

# JOEL N. BLOCK
# A Father Experiences Birth

When delivery day finally came, I wasn't feeling up to it. I had slept badly the night before and my mind felt fuzzy. I was none too articulate and my reflexes were slowed down. The next day would be much better I thought.

But Nelly was restless. For the past ten days we had lived in suspense. When would it strike? I had grown afraid of stepping out of the house for fear of missing the event. Even my dreams had taken over my cumulative anxiety. A week before the delivery I had the following dream:

I was an observer in a delivery room half the size of a basketball court. Gymnasium lines, in fact, were marked on the floor. The room contained four beds with expectant mothers. An obstetrician was leaning over each one. In one of the beds was Nelly.

Suddenly, at the far end of the room, a doctor lifted out and held up a baby by its heel. "There goes one," said someone. The sight distracted me. Then I looked at Nelly and, with a feeling of sickening dismay, saw that our baby had already been born.

I walked up to the bed. "Ha! Ha! You missed it," the baby said. I looked closely at the baby. It was a boy and resembled the Pharoah, Akhenaten, with an abnormally long jaw and sunken cheeks. (I had read recently an article in which Akhenaten, on the basis of new medical evidence, had been described as an endocrine freak.)

Well, I thought, at least the baby doesn't look idiotic, just rather grotesque, but acceptable. I could live with it. At which point I woke up.

You see, I really felt the need to be in good shape for the delivery, to be able to deal with any situation. As it turned out, I did very well anyway and seeing our child born was, to me, the most beautiful and dramatic experience of my life. But, only one day later, I became a patient in the maternity ward myself.

This story takes place in Basel, Switzerland. On delivery day we went to the obstetrician, Dr. M., a friendly, open and approachable man of recognized professional brilliance. Nelly was on the table and Dr. M. made his external examination. Everything was fine. The baby's head was centralized. The baby was fully "cooked" and ready to go. Only the contractions were missing. The doctor gave Nelly a really good shot of Syntocinon (oxytocin), the uterus-contracting hormone, and then he ruptured the amniotic sac. He said the child would be born in the course of the day.

So there it was. This was really d-day. By the time we reached the car the contractions had begun. By the time we got home, they were occurring every two minutes. No time to pull myself together. It was happening. I quickly grabbed a piece of cake to sustain myself over the next hours and, with Nelly and her suitcase, drove directly to the clinic.

At the clinic, a wonderfully efficient midwife dressed Nelly in a white

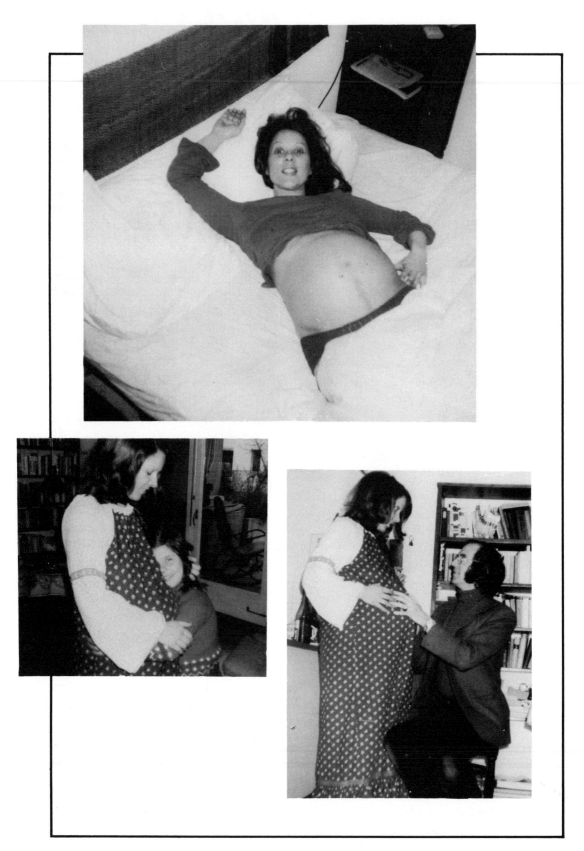

gown and lifted her into the bed. Nelly was in great pain and there was no way I could reach her through conversation anymore.

Within twenty minutes she was wheeled into the delivery room. My God! Now it was really happening. Nelly groaned in pain and clutched the oxygen mask. The midwife sat me in a chair. From time to time she rolled Nelly into a new position, away from me, causing me to grab my chair and run around the delivery table.

These moves produced a terrible sound of pain from Nelly. It troubled me a lot. Nelly had always been good with pain, very calm. Her screams were uncharacteristic. Was it supposed to happen this way?

"Schnufe!" the midwife said (which is the word for 'breathe' in the local Swiss-German dialect). I found the word 'schnufe' really ridiculous sounding. During all of this heartrending activity, my American mind had been racing with inane, manic internal monologues, like a continuous running tape in my head. "I got hit right on the schnufe," this internal voice now said. "I left my schnufe in San Francisco" came on next, to the tune of the song.

The midwife had earlier informed me that the cervical opening was the size of a Swiss two franc piece. She examined Nelly again. These cervical examinations really made her scream. The opening was now the size of a five franc piece. She called Dr. M. at his office to let him know.

At eight centimeters I gained the courage to tell the midwife I had a photographer friend, Seymour, on stand-by. The doctor had given his permission earlier. The midwife said he had better come right away. She then called Dr. M. and I called Seymour and Aiko. Within minutes, the doctor, dressed in a white turtleneck sweater, arrived at the clinic in his green Porsche. He put on a green apron, rubber gloves and was ready to deliver.

But my photographer hadn't arrived yet. To hold back the final pressing contraction, the midwife and an assistant nurse rolled Nelly back on her side. At last they arrived with cameras. Seymour and Aiko got into photographic position at the birth canal end. The midwife encased Nelly's legs in white knitted stockings. We could begin the final stage.

Nelly was told to grab her legs under the knees and pull them towards her. I was instructed to hold Nelly's head. The midwife and nurse each pulled a leg. Dr. M. had his hands open as if to receive a baseball. It was a beautiful frozen tableau. Then we all went into action. I helped Nelly pull her head forward, she pulled her knees inward, the nurse and midwife pushed her legs against her, Seymour released the shutter and Dr. M. shouted encouragement in the local dialect. "Prasse! Prasse!" he said. "Fescht drugge. Nonemol!" ("Press as strong as you can. Once again!") Nelly no longer looked as if she was in pain, only feeling relief. With each repetition of the procedure, she smiled and gave an horrendously low grunt.

What a scene! I had certainly never been through anything like this before. And then the crown of the head appeared. I was completely

overwhelmed. Seeing that tiny head make its way to the surface; seeing that there was a baby in there after all; that all these people were there to help this little baby get out and that Nelly was making such a great, beautiful, courageous, primordial effort. I started to cry. Then the baby's head disappeared.

We went through the procedure again; but now more intensely, with more smiling grunts. The head appeared again. Then an unconscious grimacing face. And then the whole body slid out! The most amazing sight I have ever seen. And the baby began to cry immediately with the off-key, somewhat metallic voice of a Munchkin from *The Wizard of Oz*. Its arms and legs were moving like mad.

"What is it?" Nelly asked. I had actually forgotten to look. It wasn't the Pharoah Akhenaten. "A girl," I croaked. It was a beautiful round-headed girl, with perfect little features, unusually long, graceful fingers and adorable miniature feet. How does it all come together like that, so complete and intricate?

I started taking flash pictures. I made certain to photograph the exact time on the electric clock for the sake of astrologers, 3:10 P.M.

Dr. M. was waiting for the placenta ("waitin' for the Robert E. Lee" my internal tape went). He tugged gently on the beautifully colored light blue umbilical cord. Nelly grabbed her legs for three more pressings and the placenta slid out. Dr. M. looked it over. It was complete; the whole babykit with removable life-support system, like a space capsule with droge parachute.

I could only marvel at the infinite brilliance, at life and I wondered the banal thought, "How could anyone kill another human being?"

It was over. By being present at the birth of our child, by sharing this with my wife, we had locked ourselves into a permanent identity with the child's life and future. No father should miss it.

The next thing, around 11:00 P.M., while home alone, I was struck full-force with the most incredible stomach pains. What was this? My turn at labor? Or, was it the exacerbation of all my stomach nerves after nine months of anxiety?

I had no medication at home. I could only suffer. At 4:00 A.M. I dug out an unopened yogurt from our garbage. I always got sick at the sight of yogurt, but now I was desperate. However, it did not help much.

By 7:00 A.M. I could only think of driving to Nelly's maternity clinic for help. She was happily eating breakfast when I lurched into her room doubled over in pain. She was quite surprised to see me that early. Dr. M., passing through, said "Ja, Ja, this sometimes happens to fathers."

# THE STORY OF KELLY

GOT PREGNANT, NEVER KNEW WHY.
HAD A BABY OUT OF CONTROL, NO POWER!
SHUT IN A HOSPITAL. CLIMBING THE BEDRAILS, THEY WOULDN'T LET
ANYONE STAY WITH ME.
SHAVED, HOT SOAPY WATER UP MY ARSE.
NURSES OVERWORKED, BADLY PAID, TIRED OUT, ILL-TEMPERED,
SHOUTING AT ME IN THE DELIVERY ROOM . . .
"PUSH!"
SO SHE CAME OUT.
STITCHED ME UP, BLOOD EVERYWHERE. LEFT ALONE AGAIN.
TINY BABY DRESSED IN WHITE. PINK LABEL, ALL READY GIRL-CHILD,
LITTLE SISTER.
HOW TO HAVE A BABY?
DON'T GO TO THE HOSPITAL IF YOU CAN HELP IT.
TRUST YOURSELF AND YOUR FRIENDS. HOSPITALS TAKE CHILDBIRTH
AWAY FROM YOU (SOLITARY CONFINEMENT, HOUSE ARREST) AND
LEAVE YOU POWERLESS.
I ACCUSE THE HOSPITAL!
I WAS IN THE POWER OF NEGLIGENT, HIERARCHICAL,
BUREAUCRATIC PERSECUTORS OF WOMEN. THEY WON EVERY
ARGUMENT. I LOST MY IDENTITY. WOMAN'S BODIES ARE PAIN AND
HUMILIATION AFTER THE DEGRADATION OF SUCH A HOSPITAL
BIRTH. SHOUTED AT LIKE A SLOW CHILD.
                    PAIN AND SORENESS.
SWOLLEN, BLEEDING CUNT, CATGUT STICKING OUT.
TOO SORE TO WALK, SIT DOWN OR LIE DOWN . . .
                    I'LL NEVER MAKE LOVE AGAIN!
I KNOW I HAVE SAID IT BEFORE.
                    "SHE NOT BUSY BEING BORN IS BUSY DYING."
THE OTHER WOMEN GRADUALLY BROKE DOWN FROM THE CON OF
FULFILLMENT TO THE DESPAIR OF HOME ALONE. JEALOUS, BITTER,
TURNED IN ON THEMSELVES. SMALL HUMILIATIONS GROWING
BIGGER AND BIGGER BECAUSE THERE IS NOTHING ELSE. ALWAYS
WAITING FOR SOMEONE ELSE—HUSBAND—NURSES—APPROVAL
OR PERMISSION. SAD EMPTY CRYING WHICH THEY THINK IS FOR
HUSBAND, CHILDREN, MISSING ROLES BECAUSE THERE IS NOTHING
ELSE. ALL BUILT UP HATE, SPITE, ANGER, BITTERNESS, ENVY.
COMING OUT OF OUR POWERLESSNESS AGAINST OURSELVES. AND
THE PEOPLE WE WOULD BE CLOSEST TO ARE TRAPPED BY WHITER
NAPPIES THAN THE WOMAN NEXT DOOR. SORE AND ACHING MINDS
LIKE CUNTS. NEVER FELT SO ALONE.
THEN OUT

                    I, SUE NO BULGE INTHESTOMACHSUE
                    ME AND KELLY, LONDON, 1970

149

# LISA LAW
# Childbirth At Home

*Lisa Law's first child was born in a maternity home in New Mexico. Here she discusses the birth of her second and third child, both were born at home.*

## The Birth of Baba

SUNDAY, OCTOBER 26th. My daugher Pilar and I woke up with slight colds so we ate lightly and drank grape juice. Took a long walk down the road in the cold afternoon. Pilar amused herself rolling on the ground and playing with the rocks. Tom was away on a trip. No daddy and the car had a flat tire.

MONDAY, OCTOBER 27th. Papaya and banana for breakfast. Potato soup for lunch. We both lie down for a nap. While Pilar still sleeps, I put the baby clothes together, the ones he will need for his birth. I seemed to be having pain on the floor of my pelvis as if my pants were too tight: I keep adjusting my pants. On the way back from the walk at three o' clock I did a lot of breath of fire to breathe away the pains. At home we start to make a red and white striped nightgown for daddy. More pains and I can't finish it. Time for dinner, a big salad. We fell asleep on the bed. At 8:00 P.M. more pains wake me up. I timed them, they were five minutes apart.

I couldn't believe I was in labor. But, I decided to get ready for it anyway. I covered the end of the bed with towels and clean sheets, put a basket of clean towels at the end of the bed, lit both fires and heated all the water I could. Fixed myself a cup of red raspberry leaf tea, cleaned up the house, lit all the candles I could find and sat down to relax. The contractions were still coming five minutes apart and now the incredible urge to shit. I took a big one and felt so much better. I also had to pee every fifteen minutes.

Here I was alone . . . and in labor! Flat tire, no way out. At 10:00 P.M. Tom drives up with a friend, Ruffin. Just in time! So good to hold him and know he is here to comfort me. Tom gave Pilar and me matching turquoise bracelets, lit incense and, sitting in his white robe, began to chant. We all chanted.

I was drinking spikenard, squawroot and lobelia tea as recommended in Jethro Kloss's *Back to Eden.* I kept peeing, the contractions were getting more intense. Being on my hands and knees, panting like a dog, felt best. The lobelia tea seemed to help me relax as the pains got stronger. The squatting position felt even more natural, less strained. I remained squatting. At 2:45 A.M. the contractions were one minute apart and very intense. I breathed through my mouth as hard as I could. Sometimes it turned into a groan-pant. Tom had to remind me to breathe, not yell. Deep breathing helps to bring more oxygen which you need during labor. I lay on my back,

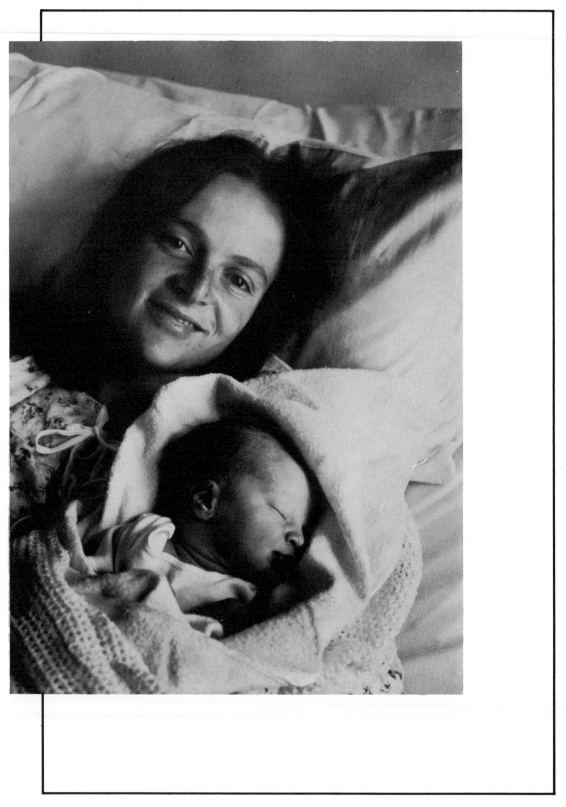

propped up by pillows, almost sitting. Tom, from behind, would lift me up during each contraction to the squatting position. Holding me with one arm, he would vigorously massage my lower back for the duration. I couldn't move from that position. During one contraction I felt a definite bearing down sensation. It was accompanied by the bloody show. During contractions it felt better if Tom lifted me up to take pressure off the abdomen. He prepared hot towels to relieve the tension in the back muscles. During the following contraction I felt the head crowning and wanted to bear down. I did, but not hard, being afraid of tearing. Next contraction I did bear down very hard, feeling that it was time. The water bag broke and his head came out.

There I was with a head hanging out of me. I was squatting and Tom was holding me up. I felt funny. Half in, half out, completely stretched. Sort of laughing and bewildered. The last two or three contractions had been accompanied by a sweating, tingling sensation all over the body, especially in the fingertips as I had finished half-an-hour of heavy breath of fire. My hands reached down and there it was indeed, the head. I told Tom. He couldn't believe it was there yet. He helped me lay back on the pillows and, with the next contraction, I lightly pushed out our little son.

Tom caught the baby and held him on his side to help get rid of the mucus. He took a good breath, cried a little getting the mucus out and made funny gurgling noises. Pilar came over when the head was out and watched the birth of her brother. Tom put the baby on my abdomen and with the next contraction I pushed out almost all of the placenta. I drank red raspberry leaf tea. I tried to push on my uterus to expel the placenta but remembered from my reading that it may take hours to entirely expel it. I just relaxed and talked with Ruffin. Tom tied the cord and cut it while the baby nursed. An hour and forty-five minutes later, the contractions from nursing released the rest of the placenta. I examined it and explained it to Ruffin. I wrapped our new son, Baba, in a beautiful blanket and we all fell off to sleep.

### The Birth of Sunday Peaches

NOVEMBER 4th, 1972. I woke up and lay in bed thinking about how I was going to clean the upstairs room, cut the corn stalks, harvest potatoes, etc. At midday Reno came over to use the saw and bring the fireworks that I was supposed to set off when I went into labor. In the afternoon I was about to milk the goats, but Tom had to because I was having cramps, very low, and couldn't manage. Victor and Linda (who was eight months pregnant) were over for a visit in hopes they would be around for the birth. We all had a light dinner and then jumped into the Japanese Furo bath. The water is heated by fire under the redwood tub and the hot water was fantastic and very relaxing. Baba and I got out and dressed. I lay down on the bed to feel out the cramps that were still happening. They were coming every four min-

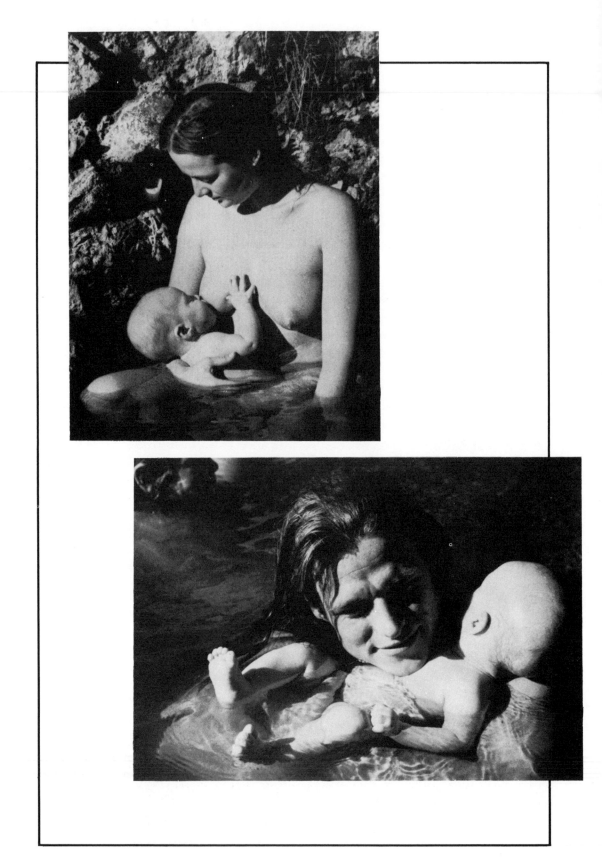

utes. I jumped back into the bath on my hands and knees and had a contraction right there in the tub. Oh boy, here it comes! The bath was very soothing. We watched television to pass the time. The contractions were now coming every two to three minutes. I called David Rosensweet, the doctor. He decided to come right away since it takes two hours to get here.

I called Stuart and Joan Pappe who had been waiting a long time for this night and told them to pack up and bring the wine and candles. The children went to sleep and the rest of us settled down for a rest. What a beautiful night, so peaceful and quiet.

Stuart and Joan arrived. Linda and Joan massaged my legs and feet. My calves were cramped; I was still having light contractions and didn't have to pant like with Baba, just relaxed. I wanted to yell, "Whoopee, I'm in labor at last!"

At 11:00 P.M. David arrived with his pressure cooker, for sterilizing his instruments, his stethoscope and doctor's bag. Just after he examined me, my bag of waters broke and flooded the towels on the bed.

Everyone was quietly sitting or standing around the house, occasionally munching on some peyote buttons or sipping wine by the candlelight.

During the following contractions, I was in the squatting position on my knees and would raise up a little bit. If I let go of my rectum and my vaginal muscles, the baby would fall down noticeably and the cervix would dilate rapidly and I could feel all of it happening. But as long as I kept those muscles tight, nothing would happen. When I did relax them, more embryonic fluid would escape and some urine too. I was doing light panting at this time, the contractions were lasting sixty seconds with two minutes in between.

Stuart was taking pictures.

David was sitting next to me on the bed taking heartbeats. Tom was walking around sipping wine with not too much to do because I had no back labor this time.

Linda fixed me spikenard, squawroot and lobelia tea mixed with raspberry leaf tea to make the contractions come faster and easier. For the first time while giving birth I smoked some grass which really seemed to help my state of mind.

Rapidly the contractions became stronger and the breathing heavier and much deeper. I started to sweat a lot and Stuart brought a wet rag for my face. Joan said many times that my third eye was showing and that it radiated violet.

I was squatting on my knees with arms straight and down, resting on my fists. Later I was sit-squatting because it was too painful to lift up. I was doing heavy breathing through my mouth and near the end of the contraction I became very vocal and let out with long yells. The louder I yelled the better I felt. It echoed around the room. I asked everyone if they were okay because I was afraid of scaring them. They were fine. During the contrac-

tions I lost eye contact which I wished I hadn't done. Keeping eye contact on something relieves pain as well as breathing does.

It was time to get the children. Pilar came right away and Baba fell asleep on the way. They both sat on the end of the bed wide-eyed and excited. Tom was sitting next to me holding my hand, coaching my breathing. I asked David if it was crowning. It wasn't, so the next contraction I had a good push and he said it *was* crowning. I wanted to see this baby coming out because I had missed looking down between my legs to see the other two. Tom got a mirror and put it between my legs. Fantastic! I could see! I really wanted to push now, I wanted to see that little baby come out and looking at the mirror lessened the pain by half. I gave another push, wanting to see the head crown and I did! This excited me so much that I pushed twice as hard again. Tom ripped the mirror away so she wouldn't hit it as she came flying out all at once. Whoops, I missed seeing it again! I guess I'll have to have another one. There she was, moving, breathing and crying, very clean with hardly any vernix at all. David sucked the mucus from her nose with a syringe and then placed her on my abdomen. We waited till the cord was flat and there was no blood left in it. Tom tied it off in two places and cut it. The placenta was still inside. To substantiate our theory, that the best way to release the placenta was by sucking on the breast, not forcing it out, Tom sucked on it because the baby didn't want to. This contracted the uterus immediately and, pop, out came the placenta!

Baba exclaimed, as it came out, "Look, another one!"

I couldn't believe it was all over. I kept repeating, "Is that all? Is it really over?" David sewed me up. I had ripped an inch being in such a hurry to get her out. During the time he was sewing me up I became very ethereal as if I were floating about on the bed. I was very high and I felt very good. I was extremely happy.

I looked over at Joan, standing next to me who was all red in the eyes from crying with big tears coming down her face.

Our baby was born at 2:15 on Sunday morning. She was so sweet that we could eat her and we named her Sunday Peaches.

# JOAN WEINER
# Stillborn Birth

*Joan Weiner prepared for a natural childbirth at home. She was in labor for a day and a half and her baby was dead upon arrival. Years later she gave birth to a healthy daughter and, at the time she wrote this account, she was seven months pregnant again.*

It wasn't something anybody ever talked about. The lean instances stillbirth was mentioned in the motherhood books, the subject was avoided like a colony of lepers. Mainly, the books stated how this probably wasn't going to happen to you anyway, how if it did it generally meant a defective baby anyway which was better off gone and not to worry your pregnant little body with something so morbid. Nevertheless, thinking about my own death in childbirth or the death of my baby was an integral part of that first long pregnancy. When it came up, I would think of how this was negative programming. But, suppress and repress as I did, it came up and up and up. In daydreams, in fantasies, in nightmares, and no list of positive statistics, no pooh-poohing by the childbirth mavens could make it go away.

I was still unprepared for it when the event actually happened. My labor was lengthy, a day and a half, only not extraordinarily long for a first baby pushing and pleading its way through unexplored territory. I labored in mid-Manhattan in the townhouse of a doctor who had agreed to let me have it in his home rather than make me take the alternative of a New York hospital. Depersonalized, redtape, 1984 assembly line tactics, gestapo nurses, accidently injected labor room sedation, milk-drying chemicals. My good friends were with me and the room was set with candles and things I liked: a picture of Swami, a bas-relief of Siva holding Ganesh, afternoon summerlight coming through the window, incense instead of alcohol in the air.

Near the end, the Sunday bells of church on Fifth Avenue were ringing and the tiny heartbeat was becoming fainter and fainter and the pushing was taking so much time (half-an-hour, one hour, two hours) with so little progress being made. At 1:30 P.M. my doctor pulled out a beautiful nine and a half pound Gabrielle. She was so perfectly shaped, so delicate, but completely void of the essence that gives meaning to such beauty and joy to the beholder. She didn't cry, except for a gurgle that was fluid being sucked out of her lungs by the straining of the doctor. After that, total stillness. No life. No cry of shock or pain as adrenaline was shot directly into her heart, piercing the bluish doll's chest. There was nobody home. The driver had gone, leaving us to cry over the perfect, unblemished, never-to-be-used vehicle.

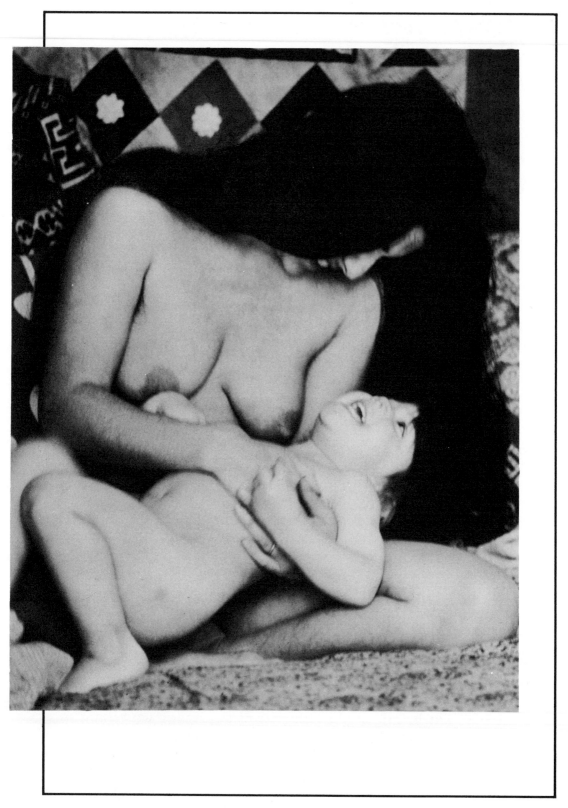

Anyway, it was easier to have this trip go down in a home, rather than in a hospital. I was surrounded by the people who loved me, who cried with me and who didn't make me feel ashamed over so much emotion. I wasn't shut away in a sterile little room with a perfect view of beaming new mothers, their arms and breasts filled with babies while I lay all empty, aching, titties abrim with surplus milk.

While I healed, physically, spiritually and emotionally, a number of people came to visit me. This was the most difficult time. They were curious and ashamed of their curiosity. They talked around the event rather than discussing it directly and though they never actually accused me of being an accessory to the death of this being, it was implied.

Could she have been saved if she was born in the hospital? One never knows. I feel certain she had repaid her karmic debt and didn't have to go any further, but there is no way to prove intuition or satisfy those who don't believe it exists.

For me there was too much time and space after the birth/death. All those hours I had projected to be filled with being a mother and taking care of the baby. I had worked up nine months of fantasy, always the child. The closer the birth came, the more I thought about my time with the baby. My whole life was cut out for me and now there was this great emptiness, the laughing void. Here and now with nothing to do. I brooded for a number of weeks. Hating all new mothers wheeling their babies down Riverside Drive, resenting each smooth swelling baby on the street, cursing the luck of every newly fertilized acquaintance, while my uterus lay fallow and discharging.

Nor was there anyone to relate to, no books on stillbirth, no magazine stories on mothers with dead babies. Miscarriage was the closest that friends had come to the experience. But it wasn't quite the same as nine months of growing, expanding, kicking, labor and term delivery. Not the same as this.

What I learned was how very precious, tenuous and miraculous life is. Truly a gift of God. When my second child, Daisy, was born, I was completely overwhelmed at hearing her cry. "Richie," I asked, "What is it?" He said, "It's alive!" We laughed and laughed. She was alive. A soft, hungry, naked, demanding individual ready to play baby to mommy, ready to let me live through that desire.

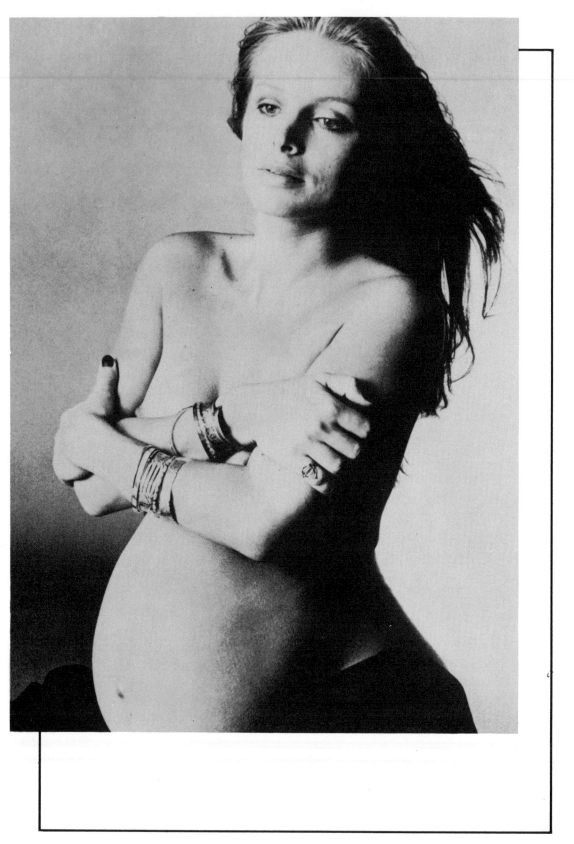

# IARA SCUDERA
## Caesarean

*Iara Scudera, 26, prepared for natural childbirth with breathing and exercises but, because of complications, was anaesthetized and had to have a Caesarean operation. Her daughter, Domenique, was born after ten hours of labor. She weighed seven and a half pounds and was twenty and a half inches long at birth.*

(The following conversation took place one month before delivery.)

**Iara:** I don't even want an injection to take the pain away if I have any.

**Caterine:** That is crazy. Why?

**I:** Well, I believe that it belongs to a mother to go through the pain. I would be terribly curious if I had to have a Caesarean, be put out straight away and never feel the pain. I'm scared, in a way, but I got to have that pain. It's like I want to have that pain! In fact, the nurse at the clinic, when I said that, told me I was a masochist. I just think that you've got to have the pain.

**C:** What an insane way to think, especially when most people are trying to figure out what triggers the discomforts and how the pain can be alleviated. You want to have the pain? It doesn't make much sense.

**I:** If I really, really cannot stand it, I will ask for medication. The same for breast-feeding. I don't want to breast-feed for a long time but I want to know the feeling and see if I like it.

**C:** How are you preparing to have your baby?

**I:** My mother had all of us at home, with the help of a midwife. She said it hurt a little but it was okay. I am taking classes in the "Lamaze Technique" and I will have the baby through the clinic services. I like it when I am attending the classes; but, when I come home I don't do it. I talk with most of the women there and they don't do it at home either. Maybe if my husband did it with me it would be fun, but I think they get more nervous about the whole thing than we do.

**C:** Maybe you would relax more if you did those breathing exercises.

**I:** In class the teacher thinks I'm very good.

**C:** I don't think it's a question of how good you are but, rather, how good do you feel?

**I:** The best thing for me about those classes is to see that all the things I have in my head, all the things I don't talk about, the other girls talk about and it's the same problems. You know, the fears, the emotions you go through; the reassurance you feel you need from the man you love. For example, I want Simon to be with me in the delivery room but he doesn't want to. He says he can't take it, he doesn't want to see it, it's too much. He feels nervous about it and it is up to me and the medical staff. In a way I understand. I have seen two deliveries; it is a very personal thing in a way.

One delivery was when I lived in Lebanon and it took place in a nursing home. There was the mother, the doctor, a nurse and me. We were all friends. As the labor progressed, the woman started to scream and I wanted to go away, but the doctor said that he had delivered her other children and this time the progress seemed to be going much faster and easier and not to worry. She told me later she had been feeling a little delirious as memories of her first birth kept coming back during the delivery. She said she was invoking God in Arabic and Kalim, the name of the first baby (who was by then a beautiful child), so that the strong pain wouldn't start again. But, in my head during the delivery, I was frightened that the baby would be dead upon arrival and I thought I would die too if that happened. I don't know why I was being so tragic, I guess I am very impressionable by external manifestations. That's why I say I can understand Simon not wanting to be there. He probably feels the same way. Anyway, the baby was being born, it was out to the waist and started to scream a healthy cry. I started to jump, cry and shout, "It's a boy, It's a boy!" I should have thought positively about life but I suppose it's something everyone thinks about. Death and birth are so close in a way. Another birth I attended was that of my best girlfriend. She wanted me to be with her and again the doctor was a friend. As she was going into the delivery room, he called me to come to the hospital. This birth went smoothly but I suppose it can be a turn off for a man.

**C:** Obviously, if a man doesn't feel good about being present, he shouldn't be there. But, how can it be repulsive or shocking? I mean, a man and a woman who decide to have a child together know each other very intimately. They can find out together about the reality of being born from books or through friends; but, best of all, by seeing their own seed come to life through the woman. Men come into this world through the same passage that we did. If they are there at conception, why shouldn't they be there at birth?

**I:** Well, some people like to see medical things and others just faint.

**C:** Birth didn't used to be a medical event.

**I:** I know but very often the medicine helps.

**C:** I never denied it, especially when it's not overdone.

(This next conversation took place one week before delivery.)

**C:** What have you been doing lately that makes you feel really good?

**I:** I enjoy staying at home with Simon the most. Cuddling, lying in bed, making love, watching television. There is a friend of ours who comes by and gives me massages with pure almond oil. That's when we are by the beach, I don't mind being all greasy there. In New York he massages me all over with Nivea liquid cream which sinks in better if you have to put on clothes afterwards.

**C:** How about walking?

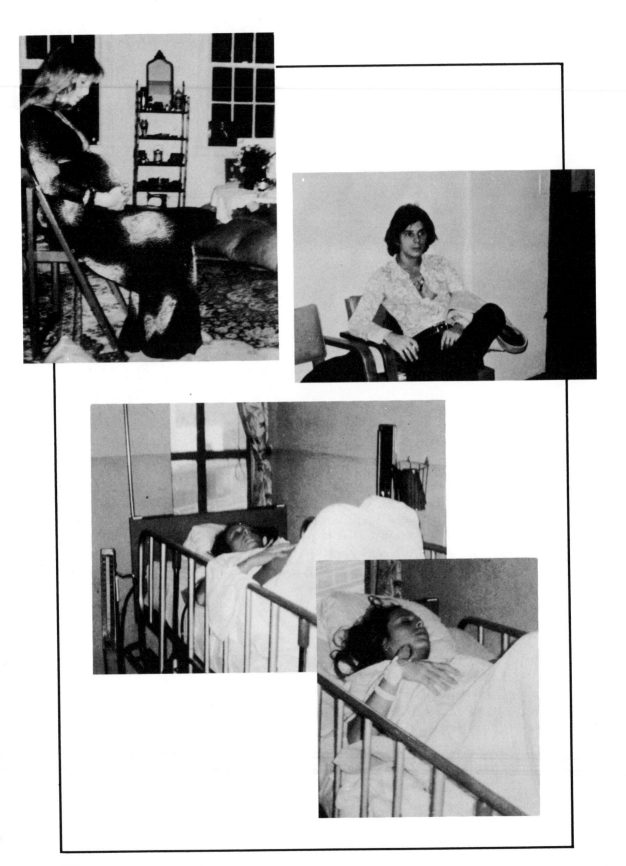

**I:** No, not anymore. The baby is too heavy. I used to bicycle a lot last month, it was like taking off on an airplane for the first time in your life. I was happy, laughing and, seeing me laugh, Simon would too. His family is of Italian descent and very protective, telling me I should be careful. A few weeks ago they had a block party in Brooklyn. There was lots of music and people, baby cribs in the middle of the street, children running around, I was dancing. People looked at me really strangely. Maybe it was the first time they had seen a nine month pregnant woman twirling about. I was dancing all by myself. I had been drinking a little rose wine and felt really good. You see, the point is that now I don't have much to do, but whenever I start dancing or working I don't think about how big my belly is as if it was the center of all my earthly concerns. You see often I feel bad because I don't do anything. I feel lazy. I did something really wrong: I stopped working. I loved making clothes and now it's a little late to start anything. I wish my mother was here from Brazil. We have such a good relationship. I know that if she were with me in the labor room I would laugh. She is such a painstaker. I am glad anyway, Simon has changed his mind and he said a few days ago he would really like to be with me all the way through.

(Simon called to say that the baby had to be delivered with a Caesarean operation. This third conversation took place three days after delivery at the hospital.)

**C:** You look well for someone who has gone through such an ordeal.

**I:** Oh! I put on some cheek rouge, when I looked at my face it was so pale. I feel kind of weak, but I'm okay. You know I broke the waters during the night. I was sleeping. I was feeling good and awake, sitting in the kitchen eating cookies. Went back to sleep and woke up in the morning with little cramps. I went to the bathroom. As I was sitting on the toilet Simon shouted, "Don't sit there, the baby is going to fall out!" (Laughter) Oh! It hurts to laugh with a fresh scar. What a crazy man! I know that babies don't come out that fast. My body kept on emptying itself from everywhere. Incredible! Around 10:30 in the morning the cramps started to happen every two minutes. They got stronger and we went to the hospital.

(We stopped the conversation here as Iara's voice got very weak and her expression got tired. We spoke again two weeks later.)

**I:** In the hospital, or rather the clinic, I was taken to a room and Simon had to stay out. This was the preparation room where they shaved me and gave me an enema. I stayed there for an hour. All the women were crying and screaming.

**C:** What was your reaction to that?

**I:** I wanted them to shut up. They were disturbing my good feelings. I guess we had different mentalities and approaches. They got scared. They were complaining about the nurses and the discomforts instead of concentrating on the coming baby. I was really dying to get out of that room. In the

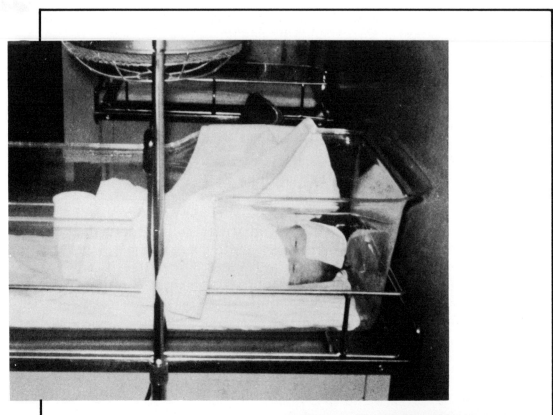

private labor room you could still hear screaming but it was from far away. Once there, it was great because Simon was with me and I had friends (doctors) who came to visit. The nurses were nice. They see so many pregnant women everyday they don't care to be especially polite. It's true they can be rude just like a saleslady in a department store but if you take time to joke with them they will laugh with you. I was in good spirits, not scared because I knew I was going to see my little babe. The contractions were really close to each other and painful. The doctor said I should have an epidural injection. I didn't want it because I thought it would knock me out, but they explained that it was just to ease the pain. The contractions got so strong I was given an injection somewhere in the lower back, but it spoiled me because when the medication wore off an hour later the pains were so much stronger. What really got confusing later on was the constant appearance of doctors who were coming around with students; looking, explaining, detailing like at school. But I was the guinea pig and I didn't like it. I must have gotten nervous because of it. I felt the pain more acutely and asked for more medicine since it had helped. They told me I was fully dilated and took me to the delivery room. Once there, all the relation with my husband started to fall apart. He said I kept pushing him away but it wasn't just him, it was anyone who came near me. Also, I hated the mask they kept putting on my face. I warned the nurse I would hurt her hand if she didn't stop it. I hated to inhale that gas. She kept on insisting that it was good for the baby to have some oxygen. I remembered that I almost died during an abortion once because I kicked the nurse so hard for putting that mask over my face. I can't take any of those suffocating gases.

By then I had been in labor for ten hours. Since the baby was not coming through at all, they started to use that suction machine or vacuum extractor. I don't remember the doctors asking me if they could do that. It was awful. I remember my husband told them to stop.

**C:** Were you fully conscious?

**I:** I was spinning. My head was full of lights, all turning around, like madness. All the words resounding. People saying, "What are we going to do now? Shall we do this or that?" Simon said that if he knew it was going to be that way he would never have come. He thought it was really ugly and scary with all those machines on me.

**C:** Why didn't he walk out?

**I:** He was trying to. There was a big confusion all around and he didn't want to leave me and I said, "Okay, let's get it over with." The doctor touched my arm very nicely and said something to me about the pelvic outlet being too narrow. "We are going to have to do a Caesarean and we are going to put you to sleep." I told the doctor, "Okay, go ahead, but make sure you cut below the line of the bikini and mine are really tiny bikinis." That made everybody laugh. Simon kissed me. I was given an injection and out!

**C:** Were you worried that something further would go wrong?

**I:** No, I am not scared of sickness or death. If I was to die now, it's okay. I don't care. But, if I live I want my body to look as pretty as possible.

I was so confused and distressed when I woke up in the recovery room around eleven at night. I was not prepared to have my baby with a Caesarean. The idea of not having been able to have my baby the natural way was unbearable. I felt like a cripple. I didn't even want to see the baby. I wasn't at my best to meet her. Slowly I reasoned with myself that all was fine because I have a lovely baby girl. Lying in that room, all night I was hearing this baby cry. I asked the nurse if it was mine and it was. Finally, at five in the morning, I asked the nurse to bring her and it was a happy reunion. When I saw her everything went away even though she looked red and blue. Domenique breast-fed straight away. In a way, it didn't matter which way I had had her, I was so glad to have her at all.

**C:** How did you feel physically?

**I:** That was something else. I could see me having a good relation with my kid; nursing, laughing and spiritually, but I couldn't get up. And, the other two mothers with whom I was sharing the room walked about learning how to change and dress the baby, changing scenery and I had to lie in bed. It was so frustrating. The pain was pretty bad, like for any operation. I had gas coming on like contractions! At least at the end of a contraction you get a baby, but those were totally useless. The bad pains only lasted five days and then it got better.

**C:** You looked so well just three days after the operation!

**I:** I was drugged, that's probably why.

**C:** With what?

**I:** I don't know. But when I had the pain I would get an injection and everything became very light and floating. I asked for so much of it that at one point the doctor said, "You have to be reasonable and handle the pain without drugs because you are getting hooked." I guess it must have been morphine or some such thing.

**C:** How long before you got out of bed?

**I:** A nurse made me get up the third day. I complained, it hurt and I didn't want to. What really annoyed me was that I couldn't handle the baby for too long because of the pain.

**C:** Is the scar healed?

**I:** It healed pretty fast. I could take a shower a week later. It is a very thin low cut.

**C:** Before you had the baby you were preparing for so much pain, did it live up to your expectations?

**I:** I would like to have another child someday. I would not be scared. It was strong pain but I was happy at the same time. If you are sick, it's a drag but labor is a different pain and you get a prize for it!

# BRIGITTE MARS
## Home Birth

We conceived January 25, 1971 in St. Croix, Virgin Islands. About my second month I did a mucousless diet to take off extra weight before I began to gain. (We had been vegetarians for five years.) I lost ten pounds while still nourishing myself and the one to come. This lasted for six weeks and then I resumed eating grains.

In my third month we moved to a farm in Missouri. We lived in a teepee like Indians. I attribute one reason for no ripping during delivery to having to squat to piss and shit rather than sitting on a toilet.

Every morning before going out into the fields, I would make a half gallon jug of red raspberry and alfalfa tea and drink it like iced tea all day. My husband, Sergai, drank it too. The raspberry leaf was to insure an easy pregnancy in general and the alfalfa was to insure milk production and vitamins as we were not consuming any dairy products.

I did the exercises from the back of Dr. Grantly Dick-Read's *Childbirth Without Fear.* I did them every night and Sergai would not let me into bed without doing them. I ordered herb formula #410 from the Indiana Botanic Gardens, Inc., Hammond, Indiana, 46325. Their catalog describes it as a "relaxant tea adopted to woman during the sensitive period of pregnancy." I remember that this formula contained black cohosh, spikenard, squaw-vine, fennel and probably some red raspberry leaves. I also drank spikenard occasionally by itself. I must mention that not once did I have morning sickness or any ill feelings at all.

Labor started on October 24th, ten months after conception. We were waiting at the airport for my friend Robin who was also pregnant at the time and had seen three deliveries. When we got home, we had dinner (which was a mistake as it made me nauseous). I did a laundry to have the baby bed ready and finished knitting Sergai's slippers. He gave me an enema and I spent a good deal of the night sleeping until the pain came. I would run to squat on the toilet (we were now living in a house in Canada) as this felt more comfortable.

By dawn it was time for heavy Lamaze breathing techniques. Robin threw the I Ching (keeping still - mountain) which was right on. During the labor I drank a tea of black cohosh and red raspberry leaf, but I couldn't hold anything down.

At 1:00 P.M., October 25th, Sunflower showed her golden head. The cord was wrapped around her neck, but after Sergai and Robin unwound it and Sergai held her upside down, she began to cry. Praise God! For such joy! After the cord was cut, I drank basil tea (which is the same as sweet basil) to help expel the afterbirth, which slid out an hour later. Sergai went and buried it in the garden for next spring. I was eighteen years old at the time and now Sunflower is nineteen months old. She was weaned as of a week ago (a process I began at one year of age).

One of the other herbs I used was camomile which worked as an eyewash for Sunflower. She had several sties which I attribute to the silver solution we used at birth and which I won't use again. Catnip helped the baby to sleep when she was teething. Peppermint with honey was a pleasant drink for the baby.

# LILIAN BRON
# Birth By Hypnosis

**Lilian:** I am not the ideal person to be hypnotized; I am too effervescent. But the woman who helped me managed to get my trust. It was difficult at first because I knew her very well and it was a bit embarrassing.

**Caterine:** Why, did you feel like giggling?

**L:** No, not really. It was more the fear of the unknown. You don't know what you are going to say when you are under hypnosis. At the beginning you feel a bit inhibited.

**C:** Why did you choose auto-hypnosis for giving birth?

**L:** Well, the idea is to teach yourself to do it and to have powerful control over yourself. That's what the teacher eventually taught me; to hypnotize myself so that I could deal with the pain. It's a form of meditation.

You lie on the bed and she tells you time and time again that your hand is very heavy. Your eyes are closed. She keeps on saying it until the rhythm and suggestion is well imprinted. Then she says, "Now try and lift your hand and you won't be able to because it feels so heavy," and sure enough, you can't. It's incredible, it really works. Your hand is feeling very numb and she says "I am going to prick your hand and you aren't going to feel a thing." It's really peculiar because you are not in a deep hypnotic state. You are fully conscious. You concentrate so hard on that one thing being heavy that it becomes heavy. It's like anything else really; you can talk yourself into anything. With concentration you can alleviate tension. I learned with my teacher to control most parts of my body and eventually I had to give myself the commands. It applied to childbirth at that point.

The teacher came along to the hospital and helped. It's all very well in theory but when it comes to practice, it's not that easy. She sat there, smoking, and we went through the motions together and eventually I was on my own. It really worked. I did not exclaim at all about the pain.

**K:** What do you mean, exclaim?

**L:** I didn't cry out in any way, wasn't fearful or uncomfortable. With my first child it was much harder. Mind you, with the first child it's never meant to be easy. For the first birth I was doing breathing exercises. Those are okay if everything goes all right but if something goes wrong you forget the rhythm. For the first child I had something called Uterine Inertia, where you keep on having the contractions but nothing happens. It was hell. I was in a nursing home and they decided to cart me off to the hospital. They thought they might do a Caesarean or a forceps delivery. The jerking of the ambulance did it, I almost gave birth during the ten minutes between the time I got in the van and the time I arrived at the hospital.

The second child was no trouble. I was sitting up all night talking to various people, sitting for some time in the room where the nurses were feeding the babies and they would tell me funny stories. In fact, I was having a laugh during labor. And, you know, most people have the most apprehension about the pushing but I found it was the most satisfying part, especially after being cooled off with the hypnosis.

# CONNECTICUT STATE. DEPARTMENT OF HEALTH

### Public Health Statistics Section—Hartford, Connecticut U.S.A.

## MARRIAGE LICENSE: TOWN OF ___New Haven___

| | |
|---|---|
| 1. Groom's Name ___Michael Margetts___ | 11. Bride's Name ___Barbara Margulies___ |
| 2. (a) Date of Birth ___11-13-1938___ (b) Age ___31___ 3. Race ___White___ | 12. (a) Date of Birth ___6-7-1947___ (b) Age ___22___ 13. Race ___White___ |
| 4. Occupation ___Film Director___ | 14. Occupation ___Stylist___ |
| 5. Birthplace: (Town) ___Camberley, Surrey, England___ (State or Country) | 15. Birthplace: (Town) ___Miami___ (State or Country) ___Florida___ |
| 6. Residence ___853 Lexington Ave. New York, New York___ | 16. Residence ___853 Lexington Ave. New York, New York___ |
| 7. (a) Previous Marital Status — Never Married — Last Marriage Ended By: Death ☐ Divorce ☒ Annulment ☐ (b) Number of This Marriage ___2nd___ | 17. (a) Previous Marital Status — Never Married ☒ — Last Marriage Ended By: Death ☐ Divorce ☐ Annulment ☐ (b) Number of This Marriage ___1s___ |
| 8. Father's Name ___Horace Winston Margetts___ | 18. Father's Name ___Irving Margulies___ |
| 9. Mother's Maiden Name ___Marjorie C. Rowlands___ | 19. Mother's Maiden Name ___Esther Feldman___ |
| 10. Supervision or Control of Guardian or Conservator ___no___ | 20. Supervision or Control of Guardian or Conservator ___no___ |

We ___Michael Margetts___ AND ___Barbara Margulies___ THE PERSON NAMED IN THIS MARRIAGE LICENSE, DO SOLEMNLY SWEAR THAT THE STATEMENTS HEREIN MADE ARE TRUE

SWORN TO BEFORE ME THIS ___4th___ DAY OF ___March___ 19 ___70___ SIGNED ___

SWORN TO BEFORE ME THIS ___4th___ DAY OF ___March___ 19 ___70___ SIGNED ___

THIS CERTIFIES THAT THE ABOVE-NAMED PARTIES HAVE COMPLIED WITH THE LAWS OF CONNECTICUT RELATING TO A MARRIAGE LICENSE, AND ANY PERSON AUTHORIZED TO CELEBRATE MARRIAGE MAY JOIN THE ABOVE-NAMED IN MARRIAGE WITHIN THE TOWN OF ___New Haven___

THIS LICENSE MUST BE USED ON OR BEFORE ___5-3-1970___ 19___ NOT GOOD AFTER THAT DATE.

Date Issued ___March 4th___ 19 ___70___ Attest ___Michael V. Lynch___ Registrar

## MARRIAGE CERTIFICATE

I HEREBY CERTIFY THAT Mr. ___Michael Margetts___ AND Miss ___Barbara Margulies___ THE ABOVE NAMED PARTIES, WERE LEGALLY JOINED IN MARRIAGE BY ME AT ___New Haven___ THIS ___8th___ DAY OF ___March 8___ 19 ___70___ Signed ___Hugh Romney___ ___Hugh Romney___

Address ___214 Cosey Beach Ave., East Haven, Conn.___ Offical Capacity ___Clergyman___ ___Clergyman___

THIS CERTIFICATE RECEIVED FOR RECORD ON ___MAR 16 1970___ BY ___Michael V. Lynch___ Registrar

Form VS-3

---

I certify that this is a true transcript of the information of the marriage record as recorded in this office.

Michael V. Lynch
Registrar Vital Statistics
Haven, Connecticut, U.S.A. Attest: ___Michael V. Lynch___ ............ Registrar of Vital Statistics

Dated ___March 18, 1970___ Town of ___New Haven___

## NOT GOOD WITHOUT SEAL OF CERTIFYING OFFICIAL

Form V. S. 14B (1-51) 20M

# BARBARA MARGETTS
# Prepared Childbirth With
# Complications

This was something that may only happen once to me. I wanted it to be right all the way through, from the very beginning. If I never did anything right before or ever again, I wanted the preparation and the actual birth of my child to be exactly as my instincts directed me. I wanted my child to be born into a quiet relaxed atmosphere where I could control my own environment and set up my own vibes. A place where I could piss on the floor, shit on the bed or curse and scream if needed; a place where I could do whatever felt good at the time. Home was the only place I could have all of this. I wanted a natural home delivery using the Lamaze method of breathing, free from any drugs which the baby would acquire if I was drugged. This baby has been warm and secure, floating about in amniotic fluid for nine mohths. It must be a strange and very alone feeling to decide to come out, trying to be "born." Then, to be washed and fooled with and slapped upsidedown on the ass and have silver nitrate on the eyes! Oh no! I wanted Michael to deliver his own child. I wanted the baby to be put on my belly and suck my breast right away. I wanted him to lie on my chest and hear the familiar and comforting sound of my heartbeat.

I chose England for the ideal place since we had a house in the country, ninety miles northeast of London. It is illegal to deliver your own child in England. They say you are tampering with a life other than your own. I saw a doctor there and told him my story. He advised me to have the baby in a hospital because I was anemic and couldn't afford any loss of blood for fear I might go into shock. I still insisted on a home delivery and started getting iron injections to bring up my red blood cell count. I received a shot every other day for a month. We booked a midwife, which is normal procedure in the rural areas. She comes to your house twice. The first time she checks on your facilities and gives you a list of the supplies she needs for the delivery. Empty jam jars (for alcohol, thermometers, etc.,) cotton wool, boiling water, etc. She comes once again to make sure you have everything and to examine the position of the fetus. When you start labor you are supposed to call her again and she will come to check you out. Then she goes on other calls and comes back to you later. This is her usual procedure. Mine was unusual for her.

I started labor at 7:20 A.M., after a restless night. I checked and found some spotting of blood, one of the signs and thought, "Oh no! Not now! I'm so tired!" I tried to sleep some more, but couldn't. Went downstairs to make tea, lobelia, to help calm me. I was getting very excited by now. I ate a mixture of liquid senna and herbs with honey as a laxative. It's good to clean out all of your passages to leave more room for the baby. Mike lit a fire

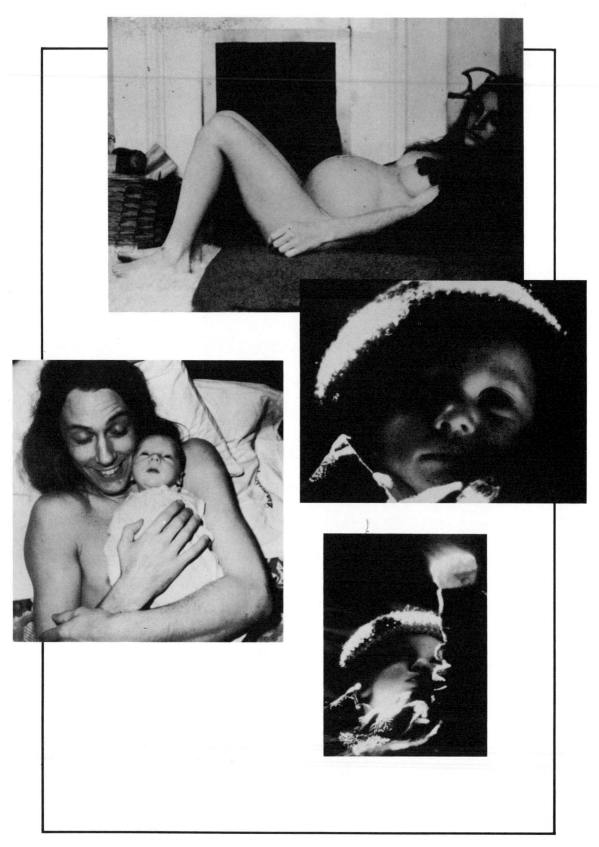

in the living room and I sat close until I felt uncomfortable. Upstairs again, to my bed and a cosy warm electric blanket. I stayed there for about three hours. I did not move nor speak. When I did, the contractions felt more painful. When they were getting really strong, Mike filled up the tub and I floated in there for awhile. It was easier to handle the contractions when I was suspended in water and weightless. I had "backache" labor which means that between each contraction you have shooting pains across your back. The best position for this type of labor is to lie on your side with pillows to support your head and shoulders, one under your belly (this one is quite important so as not to have your belly hang down and cause it to feel as if it were stretching), one between your legs and one under your feet. By this time the senna had been working for quite some time and I had moved my bowels at least six times.

Mike was upstairs reading "The Emergency Childbirth Manual" from the New York Police Department. It was the tenth hour and we still had not called the midwife. I had been bleeding quite a lot and Mike was becoming quite concerned. I still did not want to phone her. Another thirty minutes and we decided that it was probably best that she be there. You see, our personalities had conflicted from the very start. She was very prying and asked too many personal questions about which religion the baby would be (Michael and I are from different religious backgrounds), if the baby was to be circumsized, how we earned our money and so on. But, I had no other choice, she was assigned to my district.

When Mike went to phone (a quarter of a mile away) I was alone. I felt the baby slip down my back. What a feeling! "Will I have to deliver this baby by myself?" Mike was back, unable to reach her, but had left word. Half-an-hour later she arrived, big and mad, with her assistant. She changed the red bulb in the bedroom for a bright white one and ran around yelling and calling me irresponsible. I paid her no mind. I just told her that all she had to do was what she knew best, deliver my child. When she examined me, the waters broke. With the head crowning, she arrived just in time. I felt the urge to push, as if a vacuum was sucking all my insides out from under me. It was uncontrollable. "No," she said, "not now." By that time the doctor had arrived. Doctors don't usually deliver babies at home in England unless there are complications. He was standing by. "Let her push," he said. I pushed again and almost had it. Then, through the window I saw a red flashing light. "What's that?" "We called an ambulance," she said. "If the baby isn't born soon you will have to go to the hospital." This woman was determined to make me have my baby in the hospital. I sat up and started yelling at her. "I will not be moved with these contractions! Come on baby, let's show 'em! PUUUSSSHHH!" "We have to cut her." "What?" PUUUSSSHHH and out he came! PHEW! A boy, all beautiful and wet with liquid. They pulled on my cord. "We believe in an active third stage," they all said. "Good God, what are you doing down there?"

179

Michael and I were crying, almost totally unaware of their presence. I gave him a son, Noah, and that was all we were aware of. Then, because of my anemia, I felt very weak. Michael thought it would be a good idea for me to spend the night in the hospital for my own safety. So, off to the hospital with Noah. I stayed there for three days resting and recuperating. I took long baths in their six foot tubs. When it got to feeling uncomfortable again, back to the baths. I was in a room with six other women although there were 20 beds. We exchanged stories and I learned how to care for my new child by watching the nurses and the other women. By the time I returned home I felt much stronger and even happy to have been able to get some rest.

Noah is two and a half years old now and is very healthy and active. He was breast-fed for a year and a half. Although the whole point to having him at home was to establish a close family unit in familiar surroundings, I don't think my stay at the hospital altered us at all.

# MAXIME DE LA FALAISE McKENDRY
# Childbirth At Home

We were all born in the same house in St. John's Wood, England. It was built for my father by his mother. He was already established as a portrait painter. It was an incredible house, like a country house in the middle of London. A garden on each side, huge kitchen and pantry, sitting rooms, bedrooms, studies, corridors. My mother was married in that house. She swears that no one ever knew she was pregnant except my father. She was very slim and wore floating dresses. One day in the middle of a luncheon party she suddenly left the room, went upstairs and gave birth to me.

At the time I was expecting Loulou, Alain and I were living in Paris. I was working for a magazine as a fashion editor, painting backgrounds, modeling, drawing fashion sketches, and doing English translations of the captions. By the time I arrived in London, my mother had arranged everything in the house for the birth. The gamp (midwife) had already moved in. A huge woman, she gave me a book to read about other people's deliveries. But they were all tricky experiences, especially for women with ballet training like me. It told of their twisted muscles and narrow passages as the worst for giving birth. The gamp had also brought a mass of rubber tubes into the house. When I started to have birth pangs, I set fire to the medieval looking rubber implements. It gave me a lot of satisfaction. I didn't know what they were meant to do but it relieved me knowing that they wouldn't be used on me. There was this acrid smell of burnt rubber all over the house and a little heap of black mess on the bathroom floor.

The gynecologist, who had been checking me out in the last days and was supposed to deliver the baby, was unavailable. He was playing golf. The midwife sent my husband to buy some ether.

First, I drew a hot bath and stayed in it with a book and a large dose of whiskey. The birth pangs were mild. I had brought my old French maid with me from Paris. She would come in the bathroom crying, "Oh! I never thought I would see Madame in such a state." Finally, very soaked, I got out of the bath, completely relaxed. Having been myself in the same state as the baby inside of me, I could sense it would just swim out. There was a portable table set up in the bathroom. I got up on it for the gamp to look at the dilation stage. Alain put a little bit of cotton wool with ether under my nose asking me at the same time to translate French captions. The pangs got stronger . . . "Ce petit chapeau divin en feutre de calais cache un petit nid ou un rouge-gorge tient des cerises dans le bec . . . cette adorable chasuble bleu rayé . . ."

I was lying on that table (it was padded with all sorts of pillows) feeling totally relaxed from the bath when the doctor arrived. I became really curious to see who would come out of me and got interested in the whole birth. They strapped me loosely to the table. I guess they were afraid I would fall off. I didn't have time to protest. In half-an-hour, after a lot of tam-tam like the beginning of a really good dance, Loulou was born. I didn't tear or need to be sliced, being so stretched from the hot water.

Even after the umbilical cord was cut, the spiritual connection was so strong. We shared the same bed. It was so important. Hospitals are not concerned with the spiritual side, they even hide your insides from you, for them it's garbage. I wanted to see it all, feel it all.

Alexis, my second child, was born in the hospital by induced birth. It was so boring waiting in this blank room. The induction seemed to spoil the whole natural rhythm of birth. I felt rather like a hen laying one of a million supermarket eggs. After the birth I was led to my room, he to the newborn ward. It all felt very abstract. Alexis only became real and personal after we had gone back home.

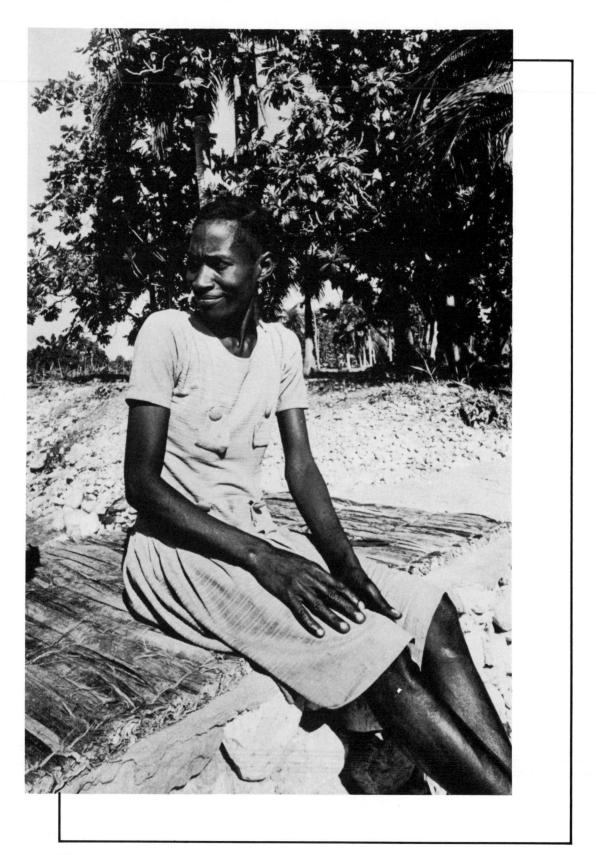

# ZILINA LUC
# Childbirth As It Comes

*Zilina Luc lives in a small village in the countryside of Haiti. She has five children and works as a housekeeper at the Episcopal Center.*

I had Wilfred, Sheila, Leslie and Madeleine at home with the assistance of a midwife. Nene, my husband, was there too and a neighbor friend who held me under the arms when I felt weak. I always gave birth standing up except for Leslie. With Leslie I sat at the edge of a chair, one knee down, the other up, legs apart. It was all quite easy except for the first one. There I had pains. After the fourth one I was soon pregnant again. I went to the dispensary because I was feeling very ill and when I was examined they said I had to have an operation because this was an ectopic pregnancy. So, when I was pregnant with Zulimen I thought it would be better to have the baby in the hospital.

When I was ready to give birth I went to take the bus. As I was walking to the stop place, the baby decided to come out. After she was born, I sat down by the side of the road in a ditch. It was late afternoon but there were quite a few people walking to the village. Somebody went to get the midwife. She cut the cord; she always does it with a Gillette razor blade. Someone else took the baby to our house and I walked back holding my skirt between my legs. I was bleeding so much! But I was feeling all right. The midwife is paid ten gourdes ($2.00) for her services. Besides helping in the delivery, she prepares three herbal baths to be taken the following days. The palma Christi leaves mixed with various other leaves helps the contraction of the body's dilated parts and keeps the body warm.

# MINIUM CAYEMITE
## Yoga Instructor

*Minium Cayemite is a teacher of Hatha Yoga in Port au Prince, Haiti. He is the father of twelve children, many of whom he delivered himself. He teaches controlled breathing to pregnant women.*

I am convinced that childbirth can again become a natural phenomenon for city women, as it still is for the women of our countryside. The latter are closer to the earth than the city women. They eat fresh food prepared simply and lead a physically more active life, enabling them to breathe with more efficiency and to remain limber. Also, they are less informed than the city woman who is gripped with fear, anxiety, doubt and nervous tension. The peasant woman, luckily for her, still has the soul, the simplicity of a child, the kind that acts without reasoning which is quite a valuable state from a psychological point of view. They are therefore more apt than the city women to have confidence in their own body's processing of natural events. It is not uncommon in Haiti for these women to give birth, with great facility, as it comes. On their way to the market, for example, and two or three hours later, with the help of people passing by, they get back on their donkey with their new babe and head for home without fussing.

So, for women who have lost the basic instinct by living in an artificial environment, it is necessary to study the natural phenomenon that is birth and re-adapt themselves through controlled relaxation and controlled breathing.

Controlled relaxation does not entail drowsiness. Rather, it is an extreme awareness and a good muscular and mental control during labor. As for controlled breathing, it is best applied for the periods when the uterus contracts.

As of the third month of pregnancy, the woman interested in learning such methods should find a qualified person who can coach her and the father. If they happen to live too far away from such centers, they can inform themselves in detail from specialized books.

# GLADYS ST. LOUIS
# Yoga Breathing

**Gladys:** Vanilo is now six days old. I don't know if it's because I haven't had a baby in four years or because he has been benefiting from the breathing exercises and the vegetarian diet I have been following, but this baby seems so much calmer. He doesn't cry as often as the others did. Maybe because I am much calmer myself. For instance, now he is sleeping, he lies happily in his crib. It's not at all the same as the others, there is a difference.

**Caterine:** What method had you chosen to give birth to your other children?

**G:** When I was expecting my first child a friend gave me a book about natural childbirth by a French doctor, Jacques Gaillard, I think. I tried the exercises, not with regularity, but enough to get me through the first three births in a conscious state (but not exactly without anxieties). However, this time I went to Professor Cayemite in my third month of pregnancy, as required, and started training with his breathing method and a few basic postures.

I think it helps. I have seen friends suffer needlessly for days because they were not prepared. You can control your own body with your breathing when the contraction happens and then the doctor knows when you are having a contraction. But, if you haven't any control over your body and you just twist and grimace without giving yourself a rest, it's difficult to figure out what's happening. And, if you don't know, how can you let the doctor know?

**C:** And how did the birth go with this child?

**G:** The day I felt ready I said to Professor Cayemite that I would see him tomorrow at the hospital. This time I didn't feel that what was going on was pain. It was more like something was in the making. I waited until 3:00 A.M. to go to the hospital. When I arrived, the doctor said I was 3 cm dilated. I would feel the contraction coming and I would breathe slowly in rhythm and it would all go well. It may have been because I am now used to having babies, but it was more likely due to the breathing. No pain. A few minutes later I felt like pushing. I told the doctor. At 5:38 A.M. the baby came without great efforts or problems. It went so fast this time. Before, for the other births, there were many moments when I didn't know what to do with myself and I wished the process would speed up.

**C:** Were you given a local anaesthetic?

**G:** What's that?

**C:** A drug that numbs part of your body against pain.

**G:** No, nothing medical except for the incision. I didn't want to take any of the herbal teas women here (in Haiti) usually absorb because I wanted to be able to evaluate the strength of the contractions and how the method works for it. I wanted to be able to tell the others first-hand if the breathing really works and how. With the herbal teas the sensations might have been

covered up. But, for the incision which had to be sewn I still followed the traditional local custom of taking a bath of palma Christi leaves (ricin oil). The doctors don't approve of it. They say it's empirical, but it works for me and that's essential. I felt so much better afterwards. I think it's one of the good customs that has been passed on through the generations and I will recommend it to my daughter.

**C:** Did you have your other children in the hospital?

**G:** Yes, always in the hospital because I always consulted with a doctor and they want to deliver children in well-equipped hospitals. But going along with Professor Cayemite's method, I could have had the child at home if my husband had been prepared to receive the baby. I couldn't take the risk. He wouldn't have known what to do with the umbilical cord.

**C:** Isn't he interested?

**G:** He is. In fact, he wanted to go with me to the hospital and stay. He drove me there and the doctor told him it might be up to twelve hours till the baby came. I knew it would be any minute but we thought it was best if he went home. Anyway, the children had to be driven to school the next morning. A yoga teacher came by a few months ago and said that he had delivered his own baby. My husband told him that it was too bad that he couldn't have learned from him.

I do not intend to have any other children. People in Haiti have twelve to fifteen children but I think that four is more than enough. But, if I ever change my mind I will have the next one at home. I went to the hospital for fear of complications and because there is no one at home who knows how to receive the baby with basic first care knowledge. I would rather stay at home any time. It's cosier, you are more at ease. I don't much like going to the hospital. When I was there I spent a sleepless night thinking about my other children.

**C:** How long were you in the hospital?

**G:** Two days! I had the baby early Friday morning and I got out Sunday morning. There were no complications, the child was very healthy. A funny thing happened when I arrived at the hospital. One of the doctors asked me if I was calm and relaxed and I said yes and then he told me that my regular doctor was away for a couple of days. I guess he thought that that would worry me but all went very smoothly. It's really worthwhile to prepare for your baby!

**C:** How do you feed him?

**G:** I do mixed feedings. I do not have enough milk so I also give him formula. There is another thing I noticed with the other births. Two days after giving birth I always had fever. I was told that it was because of the coming of the milk. This time I did not have fever and the milk came easily.

However, I experienced something I cannot recommend. I was completely breast-feeding my second child and around the sixth month after I had her I was still not getting my period back. In the early months I thought it was normal because of having a new baby. I know it does happen, but, when I went to see the doctor, he told me I was five months pregnant! I don't wish that on anyone. No sleeping at night with the new baby, tired during the day with the two of them. Oh! It was the most exhausting time of my life. But, anyway, I think that when you know how to breathe "well" a lot of things get easier.

# ANN SIMON
# A Personal View of
# Nurse-Midwifery

"Why not?," I asked myself as I considered the possibility of having a nurse-midwife deliver my second child. Through local publicity and the first-hand report of a friend, I had recently been hearing about the Maternal Health Service (Springfield, Ohio).

As I thought back on my experience with a private obstetrician during my first pregnancy, I realized that I certainly hadn't needed a highly trained specialist to conduct the routine pre-natal examinations, or during that particular (unusually easy) delivery either. Let me make it clear that I was very satisfied with the obstetrician whom I saw during my first pregnancy, but by the time I was pregnant again he happened to be delivering at a different hospital which did not have some services I wanted. So, why not place myself in the care of nurse-midwives? There would be a doctor to double-check that the pregnancy was normal, and one of several specialists would be on call for delivery if any complications were to arise. I was satisfied that I would receive good quality medical care and I liked the idea of trying out something new. So I did.

As it turned out I was delighted with my decision. I had certainly concluded correctly that I would receive good medical care. But it wasn't until I entered the examining room on my first visit that I received a glimpse of what has turned out for me to be the real outstanding benefit of the program. There on the bulletin board above the desk were prominently and proudly displayed several dozen snap-shots of newborn babies. I was delighted and astonished: the nurse-midwives had cared enough about these babies and their mothers to put their pictures up! The nurse-midwife entered the room, sat down comfortably, and asked if I had any questions. After discussing all my concerns, she usually had some information or suggestions of her own to add before asking me to lie down so she could examine me (gently, I might add). Revolutionary procedure. I always had to wait until after being examined in order to ask my doctor questions. I was left lying on my back to shout my inquiries to his retreating figure.

That the nurse-midwife volunteered information I didn't even ask about was even more amazing. I later learned she was following an informal agenda of topics to discuss at each visit if the patient hadn't already brought them up. The topics included general information that would satisfy the woman's natural curiosity about what is going on inside her body during pregnancy and what to expect during childbirth and her hospital stay. Instructions were also given about crucial aspects of maternal care, such as nutrition (with more individual attention than a list of foods passed out casually at the first visit), the importance of rest and naps, future plans for birth control, and the necessity for giving thought to organizing the home and meeting the needs of all members of the family at the time of the new baby's arrival. Incredible.

By the time I learned that I would be joined early in labor by a nurse-midwife who would remain present until the birth, I knew enough about the Maternal Health Service not to be surprised again. My husband and I were well-prepared by our previous childbirth experience (and a refresher course) to work together to keep me comfortably participating during labor and delivery, and we were expecting to do it basically by ourselves. But the encouraging presence of the nurse-midwife made the job much easier and more enjoyable for us both. I was so confident of her sincere dedication to me as a person that I was able to relax and trust her absolutely. She interpreted the progress of labor much more accurately than we could have by ourselves, and she supported both of us—emotionally and physically—through a period of fatigue and discouragement. By the time she held up our new daughter for us to see, my husband and I felt a real bond of intimacy and gratitude to the woman who had assisted and joined us in the joy of giving birth.

The nurse-midwife regards pregnancy and childbirth as a real, living heart-felt experience, as well as a series of important physical signs and events scientifically to be observed and dealt with. She is concerned with the feelings and the life of the pregnant woman, as well as the condition of her uterus, blood pressure and related physical details. She regards the mother as a human being in the midst of one of the most exciting moments of her life, rather than a body to be manipulated through a series of procedures designed to promote optimum efficiency on the part of the doctor and the hospital staff.

Any woman who is regarded with such consistent respect and individual concern throughout pregnancy and childbirth could not avoid liking herself and her baby as a result. Given the choice of selecting obstetrical care again at any time in any place, I would go far out of my way to find a nurse-midwife if I possible could. I enthusiastically encourage my friends to take advantage of the benefits I enjoyed so much, and I look forward to my own two daughters having the opportunity to do so much some day.

As I anticipate the increasing participation by nurse-midwives in obstetrical care throughout the world in the future, two concerns come to mind. I think it should be made widely known that nurse-midwifery programs provide unique advantages of warm and comprehensive attention above and beyond meeting standards of medical excellence, so that women will be informed about the nature of care available to them if such a program is established in their community. Even more important, I hope that the established professions will share my conclusion that the nurse-midwife has far more to offer than an additional pair of arms and eyes to aid the busy obstetrician, and will incorporate the mother-centered attitudes and approach of nurse-midwifery into their own established office and hospital routines.

# BARBARA JOHNS
# Breathing And
# Exercise Training

**Caterine:** Did you decide when you wanted to be pregnant or was it just something that happened?

**Barbara:** No, I hadn't planned it.

**C:** Did you want to keep the child or have an abortion?

**B:** Oh no, I was very curious about having a child, I just wasn't very ready. I figured fine, but it wasn't, you know, a "why not" kind of thing.

**C:** How old were you then?

**B:** Well, it was four years ago, I was 28.

**C:** And were you aware of the different choices available to you at the time?

**B:** Not really, I had heard a lot about natural childbirth but I hadn't really gotten into it at all. I knew I was pregnant almost immediately after conception. I mean I remember when I think about it. I am sure it was the day that these friends of ours got married. Hmmmm, it was really nice. And then I knew for sure that I was pregnant because I started to retain water; I gained weight immediately. I mean like straight away I gained about three or four pounds within days. I didn't go to the doctor to find out until I was about two months pregnant because I just knew and there was no reason to go. All was fine.

Sam, to whom I was married at the time, and I were going to Europe that summer because he was doing a film and I was going to do the still photography on the picture. It was just a wonderful pregnancy because we were in France for four months during the middle of the pregnancy. It was very relaxing and we were both working together and we were with people we loved. It was really one of the nicest times of my life. I wrote to Dr. C. (I had decided to use my sister's gynecologist) and he wrote back instructing me to have monthly check-ups in France. Well, I had this incredible water retention problem and sometimes my legs would swell up two or three inches. After a meal, for instance, and then I would put my feet up and it would go down. But it scared me, I thought it was toxemia. I kept on going to the doctors and they would say, "Oh! You are going to have a baby! How nice! Oh, Don't worry about anything." I went to one doctor in Nice, in the south of France and I got on the scale. It was in kilograms. I asked how much it was, did a little addition. I weighed 137 pounds and I thought Dr. C. was going to kill me! How funny that I should have been frightened by a doctor. The French doctor said, "Très bien!" He crossed it out and put down three kilograms less. The French doctors are very casual. They just keep telling you to take it easy. But, on the whole, it was a wonderful time and then I came back to America.

I had written to Dr. C.'s hospital and told them I would be back on the fifteenth of November and they wrote me in Paris saying, "We are terribly sorry but if you want your husband to be in the delivery room, you'll have to be back by November first. That's the last time we'll have classes for people of your due date." I came home on November fifteenth and called Dr. C. and asked him to make arrangements for me. He told me to call the woman in charge of giving the lessons at the hospital. I called her and told her I would be happy to pay extra for special tutoring and all she could answer, as if she were a broken record, was, "I am sorry but you have to have your school diploma after all the classes have been attended and you are two weeks late." I said, "Fuck you very much, I am changing doctors, changing hospitals and I am having my husband in the delivery room with me. Your rules are not going to dictate to me how to have my baby." And I did it. It was getting towards the end of the seventh month and I changed doctors. I went to Doctor Chabon and, for the exercises, to Verna Dashinger. She is a wonderful Indian woman. She told me that at Roosevelt Hospital they only give you a poodle cut, not a complete shave, and it doesn't itch so much when it is growing in.

**C:** What's so great about that? Do you know that you don't really have to be shaved at all?

**B:** Yeah! Yeah! I know. But, for a hospital, this is really as far as you can go.

　　Anyway, the Tuesday before Thanksgiving, I went in for my examination at Dr. Chabon's and he told me I was seventy-five per cent effaced. He also said, "I am going to Puerto Rico for the weekend but there is Doctor So-and-So (I forget his name) who is taking over. If you go into labor, don't worry, he is fine. He's cool." So everybody in the exercise class expected me to be the first one, right? I had Jamie two months later. I was due at the end of December, but it looked like I was going to have the baby in November and I didn't have it until January. What suspense every night! For two months I thought, "Tonight is the night!"

**C:** Why at night?

**B:** I don't know. I always thought I would go into labor at night. To me babies are always born in the middle of the night. Isn't that crazy?

**C:** What time was the baby actually born?

**B:** At 8:55 in the morning.

**C:** And when did your labor start?

**B:** I started labor at about six o'clock the morning before, but it was very soft labor. I thought, "Oh, this is no problem at all." And then the hard labor started.

**C:** Did you feel that labor was painful?

**B:** No, but thank God for the breathing. I was in labor for a long time and I spent the whole day walking around New York sort of in soft labor. I was really exhausted, I mean I was so physically tired by the time I got to the hospital.

**C:** Had you visited the hospital beforehand?

**B:** Yes.

**C:** What was it like?

**B:** It looked just like any other hospital, I mean hospitals depress me.

**C:** What depresses you about hospitals?

**B:** Well, the same thing that depresses me about a dishwasher or an air conditioner. I don't like the noises and I don't like the artificial air. But you know it's all very functional.

**C:** What changes would you like to see in the hospital's childbirth procedure from your experiences there?

**B:** At Roosevelt I didn't have any complaints at all, none. All the nurses were from Trinidad or Jamaica. It was like a dream, they were so kind. The labor room was ugly but they are not going to make a pretty labor room you know.

**C:** Many people say that they would like it to be nice.

**B:** I think that I would hate it even more if it were that institutionalized prettiness. I mean like the prison cells at Riker's Island are "decorated" and they are really obscene. I'd rather have the cockroaches! I really wouldn't, but there is something about their sterility, I don't want them prettier. A hospital is a hospital. What I would like them to be is less pretty if anything. More chrome and more design; instead of aqua walls, make them white. Make it hospital white and chrome and make it more what it is instead of trying to take the edge off and make it something else. A hospital is a hospital. In the old days they used to have wooden beds but wooden beds were not functional.

**C:** Did you feel nervous during labor?

**B:** No, not at all. But it was endless, endless, endless.

**C:** Were you frightened?

**B:** I was frightened thinking that it would never end and that the birth would be difficult.

**C:** What did you concentrate on that made you feel more relaxed?

**B:** I focused on a spot in the wall and I focused on the breathing. I was very actively involved in having Jamie but, at the same time, I was also very passive, letting it just happen I guess. But now I think that if I had another child, it would be a different experience.

For one thing, I was afraid to hope that a baby would come out. I remember thinking, "What comes out of people? Nothing but shit, mucus, urine, blood. Just ugly things come out of people. What can ever be beautiful that can come out of me?"

**C:** Do you really think that all of that is ugly?

**B:** Yeah, I don't think it's gorgeous. You know it is nothing that I would get all excited about like Jamie. I couldn't believe it when I went to the doctor once and I first heard that heartbeat, it was so fantastic. I just could not believe that there was really a baby in there. I mean there was some part of me thinking that I was just getting fat and just eating too much. And I was getting very fat anyway. So I looked at the spot on the wall and I did my

breathing. I never really had pain. I was on top of the tension. Sam woke me up, I was asleep for three seconds between contractions and it was just once that I forgot to breathe in and then it was painful because I wasn't prepared for it.

**C:** Did you get any medicine?

**B:** I was given a little medication, not very much, but something in the arm intravenously.

**C:** Do you know what it was?

**B:** Sugar? Something to speed up the labor because it was going on too long. Jamie's head was turned around towards the back and that slows down the process. I had been in labor for twenty-seven hours.

**C:** Did you decide when to go into the delivery room?

**B:** No, the doctors and nurses check on how advanced the dilation stage is. When it was time, the doctor asked me if I wanted to walk into the delivery room and I said okay. I walked from the labor to the delivery room and it felt like I had a basketball between my legs, it was unbelievable.

**C:** Were you in the labor room with a lot of other women?

**B:** No, each person in that hospital has a labor room to themselves. It is specifically a labor room. Then I went into the delivery room and had the baby without any problems and a lot of hard pushing. Afterwards, I was wheeled back to a regular room, a semi-private room that I shared with another woman. I felt like getting up only an hour later.

**C:** Considering everything, how were you treated in the hospital?

**B:** Being in a hospital is more impersonal than anything I know. Jamie was sleeping in the same room as me but for the first twelve hours they had him under observation, cleaned him up and kept him in another room. This was three years ago, but I remember this one nurse, she kept looking at me. She was black, had an afro and kept looking in my eyes. She was so beautiful and soothing. She understood, you know. When she brought in Jamie after the twelve hours, or whenever, when it was time for me to feed him, she handed him to me and said, "Feeding time!" "What should I do?" "Oh honey," she said, "You'll think of something!" And then she walked out of the room. And there was no nervousness. I put him to my breast and that was it. I never had problems with the milk. None, and I am sure it is because of that nurse. If she had said what you do is hold him here and so on I would have been a nervous wreck and it would have been a performance. But she handed him to me and split and that is the way they are there. I mean for a hospital, if you want to give birth in a hospital, it really was wonderful. They let the men come in for breakfast. They are so considerate. How nice to have a place where the man stays with you. Sam was there for the whole birth. That is pretty fantastic. In fact, at Roosevelt they encourage that, they really want the man to be there.

**C:** In this photograph you are in the hospital corridor looking behind a glass at a lot of babies. Doesn't that freak you out to see all these babies in a cage like this? Doesn't it look like the setting for a science fiction picture?

**B:** Yeah, I can understand why it would seem that way to you but to me it doesn't. I saw the babies, you are seeing the hospital. That is because you had your baby at home, the way I would love to have had it. I think that the emphasis in hospitals should be to treat women like adults and not have all those fucking rules. If a woman does choose to have a baby in the hospital, since she is paying for it, the experience should at least be pleasant and mine was. My next child, for example, I would definitely have in the hospital. Not so much for my sake but for the kid's sake because maybe it would be a difficult birth. Who knows? Then that kid is going to need hospitalization right away. Anyway, I had a terrific time but I know that if I had gone to that other hospital, although it probably wouldn't have been a disaster, it would not have been such an interesting experience. It would have just been nothing in my life.

**C:** How long did you breast-feed?

**B:** I only did it just for two months because I went down to Texas to do an assignment for *Mademoiselle* magazine and for four days I was away from my son. This was another thing. I called my pediatrician and told him I had an assignment in Texas and asked him if I should go.

"Can you take him?"

"No, I have already asked them and they said no."

"Well, is it important?"

"Yes, it is, it is very important."

"Then go. Yes, never give up anything for that child."

I left him with my housekeeper and I went. Every four hours I was with the breast pump trying to keep up the milk but it was really complicated.

I want to tell you another thing that was really incredible. I made friends with my gynecologist and his wife. They came over for dinner a week after the baby was born and his wife said something to me that has been my motto ever since. She told me what she had said to her daughter the night before:

"Brenda, I have never sacrificed anything for you; you've been nothing but a plus for me."

And I can say the same thing to Jamie now. I hope that I can say that when he is ten years old. So for me, meeting Dr. Chabon was much more than just having a baby, it was an education. I know that Jamie is who he is today because of meeting Dr. Chabon. I read his book and it made a lot of sense. His attitude was very pleasant but I don't know about that chair that he invented! That chair was a bit weird. I was very uncomfortable on it. He has this theory about the law of gravity.

One thing more I would like to say. Whoever I am today, not that I am anything special, but I am closer to myself than I have ever been. I mean I know myself more than I ever have. But whatever I am, that was the beginning. That was the turning point in my life.

**C:** You mean having a child? Giving birth?

**B:** No, no, it wasn't just giving birth. It was also having my child totally aware of what was happening. If I had gone to the hospital and had been knocked out, it would not have been the same.

Natural childbirth was like the first inkling to realizing myself. Even though I was a success and had lots of credentials to my name, before I had Jamie I was always operating on someone else's time schedule. I was doing things because they were expected of me. I wasn't really doing them for myself and now is the first time in my life that I am doing for Barbara. I was not doing for Barbara, I was being Barbara. But it was the beginning and then a year and a half later I got into the woman's movement and that was another turning point in my life. Very important. Some people are born understanding what I am beginning to understand now. But I know that nothing would have been possible if I hadn't taken that step to be conscious every minute when I gave birth to Jamie.

# FREDERICK LE BOYER
# Welcoming The Newborn

*Frederick Le Boyer is a French doctor, author and filmmaker who has developed some revolutionary techniques for welcoming a newborn into the world. From intense observation of newborn reaction at birth, F. Le Boyer (who prefers not to be labeled as a doctor) has devised various ways to make the passage from life in the uterus to life outside a smooth episode. His prime concerns, besides safety for mother and child, are breathing, light, sound, touch and the spine. Gentleness is his primary objective. He has made a half-hour film, "Blissful Birth", documenting the evolution of the newborn from a state of primal panic to one of calmness, written a book on the same subject and produced a record especially for future mothers to play for soothing the newborn. Here he discusses how he developed his theory, what he does during and after the delivery and the astonishing results of his work.*

**Caterine:** What made you become so interested in the newborn?

**Frederick:** It's a long story, a long road. I realized that modern medicine had concentrated on the woman giving birth. The technical snags, that is, have been resolved for the most part and a lot of care and attention has been showered upon the mother. Methods and drugs have been developed to alleviate her suffering (if any) and most women feel much more secure now about giving birth. This is probably the reason why so many women today want to be active and conscious participants in the birth of their children. So-called "painless childbirth" in fact aims at birth without fear. Women learn about the process of birth and gain a better understanding of human reproduction. At the centers associated with birth, anxieties and fears are aired and eventually disappear.

Each of us carries within, throughout life, the imprint of birth. As I was delivering those thousands of children I kept on wondering why those babies cried so much once they were born.

One day I started to get very interested in the newborn baby. This baby is born, cries and often the more he cries the happier people are. They say, "The lungs are developing," or "This is a sign of strength," or some such inconsiderate conclusion. So I started looking at the newborn with a different eye. I thought this child should be content, feeling good, since at last he can move freely again as he did before he was in a tight prison.

**C:** What do you mean by a "tight prison?"

**F:** Well, there are two different periods for the fetus in the womb. In the first period of pregnancy the baby feels at ease. The egg and fluid develop at a faster rate than the fetus and he has lots of room to move, he is weightless. During the second half, movement becomes more difficult. The baby is still growing but his environment does not expand anymore at such a rate. The little one's universe gets smaller and smaller. It is a constriction after the early freedom. He has to bend over, fold arms and legs. The pressure on him comes to a paroxysm when labor starts. He is pushed all around, his head is squeezed and at last he is born! At that point he should be able to feel relief and enjoy his new freedom. It seemed to me to be an extraordinary paradox, that life should begin with such a contradiction. It must be an error on our part somewhere!

How could we make this newborn feel well upon arrival?

How could we let him feel that his new condition is so far better than his previous one?

All right, we each interpret other people's actions and reactions according to our own social structure. Some people will see a newborn's cries as a manifestation of triumphant life, others as cries of torture. All I can tell you is that I have seen and listened to a lot of newborns. It became evident that what we have there is a kind of heavy sobbing. I wondered why the baby breathed so well but cried and cried. Why such screaming and lamenting? It was like an unlimited sadness. So I tried to understand what the suffering of being born was all about and how it could be helped right then and there. There is no doubt that the suffering stems from the huge contrasts between what the infant has been through before and what he experiences at birth. But also, I am convinced that the lack of understanding with which the newborn are welcomed is one of the prime causes.

Most of the time babies are regarded as if they were living objects, something that does not see, hear or have a consciousness, and because of this there is no need to treat them with the respect due to a human being. I thought again and again, if this child in his mother's womb can hear, see and feel he must continue to do so when he emerges outside of his mother. It is as if, without preparation, we found ourselves on the moon. It is total anguish, first degree panic. Out of the uterus, the body has a different weight and density. Its surroundings are vast and unfamiliar. The sounds it hears are tremendous and the air it breathes is different in substance. From then on it came to me that this child was frightened by all this. Fear is mostly brought on by the unknown, something that we do not recognize as being familiar, such as in the case of the newborn.

I sought to make the transition from internal to external life a gradual development by prolonging some of the sensations felt in the uterus, and by slowly introducing the baby to the new ones.

All new babies are, in fact, hypersensitive through the skin, the eyes and the ears. They are in a raw state.

From the moment one realizes that being born is a tidal wave of sensations, it becomes very easy to help the newborn. Let him have the new sensations as slowly and progressively as possible and not all at once.

**Light and Sound.** To begin with, I deliver babies in dim light, indirect light to save the eyes. My whole film was shot in black and white in extremely low light. I ask for silence from all of the people around. In the womb the sounds are absorbed and softened by the amniotic fluid, but when the baby is born sounds and noises are explosive. A newborn perceives sounds the same way that a fish does; all over the skin surface. The whole body is one vast ear.

**Breathing and the Spine.** At the same time I let the newborn slowly enter the world of breathing. Air is brand new and it burns as it goes down. I wait awhile before cutting the umbilical cord to allow him two ways of breathing. He still receives oxygen through the blood pulsating in the cord while he is getting used to the air outside. Another very important area to the newborn, very often overlooked, is the spine. All the life energy goes through the spine. You become very conscious of this doing yoga, any of the martial arts or Tai-chi. The spine should be handled with the greatest of care. A newborn is held delicately and not jerked upside down as a welcome! The first gesture shouldn't be one of brutality. Whatever the treatment given to this little person at birth, the first contact outside the womb is bound to stay in a corner of his mind all of his life, and even though we cannot remember it in words, it becomes part of us.

We have quite a hard time understanding each other as adults. Children we understand even less and babies not at all. We cannot enter a baby's mental structure. I went through psychoanalysis and retraced many decisive moments in my life, all the way back to birth. Freud, W. Reich and Rank expressed it well in their work: distress stems from that first anxiety brought on by the separation from the mother. It is manifested in two aspects: one physical, through oxygen deprivation when the cord is cut too soon and secondly by the emotional separation.

**Touch.** It is considered normal to put a baby into cloth wraps straight away. But, after having been in such a slippery environment, the contact with clothes for the infant is as if he were being scorched. I put the newborn on the mother's abdomen, naked, since only skin is alive and sensitive enough to be bearable. He first lies on his tummy, so he will open very slowly from the fetal position, following his own speed and rhythm. The mother puts her hands on his back and so does the father (or myself) and the newborn feels security, being held closely once again as it was in the uterus for such a long time. The baby, once outside the uterus, suddenly feels that nothing is holding him together and has a sensation of bursting at the seams. Figuratively speaking, we are holding all of the pieces together. When he begins to stretch, I turn him on his side and only once he is comfortable in that position do I turn him on his back. A little later the mother props up the baby in a sitting position. His internal attitude has changed in some way.

I am dealing here with the first few minutes of his life when all feelings are so overwhelming. His first problem is with breathing. He should be allowed to tackle it by himself within his own rhythm. Therefore, he can slowly come to terms with breathing. When the cord has stopped pulsating and is cut, I make sure that the first separation from the mother is associated with something wonderful. This is so important because it is this very separation that causes human beings the most problems. Ninety-five per cent of all people are still children hung up with their mothers; it has been replaced by other things like offices and cars but they are all dependent!

I thought for a long time about what could be the first pleasant thing for a baby besides a kind hand. It became evident that the only acceptable element was water.

A bath is made ready, the water is a little above body temperature. The newborn is slowly immersed up to his neck. What happens then is wonderful: the child truly relaxes. You can see he feels at ease, often a real smile appears on his face. The child, having experienced this heavy new world, suddenly regains some of the liquid weightlessness he used to know. His eyes open and he starts looking all around. All I do at this stage is to hold him under his head at the nape of the neck, he does the rest.

**C:** Do you mean that the umbilical stub is immersed as well?

**F:** Yes, that's quite all right. The dangers of infection nowadays are minimal. As the child is taken out of the bath, a little antiseptic can be applied on the umbilical stump as a measure of safety. I have bathed over a thousand babies at birth and there has never been an infection. For the bath, hot water from the tap is fine. If it seems too hot simply pour cold water in it. Dip your elbow in the water to check the temperature. The baby in the warm water literally begins to play and to discover inner and outer space, moving arms and legs. You look at him and you really get the feeling of someone discovering the world. Often I turn my eyes away so as not to impose my gaze upon the child, their searching is so great that it almost brings tears. Some babies become calm straight away, stop crying and play at stretching their arms and kicking their legs; others take longer. The baby remains in the bath for three to six minutes. You can see the tension disappear, the spine is loose, a smile appears. We then take him out, dry him and wrap him very loosely in cotton cloth. Then another important moment comes: we let him experience stillness. It is quite an unknown feeling for the baby since he has lived in a storm for nine months.

**C:** What did you say?

**F:** In a storm. In other words, aboard a ship constantly in movement. Even when the mother is sleeping the diaphragm is moving. So for nine months the little being has lived in a tumultuous environment. He has never known one moment of respite. His sea of amniotic fluid is always in movement whether it is calm or stormy. So we lay him flat and suddenly nothing is moving anymore. Since the baby has gone through all these experiences slowly and lovingly he accepts his new stage, even being immobile which is one of the reasons why whenever the baby cries in the following months he will have to be picked up and rocked each time this primal panic seizes him. Often this panic is provoked as the child wakes up and realizes the world is still. This and the breathing factor are the two main contradictions between life in the uterus and life outside. But in this gradual coming to life you can really see the difference in the infant's reactions: the eyes open wide, he touches himself and the things around him. No more screams and tears but a smile. When a child is born this way everything becomes voluptuous instead of painful. Not only do the babies not scream, but there is a whole special newborn language going on, babbling and funny little noises.

# Lisa Law giving birth to Sunday Peaches

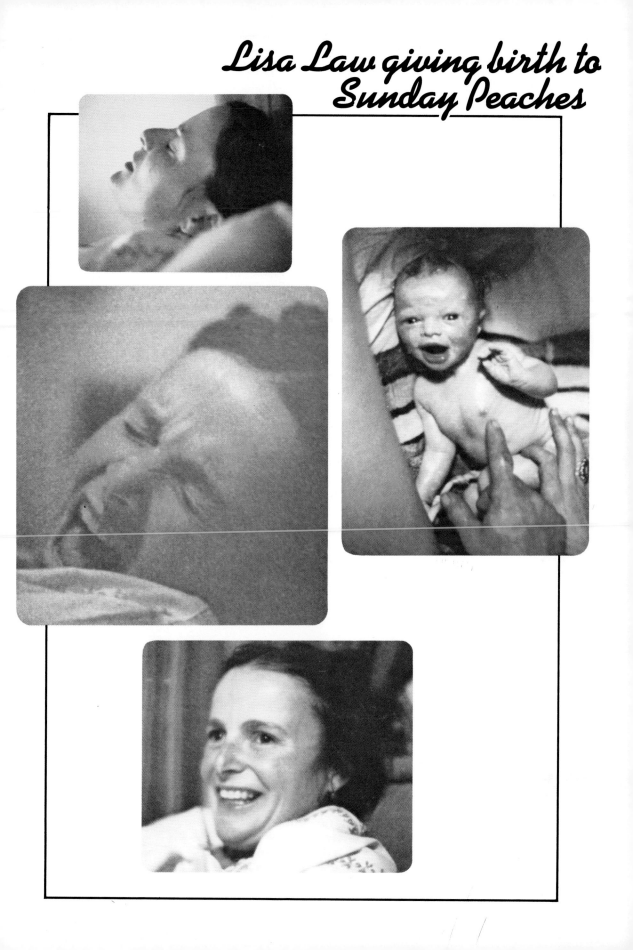

# Caterine Milinaire giving birth to Serafine

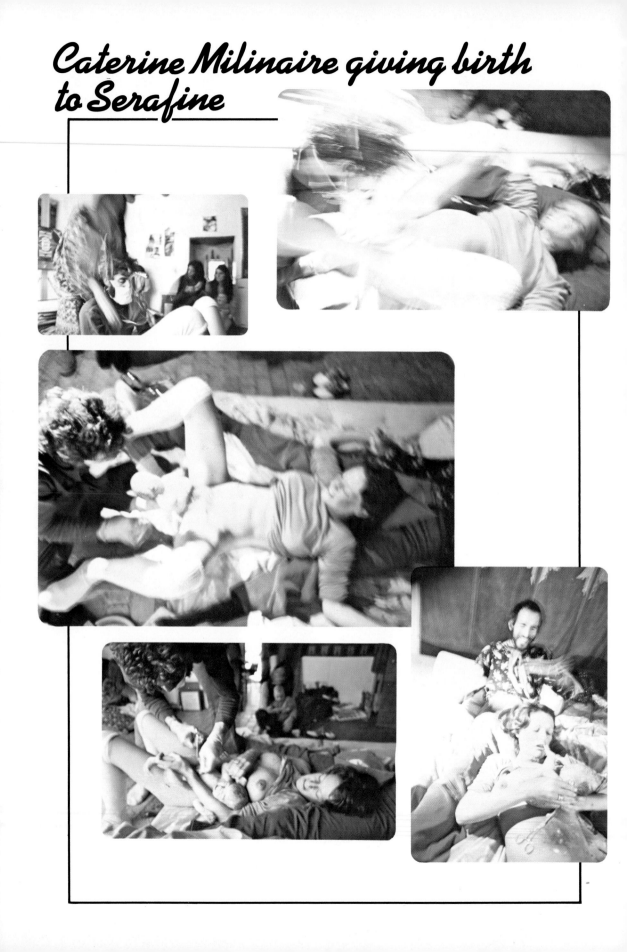

# Barbara Johns and Jamie

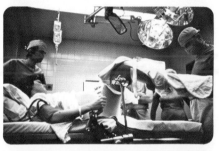

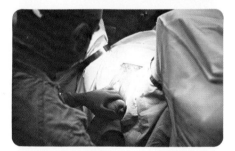

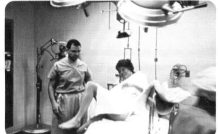

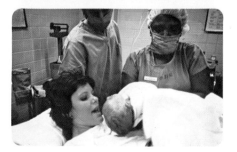

# Painting by Mati

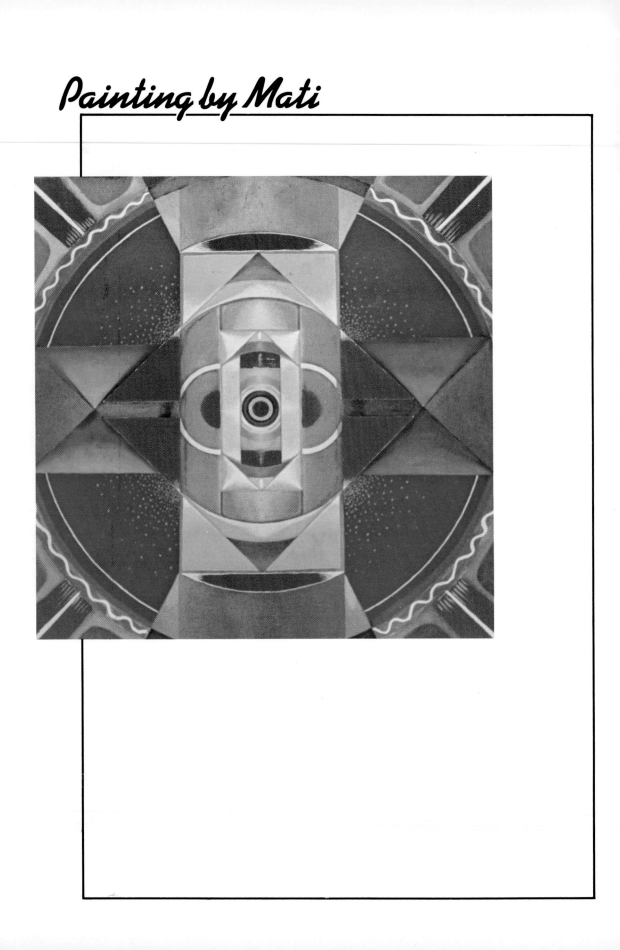

# fathers

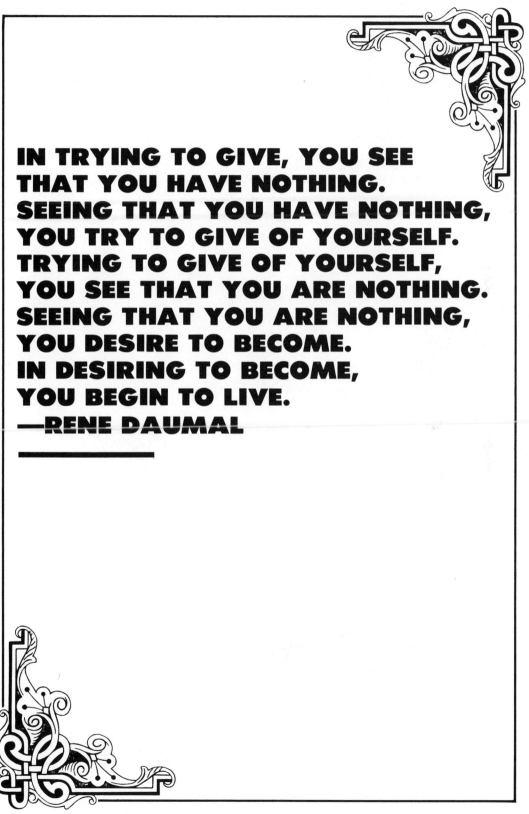

IN TRYING TO GIVE, YOU SEE
THAT YOU HAVE NOTHING.
SEEING THAT YOU HAVE NOTHING,
YOU TRY TO GIVE OF YOURSELF.
TRYING TO GIVE OF YOURSELF,
YOU SEE THAT YOU ARE NOTHING.
SEEING THAT YOU ARE NOTHING,
YOU DESIRE TO BECOME.
IN DESIRING TO BECOME,
YOU BEGIN TO LIVE.
—RENE DAUMAL

214

# fathers

There was a time when men did not recognize that semen contained the nucleus of paternity. It was generally believed that the source of a baby was engrained within the female, much like a seed lies in the earth. A good time was had sexually but it was not related to procreation.

Could it be that, unconsciously throughout the centuries, fathers have been perpetrating this belief by leaving the total care of the newborn to the mothers? Well, the usual answer to this question is that men were hunting for food, making war, cultivating the fields, going to the office, etc., so how could they have had the time to look after their offspring? Until recently it was almost as if babies didn't have fathers until they were old enough to walk and talk. Women were feeding, changing, cuddling and walking the little ones. It's only in the last decade that men have tried, in great numbers, to understand pregnancy and to be part of the birth and care of the newborn.

The relationship between a man and a woman who are expecting a child has a unique quality. The role of fathers in caring for their babies is changing radically, not so much because of inborn paternal feelings but rather as a result of general life-style tranformation. As people become more informed and enlightened, it becomes easier for a man and a woman to define the rules between themselves and their society. The traditional rigidity separating sex roles is fading. In this increasingly impersonal society, men may be feeling a greater need to relate more closely to the source of life.

Men gained a new consciousness when they realized that being part creator, a father, did not only mean fertilization. It also meant participation in making the pregnancy smoother, in giving strength and balance at birth and in caring for the newborn. There is the case of a teacher, Gary Ackerman, who claimed his rights to a paternity leave when his second child was born. This time he wanted to get acquainted right away with the new member of his family and share with his wife in looking after the infant. He won a three year legal battle reversing the policy of the Board of Education to grant child care leaves to fathers on the same terms as it does for mothers.

Assuming that this is the first baby, the new father has been learning, along with the mother, about the baby growing in her, following paternal classes or reading the same books as she does. Often men feel the classes are comical and they feel a little foolish being in this elementary school situation with so many pregnant women. However, as the classes progress and there isn't much else to do but listen, they begin to realize that they are learning vital information. The new father begins to understand the process through which the baby is born. It's often a very abstract learning experience as he cannot feel any of the subtle physical changes that the mother

feels. He can see, in the last months, that her abdomen moves as the baby changes position; he can touch it through the belly, and he can hear the little fetal heart. New fathers are just like the new mothers, inexperienced but eager to find out how a new person develops and to discover how to make the procedure as easy as possible.

David, a musician, and Susan, a fashion co-ordinator, had decided together to have a child. When she became pregnant, they both went to see a doctor in her third month. David stayed in the room while the doctor gave Susan an examination as she had requested. The doctor explained to both of them how the pregnancy would progress. David was very moved watching her grow. He kept on repeating, "It's so hard for me to imagine that I was once in my mother's belly like our child is in yours now. When I try to think of myself emerging into this world from her, I find it almost impossible to believe!"

Men have very mixed emotions about accepting the shape and state of pregnancy. To some it's comforting, reassuring, beautiful.

Andrew Warner, a furniture salesman in Santa Fé, New Mexico, says, "It's not every day that you see a woman carrying a child. I am superstitious, to me it's a lucky day if I pass a pregnant lady on the street. You see, I know she is in a special state of grace." Another man who was sitting in a playground told us he thinks that "Sometimes pregnant women look a little sad . . . so do women who are not . . . but somehow there is something very special, promising, in the way a pregnant woman looks which makes me feel warm towards her." To Fred Sweeda, a filmmaker in New York, "Pregnant women are extremely sexy. My wife Indiana and I have three children and every time she started to grow I thought it added to her sensuality; but some people are really inconsiderate. I remember walking with Indiana (eight months pregnant at the time) and as she was going through a door, a couple in a hurry just pushed her aside, not even excusing themselves. It hurt me too." Most expectant mothers have experienced the embarrassed, shifting gaze of someone ill-at-ease with the sight of pregnancy. A few men interviewed at random said that "It makes me uncomfortable to be next to a pregnant woman; they just look so full, I would be scared if she lost her balance and fell on me." Or, "Oh! pregnant women are so unattractive, absurd looking!" Husbands are often also put off by their wives' bulging pregnancy in making love or feeling sensual towards them. Sometimes this has to do with the attitude that the woman has towards herself concerning her own body.

Yet a man who is prepared to become a father and who wants to have a child with the woman he loves often finds the experience quite exciting. To Michael, "She really bloomed. I know it's not all easy for her, but seeing her grow made me feel more intimate, closer to the baby she was carrying."

The phase of labor ending pregnancy is a weird period for many fathers. Tom and Lisa from New Mexico chose home delivery. He remem-

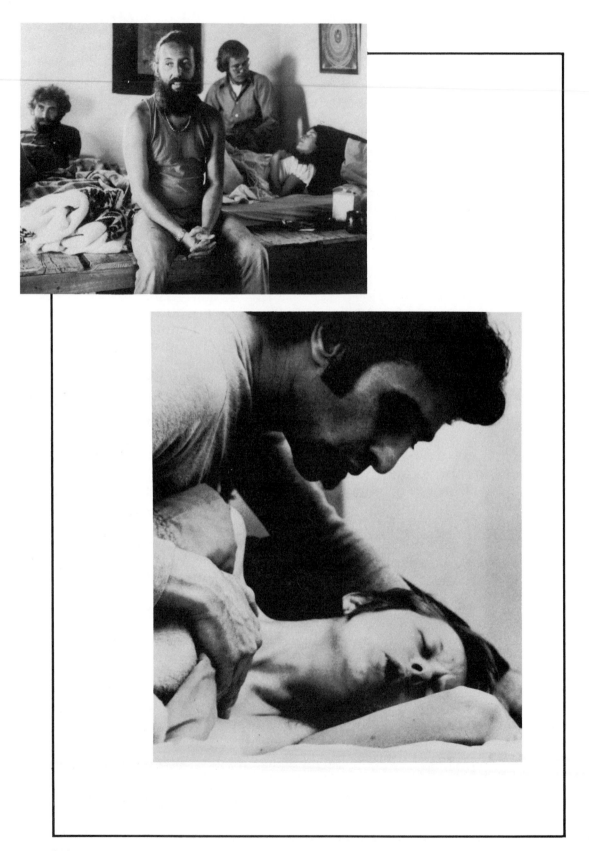

bers, "We were there, both in silence, concentrating; I felt it wasn't necessary to talk. The look in her eyes and the way she breathed said it all. There were changes taking place for which there were no words. I chanted for awhile. When contractions came, her expression ranged from tension to relaxation, from bliss to grimacing. I massaged her back and felt very close to her physically."

Steven, another father who was with his wife during labor, felt more helpless than Tom. "There we were, Jane and I, in this blank labor room. She seemed to be in pain, but when I would ask how I could help she would say she was all right and she was glad I was there. We played some games of tic-tac-toe. We had prepared together, but nevertheless I felt a little lost just sitting there. At times I would breathe along with her and that would relieve my own head cramps. Keeping in rhythm with her kept me from wanting to do something else. Between contractions, when Jane's breathing quieted down, even a whisper sounded like a cry in this empty room. Jane would sometimes grab the metal railing on the side of the bed, her muscles tensing, and then reassure me that all was fine and I could help her relax. I caressed the nape of her neck until the next contraction."

Steven was very disturbed to hear women crying and screaming in other rooms. "I thought, is this the right place? Am I in a psychiatric ward or an animal hospital? It was the same kind of attitude you get in a mental institution when somebody yells and nobody pays attention. It was a bit the same in that labor department." The comfort a father brings during labor is invaluable. Ossie had visited the hospital facilities beforehand with Vicky. Realizing that the place lacked warmth and coziness, he brought along a recorder to play soft tunes. Many men sense that the better a woman feels during labor, the more efficiently she will be able to function; and they use their ingenuity (from poems to massages) in order to achieve that state.

Not every man chooses to be with the mother during labor. Joel O. declared, time and again, that he certainly was bored, felt out of place and not at all needed in this phase of life, which in his view belonged exclusively to women. Besides, the sight of a baby being born was not particularly attractive to his eyes. He would rather see the finished product in the calmness of a bedroom instead of standing in everybody's way not knowing quite what to do. Men can be quite scared at the idea of participating in this mysterious happening. One father said "It's not as if she were going to the clinic for surgery or something. She is going to have a baby and she doesn't even know which doctor is going to help her. She says she doesn't think I should stay too long because she doesn't want to be seen in a funny state. She is darn right, I wouldn't know what to do if she started agitating or screaming!"

On the whole, however, for fathers-to-be who have prepared themselves, there is curiosity, excitement, high emotions. To fathers who realize that participating in and witnessing the birth of their own child brings them closer to understanding the meaning and the realization of a true union, becoming a father takes its full meaning. The enthusiasm, that shared intimacy of having a baby together, gives the new fathers the incentive to be with the mothers at the climax of the closest emotional and physical moment that can possibly be shared by a man and a woman: BIRTH.

There are a few fathers who have delivered their own babies at home like Tom Law: "Catching this little being in my hands was the most extraordinary sensation I ever had." And, in hospitals such as the Nesbitt Memorial Hospital in Kingston, Pennsylvania, one hundred and twenty-six fathers have delivered their own babies (from January to June of 1973). Both parents followed prepared childbirth courses. The delivery was expected to be normal. The mother was closely watched. A doctor was there in the delivery room in case he/she was needed, which of course does happen. The Supervisor of Obstetrics at the hospital reports that "None of the fathers crumple in the corner, many of the men experience deep spiritual feelings and the atmosphere creates a rapport between husband and wife." Not all hospitals, however, let the father in the delivery room as they fear he might be in the way or may faint. A bill is now pending before Congress to give "Every mother the right to have the biological father of her baby with her in the delivery room, if she chooses, and if the hospital receives Federal funds."

Fred wanted to be there; Indiana wanted him in the delivery room, but she also knew the sight of blood made him feel uneasy. He said he would overcome it. At the hospital, every time the doctor examined Indiana, the nurse asked Fred to leave the room. Finally, the doctor called the head nurse to ask why the husband couldn't stay if his wife wished it. He was told it was because of hospital rules. Fred recalls that for the first child, "I went outside of the labor room to have coffee and a cigarette and five minutes later returned to get dressed in sterile hospital clothing, but a nurse stopped me and said 'Sorry they are already in the delivery room, you cannot come in.' It didn't make any sense and there was no way I could argue. I didn't know any better, and it was my first baby. I used to think of childbirth as an operation until I expected children, and hospitals were like churches that had a monumental crushing effect on me. I know nurses, on the whole, want to do their best; but they are harassed, sometimes without being aware of it, by an antiquated code of behavior dictated by the hospital system. Kira was born without me, and Indiana didn't see anything because they removed her glasses. For the birth of Elena, our second daughter, I couldn't be in the delivery room either because there were complications. It was a breech presentation and eventually the obstetrician had to perform a Caesarean.

"For the third one, I got all dressed up again in that green surgical gear; it felt totally unnecessary. The windows in the delivery room were filthier than the soles of the shoes I had left behind. It felt dangerous because the baby was almost a month overdue. I was skeptical. Once I was in the delivery room, I felt there was nothing the doctor could do that would hasten or slow the process. Yes, I know there are all kinds of drugs, but in this case Indiana wanted to see if she could have a natural delivery before accepting anything. As the doctors thought there would be problems, there was a whole medical army on hand: the head of pediatrics, another pediatrician, a resident, two interns, an anaesthetist and two nurses.

"There we were, Indiana with her legs up in stirrups, pushing away. All was going fine. The doctor was sitting on his swivel stool, and asked if I wanted to have a look at the top of the head coming through. I moved to the side of the doctor. I became very numb, feelingless, because of the lack of words for what I really wanted to say! I returned to stand near Indiana's head. I focused on her hand, thinking how beautiful it was. I wanted to help, but there was nothing I could do. I watched Phillip come out. The white sheets draping the vaginal area made the whole thing look very surrealistic, like a painting. The nurse said, 'Some fathers feel shaky at this stage. Would you like a chair?' Once the baby was born I felt a spiritual lightness, like a sigh of relief: a lifting that is only created by death or birth. Indiana wanted to know if the baby was all right. He looked strange from postmaturity, kind of grey-yellow, but otherwise in good shape. It was strange to see him disappear so quickly again. He was taken into the special nursery for observation. I was amazed to see the internal life support system. I asked the doctor if I could see the membrane. He lifted it and it was light and weird, but the placenta and all that didn't shock me. I went back to the maternity ward with Indiana and stayed with her that afternoon feeling really good. Everything was O.K. The doctor had been really great. On my way out I stopped by to see Phillip, his yellow, sunken looks didn't turn me off. I thought good welcoming thoughts to him: 'Get better . . . everything is all right . . . Oh, gee you have a cute nose and I am happy you are here with us.' By that time I ran out of conversation and went home to feed the two girls, to tell them they had a baby brother and to collapse."

To be a father with the same meaningful sense that is implied in the word "mother" is not all that easy. The expectancy of birth has been fulfilled, the congratulations are over and suddenly there is the realization that a baby is a totally helpless and dependent being . . . alive, gurgling, twisting, crying. It's quite a surprise; the prenatal classes do not exactly prepare anyone for the anguish that grips your stomach when a baby cries and you do not know how to calm him/her. As for feeding and keeping the infant in clean diapers, it is a task many fathers have had a hard time coming to terms with. Peter admits, "I found it quite disgusting the first time I changed my daughter's diapers. It was all over the place, I had to wipe her, wash her. Once I got the hang of it there were no more problems. After all, we all started that way! The feeding was easy. Bridgitt gave her the breast

for six months, and I would give baby Monica one bottle a day because we wanted her to get used to it. When she started eating food I became pretty good at crushing bananas and feeding her with a little spoon."

Obviously, it is easier to be a full time father if the profession does not require a nine-to-five attendance. John, a painter, says, "I always thought I would like to look after my own child. Since we both work from home it's easier. We make arrangements in turn with our appointments, and alternate getting up at dawn for the early morning feeding. We are each as capable, one as the other, to look after the baby. It suits me that way." Fred didn't feel like helping change, wash, or feed his first baby. "I would play with the baby, yes, but I had a job. I was gone ten to twelve hours a day. Indiana was left alone in the apartment. I wasn't even making much money. I was trying like a good husband to provide her materially so that she could be comfortable. With the second child the situation was reversed, I had lost my job. Indiana was working in an office and I was looking after the children all day. I fed, clothed, bathed and took the two girls to the park. It was really enjoyable but at times it was frustrating because I was trying to set up a business of my own and I couldn't make any serious phone calls to organize the new business because the children would scream or pull on the telephone. With the third one we both worked at home and both looked after the three of them."

Often, looking after an infant scares a father. He feels awkward with his first child. Stanley was so intimidated he wouldn't dare go near the child in the hospital. Back at home it was worse. He would only look from a distance at the crib. This went on for two months. His wife got so irritated with his attitude that she left him with the baby for a whole day. The baby was given so much to eat that he threw up a few times and Stanley had to call a friend who knew more about babies to help him out.

To some fathers who are deeply absorbed in their daily office business, the feeling of fatherhood is superficial or doesn't gain meaning for quite awhile. "Gregory only started to interest me when he started to crawl." Or, "It's not easy to look after children; they are sweet but I have little time to spend with them because I am away from home a lot." Or, "Mary Ann is so adorable, she looks like my wife. Having a child changes your daily life. It keeps you really busy, feeding and changing at all hours of the day and night. We are lucky to have a Nanny." And, "The last of my four children is seven months old. He is fun, I give him the bottle once in a while; I even changed his diaper once or twice without wincing, but I don't get up in the middle of the night to find out why he cries. I am a heavy sleeper, my wife would hear it first anyway. I don't think it's difficult to be a father but unfortunately at the moment I don't have much time for the children."

On the other hand, more and more fathers are beginning to understand the importance of sensory ties between adult and child from an early age. The new father acknowledges that unless he lets the baby know who

he is, it's going to be quite awhile before the child calls him either Daddy or by his given name. This is no indication that fathers are ready to replace mothers in the total care of children (and who would want that anyway). It means, more probably, a coming of age of men. An evolution in which fathers are not willing to repeat the painful oversight of their own fathers. As John says, "When you have a child, it's the beginning of a love story. But it is the only kind of love in which you have no right to leave the other."

# newborn infant care

WHAT WE HAVE DONE
WILL NOT BE LOST
TO ALL ETERNITY.

EVERYTHING RIPENS
AT ITS TIME
AND BECOMES FRUIT
AT ITS HOUR.
—DIVYAVADANA

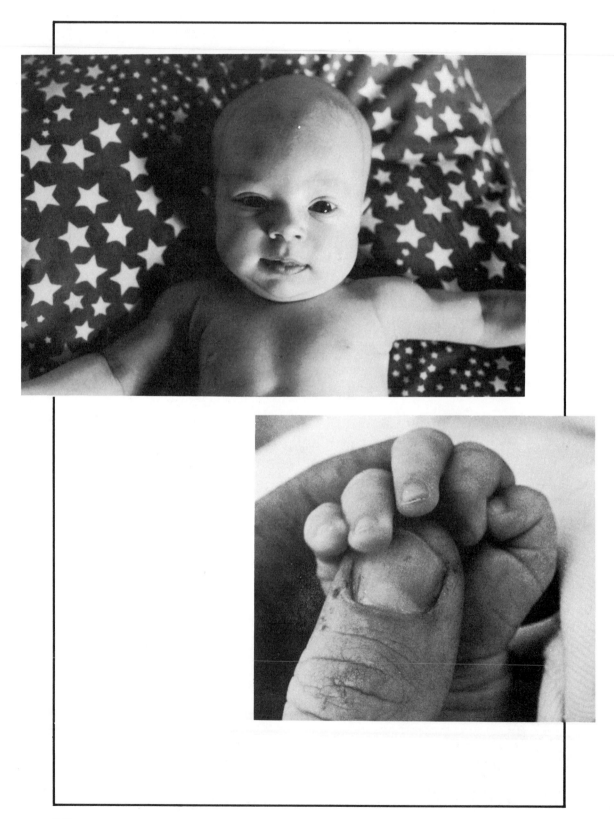

# after the birth

There is a new person in your life, a baby. What a joy, what a shock! Even though you may have done a lot of thinking and preparing for your new friend, it's not quite the same as holding the child in your arms. In all probability, the baby does not act, respond or resemble, in any way, what you had imagined it would be. Most newborns come into the world looking somewhat strange. Some infants are round and full, others may be the average weight but still have wrinkled flesh on arms and legs, and many have grimacing faces. Observing a newborn during the first few days following birth is full of surprises. Nothing can quite prepare a woman for the first meeting with her first child (except, perhaps, witnessing another woman giving birth). Many men and women interviewed for this book said that seeing even the most explicit birth films had not prepared them for the tremendous personal impact they felt when first confronted with their babe.

It's not easy to know how to handle a newborn the first time around. Even with the second or third child, it is not that much simpler. But, approached with calmness and kindness, raising a child becomes a pleasure.

The sudden change from pregnancy into new motherhood throws many women off-balance. First, there is the internal re-adaptation of the hormones, tissues and organs. Secondly, there is the recovery period from the big effort of giving birth (also, perhaps, from minor or major surgery). Thirdly, and at the same time, you must learn how to keep the non-speaking new person comfortable and happy. It's a time when emotions run high and low like a scenic railway. However, unless there are complications, a more even temperament will soon return. The best healers are sleep, fluids and nutritious foods. The doctor or midwife will make a few recommendations according to the type of delivery that took place. In general, the immediate minor annoyances are usually caused by the uterus shrinking back to a smaller size, which causes cramps; various degrees of discomfort from the episiotomy; difficulties with bowel movements sometimes increased by painful hemorrhoids; and enlargement and hardening of the breasts as the milk forms. Of course, none of these may happen in your case but one thing that does happen after every delivery is the complete cleansing of the uterus. It expels the remaining bits of tissue and liquid in the same way as a menstrual period, and as the vagina and vulva are extremely sensitive at that stage it is recommended that you wear an external pad rather than a tampon. The lochia, as this discharge is called, can last anywhere from one to five weeks and shouldn't be a heavier flow than a regular period. After the flow tapers off there may still be irregular spotting for the next few weeks.

If you have delivered at home, ideally the father of the child is with you and perhaps a close friend or two will help you during the first few days

while you rest. Your husband can hug the baby to his chest and change its diapers while you are still sleeping. He or a friend can prepare a meal and do some cleaning and shopping. The same situation applies for the mother's return from the hospital. Her companion could take a paternity leave from work and witness the baby's evolution from the very beginning of life as well as make it as comfortable for the mother as possible. In case the father is away and a friend is unavailable at the time, there are, if funds permit, specialized infant nurses who can help for a few hours a day or full-time. If you have a good relationship with your mother or with the father's mother it is often her pleasure to help and she often has the best down-to-earth advice to offer you.

Every baby has its own rhythm and its own style. Your baby is not going to conform to any time-table of growth and development. There is no set chart on how to raise a baby, but from the moment of birth every new individual has universal basic needs. Some needs the baby can fulfill by itself; but, for the most part, your help is needed in order for the baby to survive.

Each father and mother have their own way of caring for a baby. Their knowledge may come from their own family's way of doing things, from instinct or from professional advice. There is no superior way, no definite rules. The only rule is what you think is best and what makes the baby and yourself happy. The parents' care and influence during the first years is what will determine the state of health, happiness and curiosity during childhood and adolescence.

In the following pages we will deal with general common sense guidelines and family tips on infant care practices during the first three months of the baby's life.

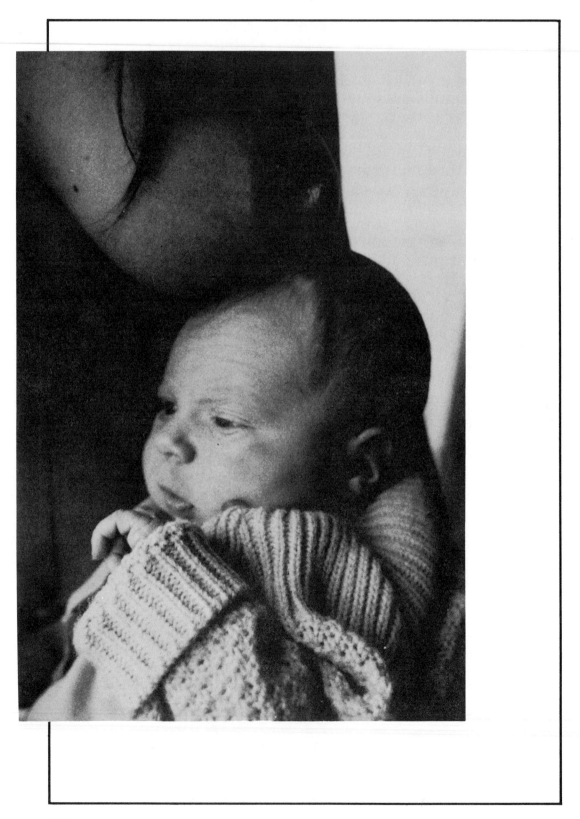

## PRAYER OF THE NEWBORN _____

*I am just born . . . listen to me!
Only a day or so ago I lay safely within the warm liquid
and quietness of your inner domain. Steer me away from
harsh lights, noisy demonstrations and whiffs of cold air.

*I am just born . . . stay close to me!
A strong force has separated me from the body that nourished
my every cell. I am afraid you may forget me in a glass cage,
leaving me with strangers — hands full of drugs — all for my
own good they say, already changing my natural equilibrium.

*I am just born . . . nourish me!
The food you took built every layer of what I am now. Give me the
best you can, as you give to yourself. Let me feed from the
strength of the sun and taste the fresh water springs. Let the
grass grow green and the sky remain transparent.

*I am just born . . . be kind to me!
The new air filling my little lungs causes me to react, the
rush of oxygen agitates my whole frame. Understand me if I cry,
it is only a sign of being alive and expressing the abundance of
odd sensations I am feeling. It is hard to be apart from you.

*I am just born . . . teach me!
Show me in playfulness what you expect of me. I will learn from
you and you can learn from my reactions where things went wrong in
your past. Re-live your life through me. Tell me where smiles
stem from and caresses go and I will learn to please, mostly
by imitating you.

*I am just born . . . give me strength!
The world you have brought me into is filled with beauty
but it is also made up of those out to kill, destroy and turn
my new brain into a machine-part. Hold me well, guide me through
each new clearing, push me through the waves.
There will come a day when I will break away, but meanwhile show me
the way.

## ELATION AFTER CHILDBIRTH

I WAS NOT I. YOU WERE NOT ME.
MY LOVE, PAPOOSE OUT OF MY THIGHS,
I ROCK YOU IN HUGE CRADLES
OF MY KNEES,
AND I HEAR YOUR FIRST
CRY IN DARKNESS.

NOW WHO AM I?
WEEPING THROUGH MY HANDS
ALL WEEDY AND YELLOW WITH
DANDELION NAILS AND DRUNKEN FINGERS,
BLOOD TUMBLING THROUGH THE
FOLDS OF MY FOOTSTEPS
FOR THIS: FLESH EMPTY
AND STOMACH ALL GONE.

I WAKE AND CANNOT FIND
YOU IN MYSELF, MY ARROW,
MY BLUE-EYED INDIAN, MY
NEW STICK, MY MARROW.

MY NUDE INDIAN
IN YOUR WOOLEN BLANKET
ON THE LEDGE OF THE WORLD.
MY LIFE. MY PHOENIX-FEATHER.

—SANDRA HOCHMAN

# feeding

We are constantly getting lectures and advice about one way of feeding or the other. It almost makes you wish there was a third method. The way you choose to feed your infant—the breast or the bottle—depends entirely on your own feelings. There is always time to bottle-feed a baby, but if you decide to breast-feed you should make up your mind in the first days following the birth (in fact you should decide during pregnancy, so you can prepare your nipples if necessary). If you leave it till later, breast-feeding could be difficult to establish and you may even miss your chance.

Both ways—bottle or breast—are good, providing it is your own choice and you don't let yourself be influenced into doing something you dislike. If you feel strong and healthy, can ignore people's objections to seeing you nurse in public, if you are going to eat well and do not have to rush, then you'll probably want to breast-feed. On the other hand, if you feel fatigued from the birth event, if you are not ready to draw your breast out at any time or any place, and if you want to resume work soon, it is better to bottle-feed the baby. Of course, these are very simple guidelines to a complex dilemma. Many women find themselves confused over the advantages and disadvantages of each method.

## BREAST-FEEDING

Breast-milk has the biological advantage of being the perfect nutritional composition for infant consumption. Along with its availability, warmth, and germ-free properties, the milk from the breast protects the baby in the first months against minor infections. Breast-feeding becomes a sensual pleasure once the milk-flow is regulated. To ensure a good start, feed for short periods and often at the beginning. A good schedule is to start with a few minutes at each breast the first day, increase the feeding to five minutes the next day, ten minutes the fourth day and quarter of an hour thereafter.

At the beginning the baby is happier if fed more often. This also prevents the ducts in the mother's breast from clogging up. If the liquid does not flow, the breasts may become swollen, hard and painful. Let the baby suck often the first days, but only a little at a time. Tender nipples which are not used to all this activity may become sore. If you haven't been able to avoid breast engorgement and they have become large, bumpy and heavy, try binding your breasts tightly between feedings with a large piece of cotton fabric fastened with big safety pins. This condition shouldn't last more than two days. The efforts you sometimes have to make in order to breast-feed are well worth it. Once the flow comes easily all you have to do is help the nipple into the baby's mouth, relax, and this weird, pleasurable, intimate sensation will take over. The first substance to come out, as the baby suckles, is the colostrum, a thin yellow liquid, full of good proteins.

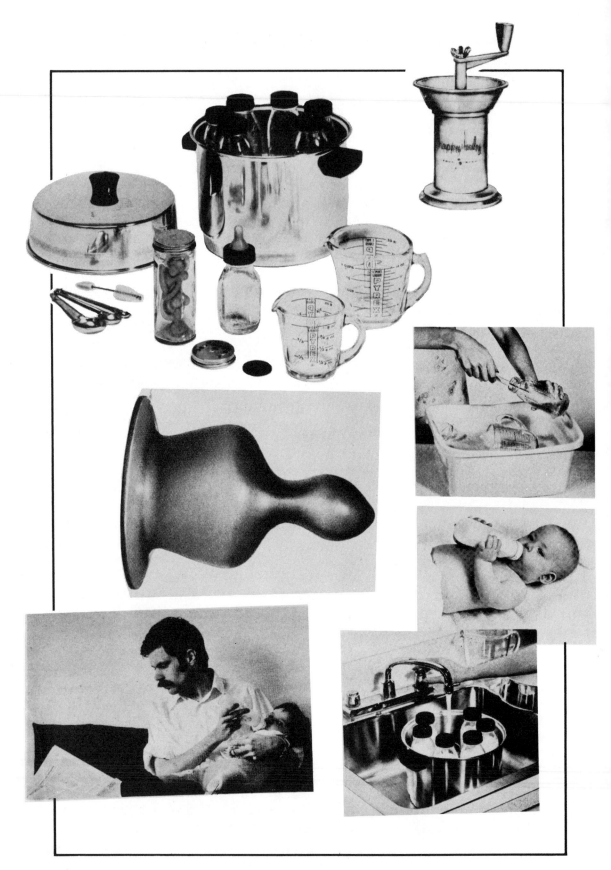

You can give the baby a little formula in a bottle if after a feeding it is crying and still appears hungry. It will get the baby used to taking a bottle at the start from the father or a baby sitter if both parents want to go out. Be careful however not to give more bottle (one a day) than the breast or you may find the baby becoming disinterested in the breast.

## BOTTLE-FEEDING

You may have tried breast-feeding but disliked it, or you may not have the time, or may not be successful at breast-feeding. Whatever your reason, it is true that bottle-feeding can nourish your baby efficiently. It means a whole lot more objects and expenses, but it also allows someone else to participate in feeding the baby. If the baby is healthy, it does not make that much difference what kind of regular formula you prepare as long as you measure correctly and follow the instructions from the evaporated milk can, powder tin, or packet. At the hospital, the doctor will recommend a particular formula for the baby when you return home.

If you think sterilizing teats and bottles is a must then do it. There are, however, many mothers who simply wash nipples, circles and glass bottles with a good soap and a bottle-brush reserved for that use. It works if you are preparing one bottle at a time and are using previously boiled water to prepare the formula. When you are making a whole day's feeding at one time and storing all the bottles, however, there is time for the germs to multiply. It is advisable, when preparing more than one bottle, to sterilize, by boiling and keeping all the equipment in the water. If you happen to be in a place without a refrigerator do not prepare twenty-four hours' worth of feeding in advance, for the same bacterial reason. Instead, make each one fresh when needed. The glass bottles may be heavier and breakable, but for the first few months they are much easier to clean. And, since at that stage it is the parents who are holding the bottle, there is not much danger of the baby hitting itself with the bottle or of the bottle breaking.

Plastic disposable bottles have become very popular in the past few years. They are often made with plastic bags inside which are filled with formula, attached to a ring and nipple and then thrown away after use. The person feeding the baby should make sure that the bottle is held in such a position so that the rubber teat is always full of milk and the baby does not swallow air. It is very important for the baby to be held closely and cuddled while feeding rather than having bottles propped up and the baby left alone to feed.

A renowned pediatrician, Dr. Virginia Pomeranz, who advocates the easy way, says: "For years, I have successfully placed infants of two months or ten pounds, whichever occurs earlier, on whole pasteurized milk." Your baby may not like an abrupt change of diet; give one feeding of formula, one of milk, alternating each over a few days and then switch completely to milk.

**Recommendations:** As the baby drinks from the breast or bottle it will swallow a certain amount of air (not always, but most of the time) and this air should be brought up either in the midst of feeding or afterwards. Hold the baby up against your shoulder and rub or pat its back until a little burp comes out.

The baby will take the amount of milk it needs at each feeding. You could begin with a four ounce bottle and see how much is taken from it and how long the baby sleeps afterwards. If the baby is still hungry an hour or two after a 4 ounce feeding it means the child needs more nourishment. Give another 2 ounces and see how much it takes. If the baby only took 3 ounces or less and sleeps two to four hours it means that this was enough nourishment. During the first weeks feed your baby on demand, and as you get to know each other better, establish a rhythm that suits you by slowly increasing the amount of liquid given and stretching the time in between feedings.

Your baby may, at times, sleep for two-hour spans and want to drink again, or it may even (more seldom) sleep as much as five hours in a row. Do not wake up the baby. Rest, work, or play but leave the baby to dream.

By the second month many babies sleep longer hours during the night. The early morning feeding doesn't have to be dreaded. Five or six o'clock in the morning is a lovely quiet hour. It takes a little while to come around to it, but once you are awake, the first morning feeding can be the best moment of the day to think, babble quietly with the baby, exercise or read and then go back to sleep. If you can do without going to work for the first three months, you should let your whole pattern of hours change without getting anxious about it. You could sleep in two shifts for a while; one at night, one in the afternoon when your babe is asleep (and the other children at school). You will be more relaxed that way than if you tried to sleep as you did before your child arrived.

After the first three months you can start feeding the baby, besides milk, a teaspoonful or two of mashed banana, finely ground cereals, scrambled eggs, crushed peaches (almost any fruit purée in fact). There is a wonderfully handy little machine, "The happy-baby-food-grinder," which can turn any meal into a purée for the baby. It comes apart to be cleaned and is so small that it can travel anywhere. The food comes through easily, unlike when puréed in a blender where small quantities of food often get stuck at the bottom.

Do not get nervous if your babe does not take much liquid at one feeding. It happens to all of us that we do not feel hungry once in a while. But, if this is a repeated problem, it may be a sign of disorder and a consultation with your doctor may help clarify the matter.

# crying

The most difficult aspect of babyhood for most parents to accept is the crying spells. Somehow, when pregnant, a woman does not think that her own baby will cry half as much as some of the newborns she may have encountered. But all babies do cry, even babes of the most calm and relaxed mothers, and there are no two ways about it.

When the mother returns home from the hospital with her baby, she begins to realize fully the demands the little one is going to put on her. At home, once the baby is born and crying a lot, you will find it very trying for your already shaken nerves. Try lying down with the babe resting on top of you, its head close to your heart. The heartbeat and the closeness of your body are two very familiar things for this little being and it often calms them all the way to sleep.

The first external day, the newborn is usually very active and certainly not likely to fall asleep very soon after the birth, as many women are led to believe. In the following few days the infant may be quieter but then may start fretting and crying again as it regains strength from food. It requires patience and understanding. As the child grows older this crying will dwindle and the tension and worry it often brings will diminish as you learn to discern the meaning and importance of each different cry. When you hear the baby cry, do not panic. Ask yourself these questions: Is the baby thirsty, hungry or wet? Too hot or too cold? Tired? Is it gas or does it need to be burped? Even after you have eliminated all these possibilities and think everything is taken care of, the baby will start again. You do not understand, there is no reason for this crying. Well, there is a lot of crying in the early months that we just cannot understand. It has to do with leaving that cosy internal life, with the body feeling strange and loose, with the new loneliness, with the food and the air, or maybe just releasing energy and a thousand and one reasons only the baby knows. All the parents can do is to take the babe in their arms and speak or sing softly until the calmness returns. If the crying persists for long periods and you are getting tired and irritated it's better to put the child back in its sleeping area and rest yourself before trying again to figure out why. It's not easy to lie down and rest while a baby is crying, but it's far preferable to feeling angry and frustrated. Almost all babies go through fretful states. When the screaming periods follow a pattern, usually after feeding or at certain times of the day, it may be colic crying and should be checked by a doctor. A change in formula or in feeding schedule may do the trick. Sometimes what may seem like day in and day out crying with little naps in between tapers out by three months of age. It's important to remember that the most common causes for crying in early infancy are certainly not permanent and the best quality for parents to have during that short (but seemingly endless) period is patience! The main causes for crying are as follows:

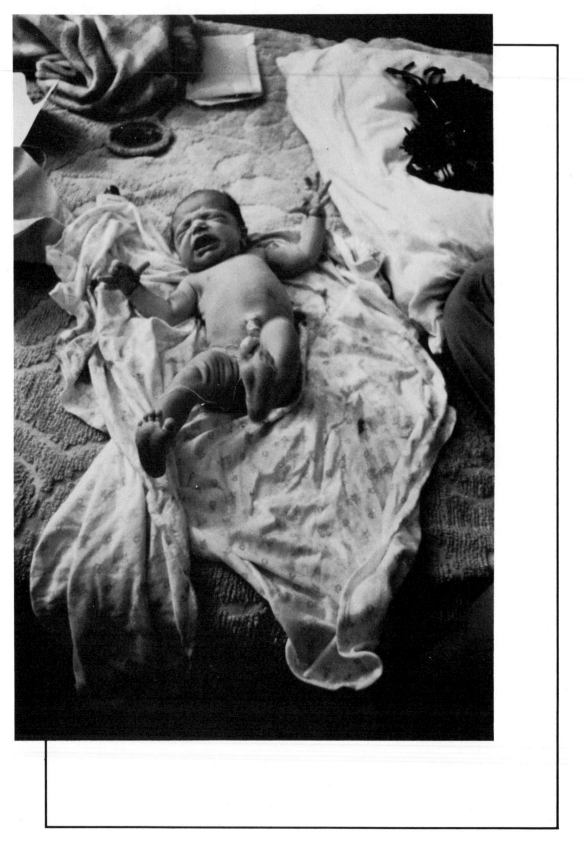

**Hunger.** It's not easy in the first few months to establish the amount of nourishment that the baby needs and this accounts for some of the crying. You will come to realize what the feeding needs are if the baby wakes up after a small feeding or if it sleeps longer after a large feeding. Breast-fed babies often fall asleep on the breast before taking a large amount. If the child usually sleeps for a long time after a short feeding, but then wakes up early, you can be sure it is because of hunger. It's not advisable to give the breast or bottle at the first sign of crying an hour or two after a feeding. Check out some of the possibilities listed earlier, then if the baby is still fretting after a while try a feeding.

**Sickness.** During the first three months of a baby's life there is a certain amount of immunity built up in the womb protecting the newborn against diseases. Acute infections are rare. However, colds are easily caught and manifest themselves through a runny nose, coughing, a change in bowel movements (generally runny). Breast-fed babies' bowel movements are generally loose and yellowish in color. Any change in consistency or color could alert you to your child's illness. Formula-fed babies' stools are usually darker and a little more solid, although no babies fed exclusively on liquid will have a really solid movement. If the long crying spells are accompanied by a change in general appearance and color of skin, take a temperature reading and consult with your doctor.

**Wetness.** Infants do not appear uncomfortable at first when the diapers are soiled or wet. It's only later, when the rejects start irritating the skin that they start crying. Check the baby often to avoid the problem of diaper rash and you will be one step closer to the process of eliminating the cause of baby tears.

**Clothes and Accessories.** Is the little blanket wrapping up the baby tight enough? Are the clothes too small? If pins are used, make sure that they are the safety ones created especially for that use. Check to be sure that you have closed them well if the baby is crying. Is there a toy in the way? Or a house pet wanting to get in the crib?

**Indigestion.** Try burping the baby again, even though you did it before successfully. If you suspect that it is gas, it should be relieved as soon as possible as it can be very painful. You can hold the baby against your chest, its head resting on your shoulder and rub or pat gently on the back. Another successful position is to prop the baby upon your lap with one hand over the baby's chest, holding it so that the face is in a down position and rub the back strongly in an upward stroke.

**Colic.** Colic, a common disturbance for infants up to three months old, is usually acute indigestion causing sharp pains in the intestines. The baby expresses this distress with shrill cries, tensing the muscles in the legs into a stiff position and agitating the arms. If gas swells the stomach it will

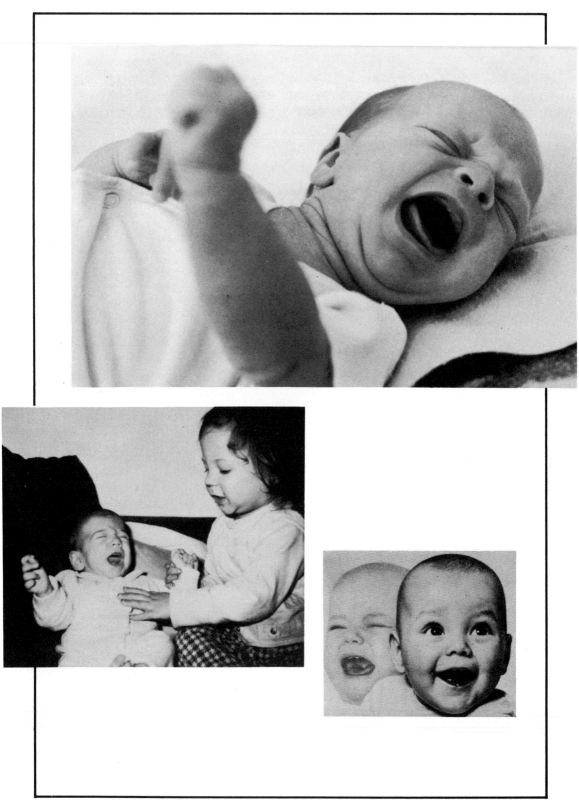

perhaps be partially relieved through the natural way. Also, try holding your babe tight against you and walk about to pacify the child. If a regular pattern of lengthy crying develops, talk about it with your G.P. or pediatrician who can suggest effective remedies.

Certain herbal teas (already mentioned in the Body Care chapter) also apply for the baby; in a smaller dose, of course. Camomile, the small yellow flower, is especially good for soothing the stomach and intestines. Mint, or spearmint, also help digestion. Catnip helps babies to sleep. It is a very distressing and helpless feeling for new parents to watch a child in discomfort and not know how to help. Herbal remedies were, at one time, the only aid our ancestors had and they are now looked upon as a lot of foolish nonsense. But, when a child is obviously uncomfortable, you want to try effective yet mild remedies to soothe it and herbal teas cannot harm anyone. Some babies only have a few attacks of colic throughout the early months, while others have a great deal of trouble every day. Colic occurs whether the baby is fed breast-milk, cow's milk or any formula. The cause is not entirely known since several conditions may be present in the immature and nervous digestive system. Fatigue also plays an important part.

**Spoiling.** An infant does not premeditate its actions, they are spontaneous occurrences. The baby is reacting to the environment and to stimulation or lack of it. Basically the baby is relying on the five senses (taste, touch, smell, sight and hearing) rather than any intellectual or logical way of thinking. Therefore, an infant will not cry in order to be picked up. The first few months of life is a stage where no amount of cuddling and special attention can spoil a child.

**Fatigue.** Infants do get tired, just like children or adults, only their resistance is lower than ours and they sometimes express their fatigue by crying. When an infant has stayed awake for an unusually long period of time, being played with, passed from hand to hand, or just being in a room or public place full of noise and action for many hours, it may fall asleep right there or it may have a hard time going to sleep and cry in frustration or whatever. Instead of just putting the baby into bed straight away after an active period, shift into a lower gear of calmness and whispers. Sing softly and dim the lights; it will be contagious, the baby will probably quiet down. You can also let the baby cry itself to sleep if the wailing gets to be too much for your nerves. But, if after a period of time the baby is still crying, it needs more comforting and a check on any possible discomforts.

Whatever you do to relieve yourself from the frustration of not being able to stop an infant from crying, just do not take it out on the baby by shaking or hitting. The crying is absolutely not done to annoy you. All babies cry and all you would be doing is adding to their anxiety. Hit your fist against the wall instead, calm your nervous system under a hot shower, breathe deeply, lie down . . . love your own babe.

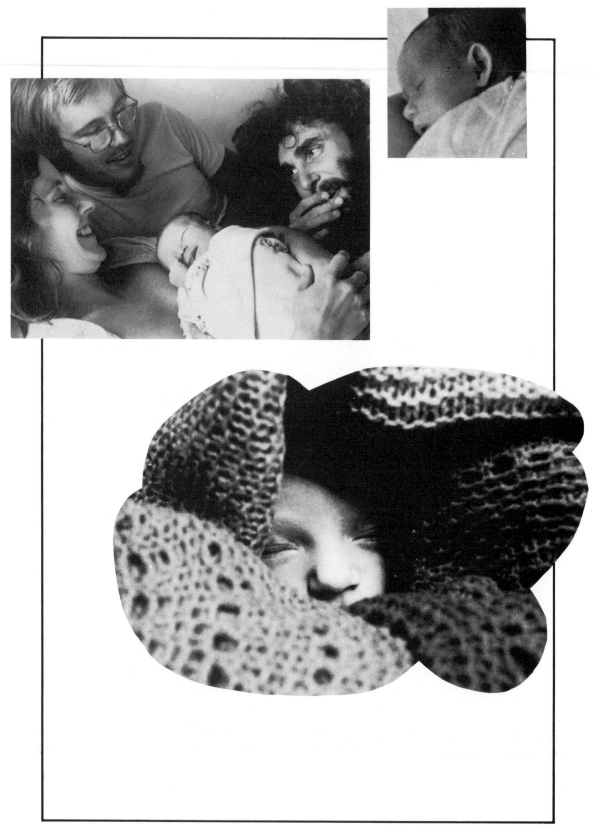

# **sleep**

In the first month of their lives, babies usually do a lot of sleeping. However, the fourteen to eighteen hours of sleeping a day are spread over six to eight short sleeping periods within twenty-four hours.

A baby will wake up, cry a little to attract attention to its state of wakefulness, then cry a little louder if not picked up straight away. Once fed to stomach's content and burped, the child will either fall back to sleep or gurgle, stare, stretch, smile, yawn or cry and eventually nod off to slumberland again.

Once you have recuperated from birth, give yourself some time out. The baby can stay in the care of the father, a friend who knows about infants or a baby minder while you go out and air your brains for a few hours. Do it after a feeding, when the baby has gone to sleep. This way you can leave knowing that the baby is well taken care of. If you are breast-feeding, call an hour or two later to check that everything is all right. In case the baby is awake and you have an appointment that prevents your return, a bottle you have left beforehand can always be given. Also, it's best not to leave a baby sitter you do not know in charge of your newborn longer than an hour or so or you may get anxious. Try the person out before you leave your baby with anyone for an evening.

Whether your baby is sleeping or not, never leave the child alone. If anything should happen while you went shopping around the corner or visiting a neighbor, you would be a lot more upset than if you took a sleeping or crying baby with you.

A baby can sleep just as well outdoors if the weather is fine. Fresh air is very important to the baby's health. If it is cold but sunny outside, bundle up the baby in woolies, blankets, bonnet, mittens and go for a walk together. If you leave your child to sleep outdoors during hot weather in a pram, box or basket, make sure that the sides are not too high and that plenty of air is circulating to let the baby breathe correctly. Hot, direct sunlight is harmful to delicate baby skin after a few minutes on first exposures. In the summer, have a little tulle-netting over the baby's sleeping area outdoors to keep the bees, flies and other animals away.

Infants can sleep pretty well anywhere, but at home it is best if they sleep in a room of their own. Keep the temperature warm (a night and day average of 70°F or 20°C). Remember, babies come from a warm place. You could keep the baby sleeping in your room at night with you in the first weeks but you may find yourself listening to the baby instead of sleeping. It is cosy, if you are breast-feeding, to have your child by your side and just take the baby in your bed when it's feeding time. But, if you are bottle-feeding and one of you has to get up, the baby may just as well be in its own room so that at least one of the parents can rest. Sometimes newborns do not cry very loudly when they wake up and they may have been whimpering for quite a while before you hear it (not a desirable situation as it makes a hungry baby nervous and fragile not to be fed when ready). Therefore, it may be a good idea, in the first month, to leave the door of both your rooms open, or, if they are on a different floors, to have an intercom system.

# POSITIONS

Once the baby is fed, changed, and ready to sleep, lay the child on its side in case it should spit up some of the feeding. An infant sleeping on its back and throwing up its food may choke on its own rejects. The majority of babies however seem to feel more comfortable and secure sleeping on their stomach. Often the pressure on the tummy brings a relief to gas pains, if any. When a baby lies too often on its back, the hair at the back of the head may rub off, leaving a bald spot. It is nothing serious, the hair will grow back later, but it can be avoided by changing the baby's position often. Lying on its stomach, a child is more likely to develop its neck muscles, and therefore be able to hold up its head sooner.

A newborn does not need an elaborate sleeping arrangement. A large woven straw basket, a padded shallow box or a folded quilt will do quite well. If you put the baby to sleep on a bed, make sure it is on the mattress and not on the pillow, as a baby could suffocate while sleeping on the pillow. Babies should never sleep on pillows at all if you want the spine to develop correctly. Also, the mattress in their sleeping area should be quite firm. By two months of age babies are strong enough to turn over. Make sure that the place where you lay them is safe, even if it's only for a minute.

Young babies, once asleep, can stay asleep quite well through all sorts of noises. It is better to get a baby used to a certain amount of everyday noises such as telephones, music, conversations, cleaning-up cling-clang instead of trying to avoid the noise and turning your child into a light sleeper. Quite a few people take babies to the movies. Until they are four months old, babies can sleep very well through the noisiest of films.

During their first six months, most babies seem to wake up at the early hour of five or six. Many mothers develop the bad habit of hardly ever falling into a deep sleep and then, at the slightest murmuring from their baby, the mother jumps up thinking that the baby is crying when in fact the child might have just gone back to sleep if it hadn't been paid any attention. During the first six weeks it is essential to be there all the time but from then on wait to see if the murmuring stops or gets louder before you go in to check. When a child is used to having company very early in the morning every day, it is going to demand such attention for a long time. Establish from the beginning of your daily rhythm that this is a feeding period after which everyone goes back to sleep, if that is what you want to have happen.

Infants' sleeping patterns change constantly. Just when you think you have established a regular feeding/sleeping pattern that has been constant for a few weeks, the baby will decide to forego the morning nap and your plans for doing a particular thing during that period are shot. As mentioned before, unless you have to go back to outside work, give yourself at least a three month period. Have a good time getting to know your own baby and get enough sleep yourself so that you can stay healthy and in a good mood to cope with all the intricacies of parenthood.

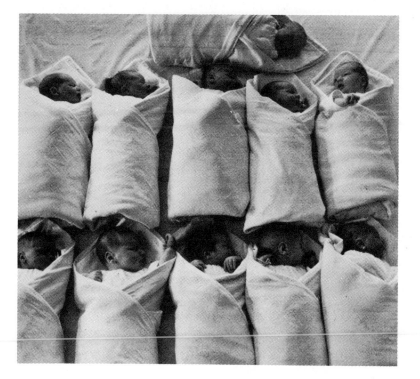

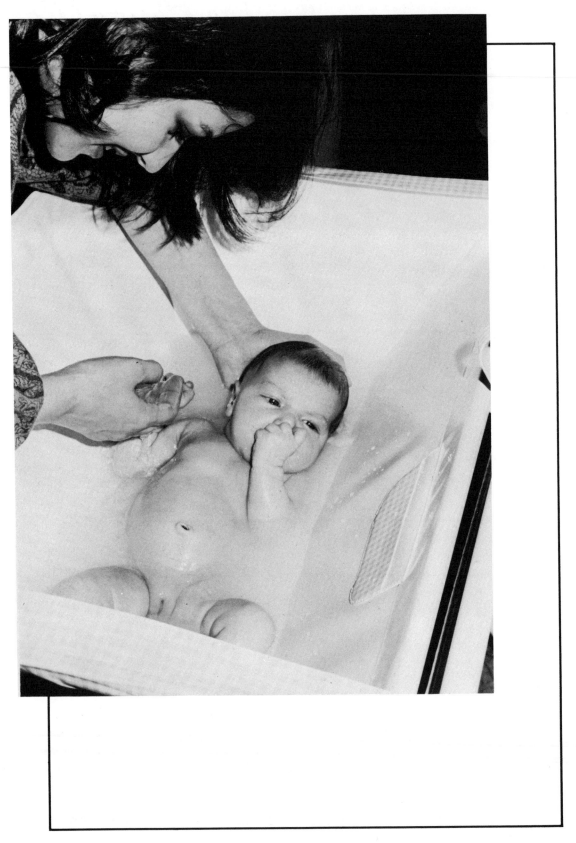

# cleanli- ness

# cleanli-ness

A baby forced to live in a totally sterile environment would have little chance of survival on its first outing. The baby would not have been vaccinated naturally by the microbial flora and fauna of our usual environment. From complete sterilization to letting the infant wade in dirt, there is a vast range of possibilities. Babies should be kept clean without exaggeration.

During the early days, a newborn's skin should not be aggravated too often with soap. If plain lukewarm water can take care of the cleaning, leave the soap aside. Soap and other products used on the baby's skin should not contain detergents or harsh chemicals.

In the hospital the baby is cleaned and dressed for you. Later, a nurse will help you to change and care for the baby, if you wish. After birth at home, the newborn can be wiped clean of blood with a cloth dipped in lukewarm water. The person doing it shouldn't rub hard as the skin is very tender. Also, if possible, you want to retain and spread the vernix.

The stump that remains after the umbilical cord has been clamped will soon dry, shrivel and fall off. It may come off three days later or remain for as long as two weeks. It will come off in its own time, do not pull on it. The stump should be kept dry and clean with sterile cotton swabs and alcohol. It can be left to dry in the air. Make sure that the diaper does not rub over that surface, or cover it with gauze. Bandages, except in extreme cases, are not really necessary. Let the doctor or midwife know at once if any blood or pus is seeping from the stump.

Start bathing the infant with lukewarm water and a little soap. Too much soaping removes the fatty layer of the skin and leaves it open to irritation and germ contamination. Fill the bath area with small amounts of water for the first baths. A few days later, when you are used to holding the slippery baby and supporting the back of the head as you are washing him/her, you can put in more water. The temperature in the room should be warm and you should dip your elbow into the bath water to make sure that it is not too hot, a tepid 95°F (25°C). Lay out a towel and a clean set of clothing nearby as it is impossible to leave the baby in the bath by itself for even a second, and walking around with a wet baby is not wise. After a good wash, going in and out of the neck, groin and underarm folds, over the face gently and around the head like a little shampoo, dry the baby well. Check the nails of hands and feet. They grow very fast and the baby will often scratch its face if they are too long. Clean the nose and the ears and then dress the baby. Choose the time to give the bath according to what suits your activities best. Some parents like to give it in the morning after the second feeding, others prefer bathing the baby after the evening feeding, saying it sets the baby off to a good night's sleep.

Quite a few babies get cradle cap, light brown scaling of the scalp. It is harmless and can usually be rubbed off with a little oil (mineral or olive). Try it, gently, once or twice a day. If the cradle cap persists, your doctor may suggest other preparations.

Some of the toilet and bathing articles that you may need are: three bath towels and wash cloths, almond or other baby oil and lotion, sterile cotton swabs, a soft brush and a diaper pail.

# clothes

Clothes have other purposes besides following fashion or making babies delightful to view! Clothes are meant to make life more comfortable, a screen against capricious weather and perilous environment.

Clothes for babies should be practical first and happy to look at second. Buy or be given what you really need, it's not all that much. You have to take into account that infants grow every day and they need clothes with a lot of room for stretching and kicking. In temperate climates, start with a cotton undershirt that snap-closes in front. It is quite disagreeable for infants to have anything pulled over their heads at that stage. The undershirts come in cotton or thin wool for winter, and some have tabs which are meant to be fastened to the diaper so it won't ride up and will keep the stomach warm. Four to six long or short sleeved shirts will be enough.

Disposable diapers have eliminated the most detested cleaning chore and a lot of diaper rash. Diapers that can be thrown away are now made in every size and instead of safety pins they are made with a special tape attachment. If you go to a foreign country, chances are that they will not have disposable diapers available yet. When traveling abroad some parents would rather take a suitcase full of throw-away diapers than a lot of cloth diapers for the babe. On the other hand, you may feel destructive about submerging the planet with so many soiled disposable diapers which do not burn and take forever to rot! Also, your newborn may have extremely sensitive skin and cloth diapers could be the only solution in the first months. There is probably a good diaper service around you that has a pick up and delivery service if you can afford it. It is always useful to have a dozen cloth diapers, a couple of baby pins and waterproof pants on hand. You are going to have to use a lot of throw-away diapers. Order or get a lot at one time to save trips with bulky boxes. A stretch jump suit, covering the baby from neck to toe, can go on next. The baby can wear it during the day and at night. It's an ideal all-around piece of clothing by the time the baby is one month old. Before that time the baby may like to have the legs and hips wrapped up tightly in a receiving blanket, giving a snug feeling of security, as it was in the womb. At night a sweater or zip-up sleeper can be added if the temperature drops.

A nightgown with a drawstring at the bottom is also very useful in the first months. It can be worn either when the baby is awake or sleeping. The drawstring makes it easy for diaper changes and sometimes these nightgowns have little mittens at the cuffs which can be put over the hands if the baby has a tendency to scratch itself.

Sweaters for babies now come in the prettiest of colors. White, pale pink, blue and yellow are certainly baby-like and adorable but a little multi-colored-baby warms the heart just as much, if not more. Knitted booties and ear covering hats are most comfortable for their sensitive skin.

Make sure that the wool they are made from is soft. Quite a few babies are allergic to synthetic fibers. When selecting an outfit to be worn close to the skin, fine cotton and fine wool material should always be favored. Dresses, as cute as they may look, are drafty in the winter and never quite as practical as shorts and a tee-shirt in the summer.

If you think a child romping around in plain disposable diapers is not the most attractive sight (Would you walk around parading your plastic underwear?) you could cover them with stretch terry cloth pants available at most dime stores. Or, you could quickly sew a few printed pants large enough to fit over the diapers. Maybe one day the companies will print motifs on the plastic pants.

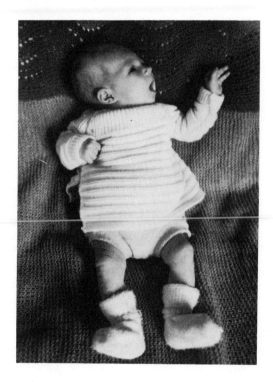

# accesso-ries

Modern nursery gadgets are numerous but if you use your imagination you need to buy very little for your newborn. If you want to go all out and can afford to buy a matching set of baby furniture, it is available. But remember that after two or three years it becomes obsolete (unless you give it to new parents or save it for your next child).

Chances are that someone around you has a crib with wooden bar drop sides or even a playpen in which your baby can sleep once the first week's arrangements are outgrown.

Other useful items you may need, depending on your life-style:

☐ A baby pouch, criss-cross strapped around you, leaving your hands free and the baby close to your warmth.

☐ A baby carriage or stroller.

☐ An easily transportable basket of woven straw or solid cloth is very useful for the car and for taking the baby out on long journeys.

☐ A high table on which you can safely lay the baby to change clothes and diapers. However, a bed with a waterproof flannelette cloth is sufficient.

☐ A set of drawers; a trunk or suitcase for baby's clothes; shelves or a box for oils, lotions and other toiletries.

☐ An infant seat of molded plastic which has adjustable heights, a safety belt and can be transported anywhere.

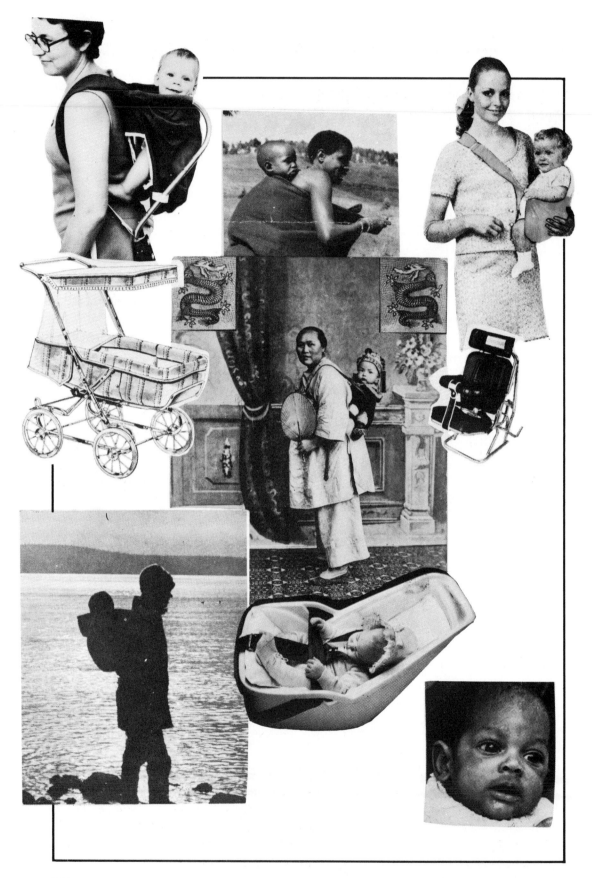

# traveling

Traveling with your baby can be easy and require a minimum amount of fussing and care, or it can be the most chaotic, hectic, and frustrating experience for everyone involved.

Whether it is a few hours in a car, a few days or a cross-country adventure, the ease of traveling has a lot to do with giving yourself ample time for preparation. An outing or a holiday should be just that and it should never be more work than if you stayed at home. If you have any doubts about your child's health concerning a trip, ask for advice from your baby's doctor.

Before leaving you should prepare a shoulder bag containing:

☐ Two to X amount of disposable diapers, according to the length of the trip.

☐ Plastic bags for the soiled bits and pieces and diapers, in case you don't have a place to throw them away.

☐ Tissues, cotton swabs, baby cream (or whatever stuff you use to clean the baby's bottom).

☐ A waterproof sheeting with flannelette backing on which to change the baby or in case you put the baby to sleep on someone's bed.

☐ A yard of printed cotton fabric always comes in handy. Use it on top of the flannelette as a sheet, to cover a rough or dirty surface before you lay the baby down, to block off the sun from a car window, to wrap the baby against you, to give a happy touch to a blank environment.

☐ A bottle of formula ready to be given and as many disposable bottles (or cans and empty bottles with bottle brush and soap) as needed for the trip.

☐ A change of clothing and a little shawl or blanket for the night or temperature changes.

If you still have some room include one of those little music boxes. Some have very quiet tunes which babies find soothing.

Another very useful item is a little foam rubber mattress of one and a half by three feet covered with cotton. The little mattress can be rolled, tied, and carried anywhere for the baby's lying comfort.

**By Air.** Call the airline in advance to find out their facilities on long distance flights. If you tell them you are traveling with an infant when you make your reservation they may be able to reserve a bassinette for you so that the baby can sleep in it rather than on you, leaving you more freedom of movement. The hostess or steward can warm the bottle if necessary. If it is not a busy period, one of the hostesses can hold your baby while you eat, take a stretch or go to the toilet. For take-off and landing always have the baby in your arms, and the same applies for when there is turbulence on the plane. If the baby is asleep during the flight you could lay it down on the little mattress, in between your feet on the floor if there is no bassinette. It's quite an experience to change a soiled baby in a narrow seat, sandwiched in

between two strangers! If it is a large plane ask to do it in the space provided as a rest area for the hostess. It's certainly not possible to do it in the toilet-bathroom as they are far too small. If it is a flight over two hours long, the temperature in the plane can get very cool, and on transatlantic flights, after the cold it sometimes becomes hot and dry. Check the baby often for comfort. On most major airlines, infants and their parents can be pre-boarded on the plane before the main crowd rush. Also, ask for a seat with the most leg room (i.e., the first row). In flight, if your child is crying, do not feel you are stuck in one spot after the seat-belt sign is off. Walk up and down the aisle, rocking the baby to sleep. A pacifier also might help or a whole box full of earplugs for your sleeping neighbors. One of those snug "carry the baby against you" trappings is a great help if you have to walk long distances in airports and wait at the customs office. It's better than a stroller because in the first few months the baby cannot sit in a stroller. Some airports now have unstaffed nurseries where you can clean the baby properly on high tables, lay the baby down in a crib and lay yourself down on a couch. On national flights infants can fly for free and on international flights the price is ten per cent of your ticket.

**By Train or Bus.** Have patience. Include in the infant bag moist towelettes as trains and buses are usually quite dirty (unless you can afford to travel first class). Don't forget food and liquid for yourself.

**By Car.** If you are driving with an infant in the car put the little carry-cot or straw basket on the floor of the car to make sure it will not fall off the seat when you drive, or strap it to the seat with safety belts. It's better not to use the little mattress on the floor of a car because if you brake the baby might roll about. Besides, there is a lot of dust flying around down there. Do not plan to drive by yourself for long hours with an infant; the baby would probably not be able to take it. If you are being driven, watch out for drafts and put the baby in a safe position, either lying down or resting on your knees. You will probably be more comfortable in the back seat with your baby.

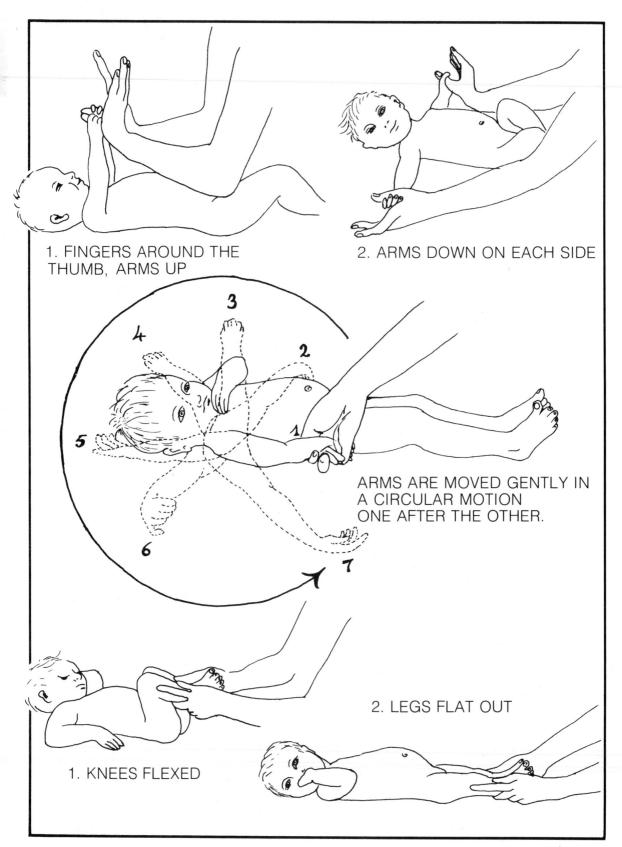

1. FINGERS AROUND THE THUMB, ARMS UP

2. ARMS DOWN ON EACH SIDE

ARMS ARE MOVED GENTLY IN A CIRCULAR MOTION ONE AFTER THE OTHER.

2. LEGS FLAT OUT

1. KNEES FLEXED

# exercise

Intra-uterine life, particularly in the last few months, is very constricting for a thriving little body. The newborn has elongated dorsal muscles and short stomach muscles. Balance will be re-established with a few simple exercises. The arms and especially the legs have been folded from birth and they are slowly extending. The baby is stretching them and you can gently help. A newborn, a few weeks after birth, can use a little exercise and stimulation. Infants are bored quite easily. In the cases where a mother or father carries the baby everywhere, little crying is heard. The child is in a different position than in the crib and is constantly stimulated by the changing view in their waking hours.

A little exercise and play stimulation started early, by the third month (according to the baby's health), will give immediate results. Better respiratory exchange, increased regularity of appetite and digestive functions, general strengthening of the body (assuring the child a good posture), early coordination and something to do besides gazing at the ceiling are the prizes for exercising.

Five to ten minutes a day is quite enough. Put the naked baby in a warm area on the little mattress and keep a towel handy to cover the child afterwards. Execute the movements slowly and easily, without ever pushing or forcing. Look at the baby's muscles at play and talk in a friendly tone as you are going through the motions. It should be a happy period or you should not bother with it.

First the baby learns to hold. Open its little closed fist and put your index finger inside the hand; the little finger will close around yours. See how strong the grip is by pulling the arm little by little towards the outside. If the baby resists, it is exercising its muscles and the goal of this exercise is achieved.

**Arm extension.** Now instead of giving the baby the index finger, try both thumbs. If the baby cannot quite grab them strongly enough, hold the wrist with your other fingers and gently extend the arms.

*First movement:* towards you and up.

*Second movement:* lower the arms down on the mattress on each side laterally and then up again.

Repeat these movements four or five times in the same rhythm. The baby will soon participate either by opposing the movements or imitating them in which case guidance is all that is needed.

This little exercise helps consolidate the strength of the ligaments in the articulation, the muscles of the shoulders and those of the arms. This exercise should be done slowly, complete extension will only be obtained progressively. Do it easily. Variations to the above exercise are moving one

arm at a time in a circular movement as indicated on the diagram, and bending/extending the arms.

Repeat—perform the exercises with great care.

**Leg extension.** The baby naturally folds its legs at the knee. Hold the ankles with your fingers, the thumb resting on the front part of the leg and the index on the side. Slowly extend the legs and bring them back to the flexed position. Do not try, in the beginning, for complete extension, the baby will not be able to do it. Flex the legs again towards the stomach and extend them. Repeat four or five times. The baby will probably resist a little. Do not force. After a few days the child will probably extend the legs all by itself, in which case replace them to the flexed position to incite spontaneous movement of the muscles. Avoid overextension of the knees which could distend the ligaments too much.

This exercise should fortify the leg muscles and encourage straight legs. A variation to this exercise is alternately to flex the legs from one side to the other.

You could also gently flex the little hands and feet. Bring the legs up and down and later check into exercises for the torso.

There are teachers who specialize in giving baby exercises. You could either take your baby there for weekly exercises or learn from the teacher the basic movements in case you are not sure how to go about it yourself. These classes are usually for babies already five months of age.

## STIMULATION OF THE SENSES

By one month of age infants respond to large moving shapes such as mobiles by staring and following the movements. By two months of age a baby can attempt to grab and hold objects. Place a safe toy, a fabric toy, a rubber animal at hand's touch. By now a bath should be an enjoyable time. By the third month the baby follows objects and people, moving its head from side to side. Fasten toys or colorful shapes to the side of the bed for the baby to look at. Hang a plastic bag filled with swimming goldfish to the crib for a while. Three month old babies stay awake longer, kicking their legs and circling their arms, doing the same kind of basic movements you are going to play/exercise with them to help develop their bodies.

Your baby at this stage may be sucking its fingers even though feeding time is finished. For an infant, sucking a nipple, a fist or toys is a very gratifying pastime. When you are breast-feeding, a lot of close touching goes on which is security for the little one. Your baby's little hand may hold one of your fingers during feeding and you can be sure little caresses on the baby's cheeks will get you a smile. Stimulate the baby's reactions with a little hand play, they are the best toys.

The more a baby is actively involved with its surroundings and stimulated to discover, touch, taste, smell (try a flower), listen (try different kinds of music), and look the greater the child's ability will be to learn how to busy itself in the future.

As mentioned before, the excitement of overstimulation can make a baby nervous and apt to cry. While you are having an active playtime with your baby, be watching for its reactions.

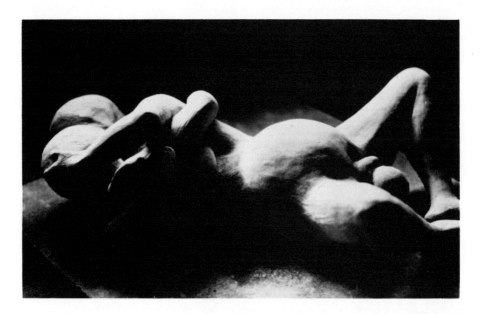

**7**

# birth customs around the world

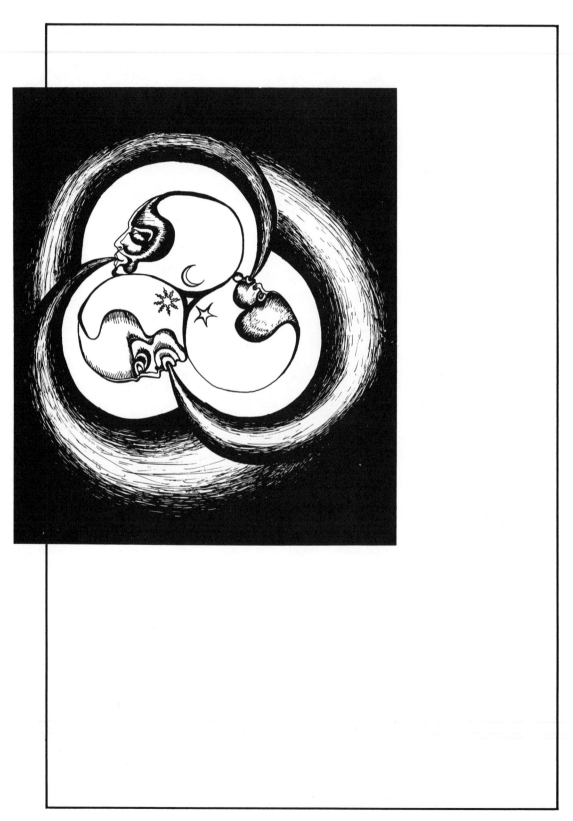

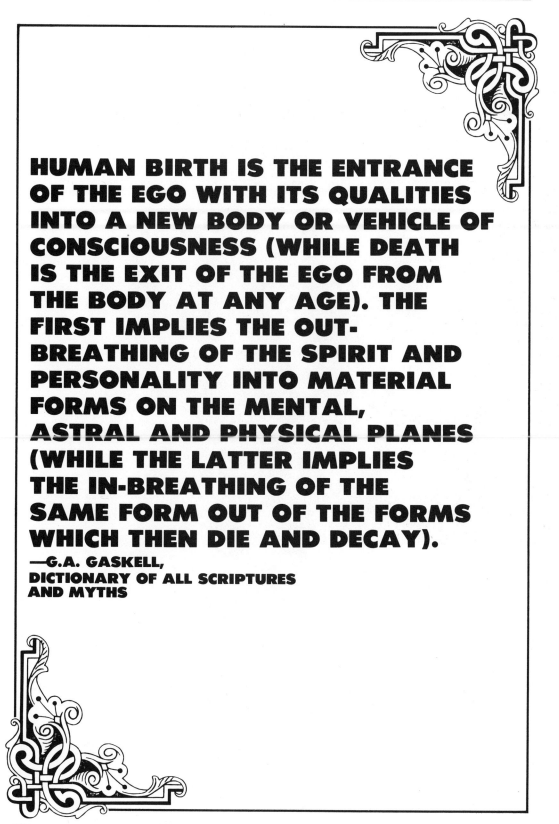

HUMAN BIRTH IS THE ENTRANCE
OF THE EGO WITH ITS QUALITIES
INTO A NEW BODY OR VEHICLE OF
CONSCIOUSNESS (WHILE DEATH
IS THE EXIT OF THE EGO FROM
THE BODY AT ANY AGE). THE
FIRST IMPLIES THE OUT-
BREATHING OF THE SPIRIT AND
PERSONALITY INTO MATERIAL
FORMS ON THE MENTAL,
ASTRAL AND PHYSICAL PLANES
(WHILE THE LATTER IMPLIES
THE IN-BREATHING OF THE
SAME FORM OUT OF THE FORMS
WHICH THEN DIE AND DECAY).
—G.A. GASKELL,
DICTIONARY OF ALL SCRIPTURES
AND MYTHS

here is a vast variety of superstitions that revolve around birth. From prehistoric times to the present, people have concocted different ceremonies, rites and superstitions concerning birth. Each region or group of people has its own peculiarity, but their aims are usually common to all: luck, success and the warding off of evil spirits.

# birth customs around the world

## SOUL

Many women need help during childbirth to protect themselves and to insure a healthy and safe delivery of their baby. But many people in many different countries also believe that the souls of both child and mother need special protection. The soul must not be forgotten or else it may escape.

In Sumatra, Indonesia, the midwife will sometimes tie a ribbon around the wrist of a woman about to give birth. This blocks the passage of her soul in case it should decide to leave her body. It would be nice to think that the plastic name bracelet you are forced to wear in a hospital serves the same purpose.

When a woman in the Southern Celebes Islands is in difficult labor and needs help, the messenger who fetches the midwife always carries something made of iron. It is usually a knife or machete which will be delivered to the midwife. The midwife must keep the metal object in her house until the birth has taken place and then give it back upon payment of an established sum of money once the delivery is performed. The knife represents the woman's soul, which at this critical time is believed to be safer outside of her body. To make sure the baby's soul doesn't escape and get lost at birth, every possible opening in the house is blocked. The household pets and the outside animals' mouths are tied just in case they might swallow the soul. All the people present at the birth are asked to keep their mouths tightly closed.

Another tribe believes that before people are born, they are asked how long a soul they would like to have. According to their answer a soul is measured out. A person's life span is proportioned to the length of their soul. A child who dies young has asked for a short soul.

Identification of the soul's earth spirit perpetrates another ancient superstition among the peoples of Mexico, Central America and some of the Plains Indians of the United States. This superstition, known as nagualism, enforces the concept that each individual has a guardian spirit that watches over the person during his lifetime. Ones' spirit, or nagual (sometimes known as tonal), is joined in another being shortly after birth.

Ashes are spread around the sleeping area of the newborn. The following morning, the father checks the ashes to identify any animal tracks which would indicate the animal spirit that has taken charge of the newborn soul. For some people the spiritual connection is so strong that they believe that the animal and the baby will share the same soul.

Other groups of people believe that they do not come from the earth in general, but from a very particular place such as a certain cave, the hollow of a tree, a bush, a rock formation or an ancestral site where souls of the unborn await incarnation and to which the dead return. The belief that women become pregnant when they come near these fertile shrines of souls is widespread. The souls are felt to be already waiting in the earth's womb and their human mother is considered a temporary vessel, acting on behalf of the great earth mother herself.

## TREES

Trees serve an important function in the daily lives of the small villages all around the world. In certain communities the biggest and oldest trees are considered the place of residence for guardian spirits. In other places, the big tree is the meeting place, the central point in a plaza, a spot where ceremonies are held. In connection with the rites of childbearing, the tree represents growing life, the continuing cycle.

It's an old custom to plant a fruit tree for a new baby. In Switzerland, an apple tree is planted for a boy and a pear tree for a girl. In Haiti, a coconut or breadfruit tree is planted. In Sweden, a lime or elm tree was considered to be a guardian tree; anyone who damaged it would certainly be punished with bad luck, but a pregnant woman who clasped it insured herself of an easy delivery. One can read in Greek mythology how Leto embraced a palm tree as she was about to give birth to Apollo and Artemis in order to facilitate her delivery.

In Africa, women from a Congolese tribe wrap themselves in cloth woven from the fibrous bark of special trees which protects them from dangers that can occur in childbearing. In Western Africa the people of the M'Benga tribe plant a new tree at childbirth time and then dance around it believing that the soul of the new child resides in that tree.

## STONES

Stones have always played an important role in perpetrating good luck: gem stones, stone carvings, and spiritual dwellings such as Stonehenge in Britain. Some tribes also believe that a ceremony involving a stone at childbirth will ease a troublesome labor for the mother.

Amongst the Dayak in Borneo, the village magician is called to help a woman who is having a difficult time delivering her child. He arrives with an

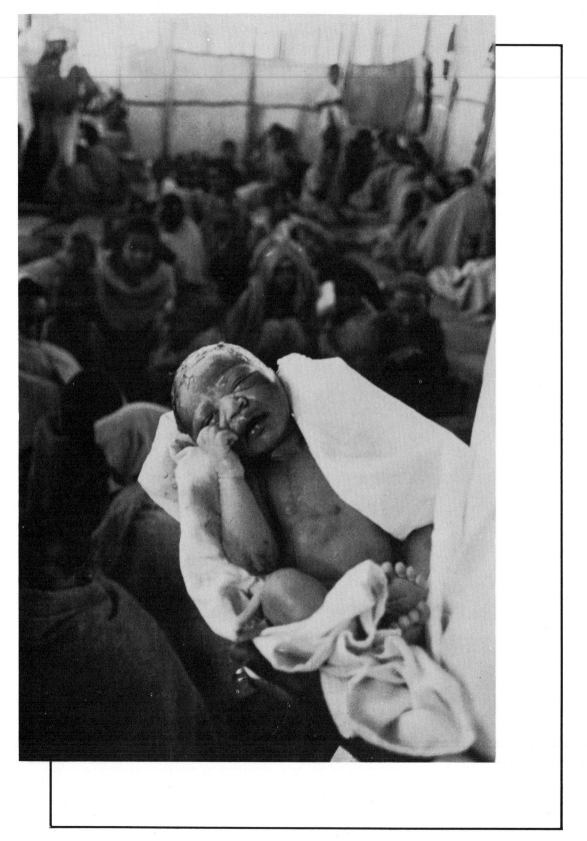

associate and a large moon-colored stone. The magician goes inside the hut to massage and soothe the woman. His colleague remains outside, attaching the stone to his stomach with a large piece of fabric (to simulate the birth) and, following the instructions shouted to him by the magician inside the hut, moves the stone in imitation of the baby's movements. Supposedly, he is absorbing the weight of the woman until the actual birth of the child.

There are also stones used to induce the flow of milk. In Greece and Crete the milk stone (probably a form of chalk-calcium) is dissolved with honey and consumed by the mother. This is supposed to produce an abundant supply of milk. In Albania the stone is worn on the body for the same purpose. In Haiti pregnant women ward off the evil eye of miscarriage by sewing a little polished stone from their magician into the hem of a seven layered petticoat.

There are still some Arab women who perform an ancient superstitious tradition when they fear difficult delivery. Three days before due date, they tie a fire stone wrapped in cloth around one of their thighs to insure an easy delivery.

## THE AFTERBIRTH

The afterbirth plays an integral part of birth ceremonies throughout the world. The afterbirth is made up of the placenta, the amniotic membrane and the umbilical cord. Many people believe that the afterbirth remains as an important part of the body, even though the physical connection has been severed.

From Baganda to the U.S.A., many parents believe that the food that has nourished the baby is very special and should be disposed of with thought and care.

There are people in America today who eat the stewed placenta in a thanksgiving meal after the birth. In New Mexico the afterbirth is planted under a new Ponderosa Pine tree. An Indian tribe in Arizona makes a bracelet from the umbilical cord. After it has dried, bead stones are threaded on it and given to the child to bite on at teething time. The Incas of Peru preserve the cord and give it to the child to suck whenever it falls ill. In Europe the midwives used to keep the cord until it was dry and then give it to the father, instructing him to preserve it safely as the child would be healthy and prosperous as long as it was kept in the family. In the countryside of France, the navel cord was never thrown into water or fire for fear that the child would drown or burn.

One of the most poetic stories about the afterbirth comes from Queensland, Australia. The natives of Queensland strongly believe that a part of the child's spirit stays in the afterbirth. It is the grandmother's role to look after it; she takes it away and buries it in the sand. Then she marks the spot with a number of twigs which she sticks in the ground in the form of a circle,

tying the top twigs together so that the structure resembles a cone. When Anjea (the being who causes conception by putting mud babies in the mother's womb) passes by and sees the place, she takes out the spirit of the baby and carries it away to one of her haunts, such as a tree, a hole, a rock, a shell or a lagoon where it may remain for years. At some later date, Anjea will put the spirit in another mud baby to be born again into the world.

On one of the Caroline Islands, in the Pacific, the umbilical cord is placed in a conch shell and treated in a manner that would be best suited for the child's future. For example, if the parents think that their son will need to be a good climber in order to survive, they will hang the conch on a tree.

In other places the umbilical cord, once dried, is reduced to powder and used as a remedy. In Iran, the powder was once used against trachoma (inflamation of the inner eyelid). It was a love philter amongst the Kalmucks, and in the Oceanic Islands some of the powdered cord was thrown in the sea to cast a good spell on their armaments at the onset of fighting.

It may seem a bit weird to eat the placenta raw, as some tribes from Central Brazil do, but it is not any more odd than using any of the facial creams or rejuvenating injections which are made from placental extract.

## KNOTS, LOCKS AND BONDS

The symbolic obstacle of a knot is sometimes associated with or believed to create a corresponding physical obstacle in the body, particularly during childbirth. For this reason, there are many ceremonies centering around knots, locks and bonds.

In Argyllshire, Scotland, for example, all the clothes of a woman in labor must be free of knots so that she will not be tied up inside. In the East Indies a woman must not tie any knots nor braid anything during the whole course of her pregnancy.

The Hos of West Africa call for their magician when a woman wants relief from a long labor. In certain cases he will declare that she cannot deliver because the child is bound within the womb. He promises to loosen the bond so that she may bring forth the baby. He orders someone to get a long creeper from the forest and with it he binds the hands and feet of the woman. He then takes a knife and calls out her name. When she answers, he cuts through the creeper saying, "Today is the day for the bonds between this woman and her child to be cut." He then chops up the creeper, puts the little bits in a basin of water and bathes the woman with the liquid.

In Chittagong, Pakistan, a woman in the same predicament calls a midwife. The midwife orders all the windows and doors opened, all the bottles uncorked, the horse is freed from the stall, the dog from the chain, the sheep and the fowl from the stable. This universal liberty accorded to animals and inanimate objects is supposed to be an infallible means of allowing the babe to be born.

When a woman is in labor on the Island of Sakhalin, in the North Pacific, her husband loosens up everything that can be undone: he undoes the plaits from his hair, the laces of his shoes and unties everything around the house and outside. In the yard the axe is taken out of the log, the cartridge withdrawn from the gun. In Toumbuluh, men abstain not only from tying knots but also from sitting cross-legged during their wife's pregnancy.

## WATER

Almost every religion has some ritual involving the use of water. As a purifying agent, as a blessing or to render fertility, the pouring of water and special ablutions are closely associated with the ceremonies performed after birth.

Ceremonial bathing in the ancient Greek civilization can be found in the Homeric story of the birth of Achilles. In the poem, the mother of Achilles took him for his first dip in the river Styx. She plunged him into the water until he was completely covered except for his heels by which she held on to him. His body was thereby rendered indestructable except for the famous Achilles tendon.

In the early part of this century, in the Chinese provinces of Kiangsu and Chekiang, a bathing custom following the birth of a baby was recorded. A member of the family would prepare the baby's bath. Two tubs were filled, the bigger one for the body, the smaller one for the head. Into the water of both tubs were put dragon's eyes and peanuts, insuring success and long life for the baby.

The inhabitants of the Trobriand Islands of New Guinea involve the sea with each pregnancy. The mother, sister, father and other members of the paternal family of the pregnant woman go to the beach and two by two enter the water. Facing each other and holding hands, they form a human bridge for the woman to walk on without touching the water. She keeps her equilibrium by leaning her hands on their heads. Each couple whose hands she has already walked on runs from the tail to the head of the bridge until, at one point, she jumps into the water and everyone splashes, rubs and cleans her. Once this ceremonial bath is over, they carry her back to the beach where she is laid on a fresh mat of coconut tree leaves. A purification ritual ensues with magic incantations to prepare her for the event of birth.

The womb is often compared to the earth-soil as the place where seeds grow. Exposure to sun and water is therefore essential for the seed to grow. In Australia and South Africa, women who wish to become pregnant will lie in a shower of rain, thinking that the seeds of growth lie within them.

In the seventeenth century, baths from fountain waters, forest springs or river water were recommended after the birth. Into the bath were thrown leaves of ivy, sage, fennel, camomile, rosemary, catnip and, for those prepared for an additional expense, two glasses of white wine were added!

During the Pre-Columbian days, pregnant women used to dye their

hair purple and then, during the fourth and seventh month of pregnancy, they took special ritual steam baths, abdominal massages and light knuckling of the back to insure a favorable position for the fetus.

## COUVADE

Couvade is a very old custom that has almost disappeared. The name couvade is derived from the French word 'couver' which means "to hatch", "to sit on." It is a custom whereby the father substitutes himself for the mother when labor begins. The ritual helps the father identify with and participate in bringing forth a new life and at the same time it is a protective measure to absorb or, at worst, divide the interests of malign powers.

When the woman stops her daily activities to give birth, she will go either to a special birth house of the village or off into the countryside to give birth by herself and return a few hours later with babe in hand. The father, meanwhile, goes to his sleeping area and pretends to be greatly shaken and in need of attention, moaning and groaning. Sometimes the father will perform these ceremonial gestures for days before and after the actual birth.

In Southern India the procedure used to be for the husband to dress as a woman when he was notified of the onset of labor. He would remain on a couch, twisting and turning until the baby was born.

Amongst the Bakairi in Central Brazil the father has to lie in a hammock with the newborn baby while the mother goes back to her daily occupation right after giving birth. He is supposed to observe a very strict fast consisting only of cassava (a flat bread which is made of manioc flour) dipped in water. No meat is eaten until the baby's navel is totally healed. During this period the father is not allowed to touch his arms. According to the tradition, it would be fatal to the child if these conditions were not fulfilled.

The requirements vary with different tribes in different countries. The Land Dayak of Sarawak, Malaysia, insist that the father stay out of sunlight during the four days following the birth. Also, he is allowed to eat only rice and salt for the next week. While the couvade is happening, the women of the compound who are not out working in the fields, look after and care for the father in the same way that most people would care for the new mother.

## GENERAL SUPERSTITIONS

There is an old Jewish superstition about not saying out loud that something good is going to happen to a person. If it is spoken, it is believed not likely to happen. If something good is happening it is paramount to keep it to yourself until it is well established. If a person says it out loud they are putting a KANAHARA on it. Many Jewish mamas, when wheeling their babies around, have a red bow attached to the carriage just in case someone comments favorably about the baby. The Kanahara is then

dispelled by the mother kissing the tip of her fingers and touching something red.

In China, a locket made of gold, silver and jade inscribed with the words "Long life and riches" was put on the baby's wrist or neck after birth. Fearing that the child would be difficult to raise, this locket was used to encase the little life so that the evil spirit could not penetrate or harm the child. This locket was supposed to remain until the child was twenty or thirty years old.

Another way of preserving the child's life in ancient China was to have the baby wear a dress made up of small pieces of different colored cloth donated by the neighbors. Those donations were supposed to keep the evil spirits at bay.

Among the Aztecs of Mexico it was (and still is) believed to be an ominous sign for a pregnant woman to gaze at an eclipse. This is thought to be a sure sign that the child will be born with a harelip. To counteract this malevolent influence, a small obsidian knife was sewn into the clothing, against the abdomen. Today, an iron knife is used in its place.

And, from Morocco, a real slapstick situation is reported. In the early part of this century, a Moroccan Jewish bridegroom would break a raw egg and fling it at his bride so that her future labors would be made easier!

## CEREMONIES

The celebration of birth with ceremonial rituals is a common practice throughout the world. In many Christian families, for example, rejoicing is manifested in baptism. In Africa, certain tribes require purification ceremonies at birthtime. Many of these ceremonies are characterized by propitiation rites on behalf of the newborn child, and also on behalf of the whole community.

Amongst the Tswana tribe, animals are sacrificed at a birth ceremony and the skin of the beasts is used as a blanket for wrapping the newborn child. The Sambas, on the west coast of Borneo, perform a ceremony for the first born child using two small figurines representing the parents. During the first part of the rite these figures are hidden beneath a veil. At a later point the veil is removed and the parents are invited to have intercourse in front of the statuettes. If the first born is a male, the old woman directing the ceremony rubs a little of the father's semen across the child's forehead, saying, "Receive from your father the gift of engendering children." If the child is a girl, she takes a little of the vaginal mucus from the mother and, signing the baby's forehead, says, "Receive from your mother the gift of conceiving children."

The Thonga of Mozambique also practice ritual coitus with emission outside the vagina so that the semen moistens a cotton cord which is afterwards tied around the infant's stomach in order to confer the gift of fecundity.

DIANA OF EPHESUS

# EARTH MOTHERS AND BIRTH GODDESSES

These are only a few of the female figures invoked at birth in ancient and modern times throughout the world.

**Aphrodite Genetyllis:** She was concerned with, and in fact embodied in, the reproductive powers and was worshipped to procure easy labor in ancient Greece.

**Artemis and Diana:** These two goddesses, one Greek and one Roman, are often mistaken for one another. Diana was an ancient Italian goddess; helper of women in childbirth. She was affiliated with Egeria and Virbius, divinities of childbirth. Later she was identified as the goddess of the crescent moon, identical with Artemis. This Greek goddess was originally a mother deity and goddess of lakes, woods and wildlife. She later developed into a goddess of fertility, marriage and childbirth, with the power of facilitating labor and delivery. The statue of Artemis at her temple at Ephesus, one of the seven wonders of the world, is sometimes identified as that of Diana. The upper part of the figure is covered with fruit-like breasts, identifying the goddess as a mother-deity and goddess of plenty.

**Astarte:** The Phoenician Great Mother — goddess of fertility — she was pictured holding a child in her arms. Her head was usually that of a bull or cow, with crescent-shaped horns which identify her as a moon goddess.

**Atargatis:** Hittite mother goddess and fertility deity. She is pictured as a mother nursing a child with a cornucopia. Like some other birth deities, she was also worshipped as a moon goddess. Syria.

**Cybele:** The Great Mother goddess of Phrygia, she was worshipped as mother earth, and goddess of all reproduction in nature.

**Demeter:** One of the twelve great Olympian deities, she was the protector of fertility and marriage; a mother goddess; the deity of the harvest; the ruler of Virgo (in the Greek Zodiac). She was usually portrayed as a tall woman with beautiful golden hair.

**Êuret-Êpet (Tauret, Apet, Opet):** An ancient Egyptian goddess who was the protector of all animals, and was pre-eminently helpful in childbirth. She was the giver of fecundity, guardian of women in childbirth, patron of the art of medicine and sender of fertilizing showers. She was represented as a hippopotamus with pendant breasts and paws like a lion, carrying a crocodile on her back. In other art she was pictured as a pregnant woman with lion's paws.

**Ishtar:** The Assyro-Babylonians believed the universe was created by a woman, and Ishtar was worshipped as the source of all life. Her name means "daughter of light", and was written with the character which stood for a house with the sign for a fish inside it; thus, a house filled with fertility.

# THE GODDESS TLAZOLTEOTL

She was also called Ban Gula, Mama, Mami and Zerpanitum. Her image was represented in phallic symbols, such as a stylized tree or pillar, as well as in the human form of a queen wearing a crown.

**Isis:** The Great Mother goddess of the Egyptian pantheon. In art she appears as a mother suckling her son; wearing a crown with a disk and cow's horns on top; standing on a crescent moon surrounded by twelve stars.

**Ixchel:** Mayan rainbow goddess and Yucatan goddess of fecundity, invoked at childbirth. Mexico.

**Kuan Yin (the Giver of Children):** The Chinese goddess of fertility and motherly love whose special attention is given to women who beseech her to bless them with children. Her figure is often draped in long, flowing white robes while she sits on a throne of lotus blossoms or stands on a tall rock with a child in her arms. Some artwork shows her riding a dragon while she holds the twig of a willow in one hand and a bowl filled with the dew of immortality in the other; and she is sometimes represented as the thousand armed goddess, showering mercy and consolation upon mankind.

**Postverta (also called Carmenta):** A Roman goddess who was a guardian of women in childbirth, and was invoked for aid during confinement.

**Teteoinnam:** Mother of all the gods; the midwives' patroness. Mexico.

**Tlazolteotl:** She is represented in the same clothes as Teteoinnam, and is therefore regarded as a manifestation of the mother of all the gods with special powers in the realm of fertility. Mexico.

**Venus Genetrix (or Venus the Birth Giver):** She was the special divinity of the childbirth bed for the Roman matron.

# helpful addresses

## NATIONAL ORGANIZATIONS

American Society for Psychoprophylaxis in Obstetrics (ASPO)
1523 L Street NW, Washington, D.C. 20005
202-783-7050

Classes in the Lamaze method of preparing for natural childbirth; films on birth; referral services; a telephone recording which is kept up to date with information about any current events of interest to parents. Write or call to get the phone number in your area.

International Childbirth Education Association (ICEA)
Box 5852, Milwaukee, Wisconsin 53220

Provides a list of books and pamphlets about pregnancy and childbirth; counsels parents interested in starting childbirth education classes in their own area; and publishes its own newsletter.

ICEA Education Committee
Box 22, Hillside, New Jersey 07205

La Leche League International
9616 Minneapolis Avenue, Franklin Park, Illinois 60131

Offer a listing of the home phone numbers of nursing mothers so that women who want to breast-feed their babies can get in touch with one another. Some women meet in groups and nurse their babies together. The League offers all kinds of information — tips and tricks of the trade which are learned from personal experience — to mothers who are nursing for the first time.

## REGIONAL ORGANIZATIONS

**California**
Haight Ashbury Women's Clinic
1101 Masonic, San Francisco, California
415-863-2790

For an annual fee of $6.00, they offer pregnancy testing, birth control counseling, abortion referral and many other health services.

Problem Pregnancy Information Center
Box 9090, Stanford, California 95305
415-226-7846

Located in Palo Alto, the Center offers free services in pregnancy counseling, adoption placement and abortion referral.

## Illinois

Chicago Women's Liberation Union
852 Belmont, Chicago, Illinois
312-348-4300
Pregnancy testing done for $1.50.

## Massachusetts

Pregnancy Counseling Service
3 Joy Street, Boston, Massachusetts 02108
617-523-1633
Information on health and welfare services for pregnant women as well as abortion counseling.

Women's Health Counseling
115 State Street, Springfield, Massachusetts 01103
413-732-1852
A Feminist counseling and referral group which includes services in natural childbirth and abortion.

## Minnesota

Women's Counseling Service
621 West Lake Street, Minneapolis, Minnesota 55408
612-827-3819
Medical information and referral service which grew out of a women's collective. Classes and workshops are held in pregnancy and abortion.

## New Mexico

Counseling and Referral Service
Women's Center, 1824 Los Lomas
University of New Mexico, Albuquerque, New Mexico 87106
505-277-3716
Abortion and birth control information.

## New York

Maternity Center Association
48 E. 92nd Street, New York, New York 10028
212-369-7300

Medical Society of the County of New York
40 W. 57th Street, New York, New York, 10019
212-JU2-5858
The Medical Society can be contacted for the referral of gynecologists and obstetricians in the borough of Manhattan.

New Yorker Films
43 W. 61st Street, New York, New York 10023
212-CI7-6110
*The Birth Film,* by Susan Kleckner. Birth at home, 16mm color, $60.00 to a group of fifty, other rates for other group sizes. It can be mailed anywhere, parcel post, special delivery, for one showing.

Women's Counseling Project
Earl Hall, Columbia University
117th Street and Broadway, New York, New York 10027
212-280-5113

Free referral services for birth control, abortion, pregnancy, childbirth and other health-related matters. Available to all women, even those not affiliated with the University.

## North Carolina

Pregnancy Counseling Service
University of North Carolina at Chapel Hill, Chapel Hill,
North Carolina
919-933-5506

Free counseling and referral services.

## Oregon

The Women's Health Clinic
3537 S.E. Hawthorne Boulevard, Portland, Oregon 97214
503-234-9774

A group of volunteer women offering, among other things, educational classes in herbal medicine, birth control and abortion. These services are free of charge.

## Vermont

Vermont Women's Health Center
P.O. Box 29, Burlington, Vermont 05401
Health services and abortion facilities.

## Washington, D.C.

The American College of Nurse-Midwives
Suite 500, 1000 Vermont N W, Washington, D.C. 20005
202-628-4642

This is the professional organization for nurse-midwives in the United States. It approves schools of nurse-midwifery and certifies nurse-midwives. The College can be consulted for referral of schools and a list of nurse-midwives. There are approximately 1,500 known nurse-midwives in this country, and the College has certified 1,000 of them.

## Washington

Aradia Clinic
4224 University Way, N.E., Seattle, Washington 98105
206-634-2090

A Feminist organization and health care clinic which encourages women to learn the techniques of self-examination. Operated by and for women, Aradia offers its services and medication free of charge and also sponsors political education.

## England

National Childbirth Trust
9 Queensborough Terrace, Bayswater, London W2 3TB

# herbs

## BOOKS

Bethel, May. *The Healing Power of Herbs.* Hollywood: Wilshire Book Co., 1968.

Kloss, Jethro. *Back to Eden.* Coalmont Tenn.: Longview Publishing House, 1939.

Schauenberg, Paul. *Guide des Plantes Medicinales.* Neuchatel, Switzerland: Delachaux & Niestle S.A., 1969.

Rose, Jean. *Herbs and Things.* New York: Grosset & Dunlap, 1972.

## SUPPLY HOUSES
## (send for catalogues)

**California**
Nature's Herb Co., 281 Ellis Street, San Francisco, California

**Indiana**
Indiana Botanic Gardens, Hammond, Indiana 46325

**New York**
Aphrodisia, 28 Carmine Street, New York City, New York 10014
Kiehl's Pharmacy, 109 Third Avenue, New York City, New York 10003

**Oregon**
Nichols Garden Nursery, 1190 N. Pacific Highway, Albany, Oregon 97321

**Pennsylvania**
Penn Herb Co., 603 N. Second Street, Philadelphia, Pennsylvania 19123

**Rhode Island**
Meadowbrook Herb Garden, Wyoming, Rhode Island 02898

**Canada**
Worldwide Herb Ltd., 11 St. Catherine Street East, Montreal 129

**England**
Culpepper, 21 Bruton Street, London W1

# bibliography

Arms, John and Suzanne. *A Season to Be Born*. New York: Harper & Row, Harper Colophon Books, 1973.

Bing, Elizabeth. *Six Practical Lessons for an Easier Childbirth*. New York: Bantam Books, 1969.

The Boston Children's Medical Center. *Pregnancy, Birth and the Newborn Baby*. Boston: Delacorte Press/Seymour Lawrence, 1972.

The Boston Women's Health Book Collective. *Our Bodies Ourselves*. Boston: Simon & Schuster, 1971.

Bourne, Gordon. *Pregnancy*. London: Cassel & Co., 35 Red Lion Sq., London WC1 R4 SG, 1972.

Briffault, Robert. *The Mothers*. New York: Grosset, 1927.

Buryn, Ed; Brown, Janet; Lesser, Eugene; and Mines, Stephanie. *Two Births*. New York: Random House Bookworks, 1972.

Chabon, Dr. Irwin. *Awake and Aware: Participating in Childbirth Through Psychoprophylaxis*. New York: Delacorte, 1966; Dell Publishing Co., 1969.

Cohen, Allen, and Walzer, Stephen. *Childbirth is Ecstasy*. San Francisco: San Francisco Aquarius Publishing Co., 1971.

Dally, Ann. *The Birth of a Child*. New York: Crown Publishers, Inc., 1969.

Davis, Adelle. *Let's Have Healthy Children*. New York: Harcourt, Brace & World, 1951.

Debray-Ritzen, Pierre. *Le Grand Livre de la Femme Enceinte*. Paris: Hachette, 1972.

Dextreit, Jeannette. *Des Enfants Sains*. Paris: Vivre en Harmonie, 1967.

Dickinson, Robert Latou., M.D. F.A.C.S. *Atlas of Human Sex Anatomy*. 2nd. ed. Baltimore, Md.: Williams & Wilkins Co., 1949.

Dick-Read, Dr. Grantly. *Childbirth Without Fear*. New York: Harper & Row, 1970.

Diner, Helen. *Mothers and Amazons*. New York: Anchor Books, 1973.

Eastman, Dr. Nicholas J., and Russel, Keith P. *Expectant Motherhood*. New York: Little, Brown & Co., 1963.

Eastman & Hellman. *Williams Obstetrics*. New York: Appleton, Century, Crofts, div. of Meredith Publishing, 1966.

Edelman, Claude. *Les Premiers Jours de la Vie*. Paris: Editions Jean Pierre Taillandier, 1971.

Eloesser, Leo; Galt, Edith J.; and Hemingway, Isabel. *Pregnancy, Childbirth and the Newborn: A Manual for Rural Midwives*. 2nd English ed. Mexico: Instituto Indigenista Interamericano, Ninos Heroes, 139, Mexico 7, D.F.

Ewy, Donna and Roger. *Preparation for Childbirth*. Colorado: Pruett Publishing, 1970.

Flanagan, Geraldine Lux. *The First Nine Months of Life*. New York: Simon & Schuster, 1962.

Frazer, James G. *The Golden Bough: Study in Magic and Religion*. 12 vols. London: Macmillan & Co., 1890-1915, abridged edition in hardcover and paperback. New York: Macmillan Co., 1951.

Gaskell, G.A. *Dictionary of All Scriptures and Myths*. New York: The Julian Press, Inc., 1960.

Gerard, Alice. *Please Breast Feed Your Baby*. New York: New American Library, 1971.

Guttmacher, Alan F. *Pregnancy and Birth*. New York: Signet, 1962.

Hall, Manly Palmer. *Man, Grand Symbol of the Mysteries*. Los Angeles: Philosophical Research Society, 1932.

Hall, Dr. Robert. *A Medical Guide for Pregnant Women.* New York: Bantam Books, 1960.

Hazell, Lester D. *Commonsense Childbirth: How to Have Your Baby Your Way.* New York: G.P. Putnam's Sons, 1969.

Karmel, Majorie. *Thank You Dr. Lamaze: A Mother's Experience in Painless Childbirth.* Philadelphia: J.B. Lippincott, 1959. Paperback, New York: Doubleday, 1970.

Kitzinger, Sheila. *The Experience of Childbirth.* New York: Taplinger, 1972. Paperback, New York: Penguin, 1972.

Kitzinger, Sheila. *Giving Birth.* New York: Taplinger, 1971.

Klein, Carole. *The Single Parent Experience.* New York: Avon, 1973.

La Leche League International. *The Womanly Art of Breastfeeding.* Franklin Park, Illinois: La Leche League, 1963.

Lama Foundation. *Be Here Now.* New York: Crown Publishers, Inc. 1971.

Lang, Raven. *Birth Book.* Big Trees, Felton, California: Genesis Press, Box 877, Ben Lomond, Calif., 95005, 1972.

Le Boyer, Frederick. *Pour Une Naissance Sans Violence.* Paris: Seuil, 1974.

Massacrier, Jacques. *Savior Revivre.* Paris: Editions Albin Michel, 1973.

Maternity Center Association. *A Baby is Born.* New York: Grosset & Dunlap, 1957.

Mayle, Peter. *Where Did I Come From?* Secaucus, N.J.: Lyle Stewart, 1973.

Montague, Ashley. *Life Before Birth.* New York: Signet, 1965.

Neuman, Eric. *The Great Mother: An Analysis of the Archetype.* Translated by Ralph Manheim. New Jersey: Princeton University Press, Princeton Bolligen, 1963.

New Moon Communications: *Proceedings of the First International Childbirth Conference,* Stamford, Conn.: New Moon Communications, Box 3488, Ridgeway Station, Stamford, Conn., 06905, 1973.

Nillson, Lennart; Ingelman-Sundberg, Axel; and Wirsen, Claes. *A Child is Born: The Drama of Life Before Birth.* Translated by Britt and Claes Wirsen and Annabelle MacMillan. New York: Dell Publishing Co., 1966.

Pomeranz, Virginia and Schultz, Dodi. *The First Five Years.* New York: Doubleday, 1973.

The Princeton Center for Infancy and Early Childhood. *The First Twelve Months of Life.* New York: Grosset & Dunlap, 1971.

Pryor, Karen. *Nursing Your Baby.* New York: Pocket Books, Inc., 1972. Harper & Row, 1973.

Rayner, Claire, S.R.N. *Child Care Made Simple.* London: W.H. Allen, 44 Hill St., London W1x 8LB, 1973.

Reich, Hanns. *Children and Their Mothers.* (pictorial book). New York: Farrar, Strauss & Giroux, Hill & Wang, 1963.

Rudinger, Edith, ed. *The Newborn Baby.* Caxton Hill, Hertford, England: Consumer's Association, 1972.

Rudinger, Edith, ed. *Pregnancy Month by Month.* Caxton Hill, Hertford, England: Consumer's Association, 1968.

Siedel, Ruth. *Women and Childcare in China.* Baltimore: Penguin, 1973.

Spock, Dr. Benjamin. *Baby and Childcare.* New York: Pocket Book, 1968.

Tanzer, Deborah and Block, Jean. *Why Natural Childbirth?: A Psychologist's Report on the Benefits to Mothers, Fathers, and Babies.* New York: Doubleday, 1972.

Thomas, Philip and Ellen. *The Natural Childbirth of Tara.* New York: Frederick Fell, 1973.

*Touching . . .the Human Significance of the Skin.* Anon. New York: Columbia University Press, 1971.

# Bibliography

Vellay, Pierre. *Childbirth Without Pain*. Translated by Denise Lloyd. New York: E.P. Dutton & Co., 1959.

Wallnoter, Heinrich and Von Rottauscher, Anna. *Chinese Folk Medicine and Acupuncture*. New York: Crown Publishers, Inc., 1965.

White, Dr. Gregory. *Emergency Childbirth*. Franklin Park, Ill.: The Police Training Foundation, 3412 Ruby St., Franklin Park, Ill., 1958.

Wright, Erna. *The New Childbirth*. New York: Hart Publishing Co., 1968. Pocket Books, 1971.

 **credits**

*Credits for the illustrations in this book are listed by page number. Where more than one credit is required for a page, they are identified top to bottom, separated by dashes.*

# index

*Page numbers for illustrations are printed in boldface type.*

Pomeranz, Dr. Virginia (pediatrician), 241
Preeclampsia, 91, 93, 94
Prenatal classes, 27, 37, 85
Prenatal exercises, 27; breathing, deep, 37-38, 101-3; breathing, pant, 37, 40, 105; breathing, shallow, 37, 39, 103-5; disassociation, 31; Kegel, 33; Lamaze method, 85, 163, 172, 177; limbering, **28**, 28, **29**, 29, **30**, 30, **31**, 31, **32**, 32; total relaxation before, **27**, 27, **29**, **33**, 33; yoga, 34, **37**, 85, 187, 189-91. *See also* Interviews
Prepared childbirth. *See* Interviews; prenatal exercises
Progesterone, 15
Psychoprophylaxis. *See* Interviews; Prenatal exercises

# R

Rh factor, 93, 95-96
Roccia, Professor (anaesthetist-acupuncturist), 92

# S

Sexual relations during pregnancy, 43
Sleep (infant), 247, 249-51
Sleeplessness during pregnancy, 55, 59
Smoking, 51

Spermatozoa (sperm), **6**, 7, **10**
Stillborn birth, 159

# T

Tension, 55
Thermogram sonar wave test, 95, **141**
Toxemia, 89, 93-94, 110
Traveling with infant, 261-63

# U

Umbilical cord: care of, after delivery, 208, 253; development and function of, 9, 13, 15, 17; during delivery, 105, **107**, 207, 208; role of, in birth customs, 279, 281
Uterus: during pregnancy, **6**, 7, **8**, **11**, **18**; during labor and delivery, 103, 105, 109, 153

# V

Vacuum extraction, **88**, 91, 169
Vernix, 17, 109
Vomiting during pregnancy, 57

# X

X-rays, 13

Publisher: Bruce Harris
Editor: Linda Sunshine
Production Manager: Murray Schwartz
Book and Cover Design: Stephanie Tevonian
Cover Photograph of Penny McLeran : Caterine Milinaire
Research: Maria Iano
Proofreaders: Ellen Leventhal, Dave Stamm

*The Beginning*